CHRIS STR

WIN LOSE REPEAT

My Life as a Gambler, from Coin-pushers to Spread-betting

Ortus

First published in 2017 by
Ortus Press
An Imprint of
Free Association Books

A CIP Catalogue of this book is available from the British Library

ISBN: 978-1-9113830-8-6

ebook also available

Mobi ISBN: 978-1-911383-10-9
ePub ISBN: 978-1-911383-09-3

Front cover images sourced through royalty free photo libraries:
© Hamara | shutterstock.com, © mrmohock | shutterstock.com,
© Antonio Gravante | shutterstock.com, © corund | shutterstock.com,

Cover design and typeset by
www.chandlerbookdesign.co.uk

Printed in Great Britain by
TJ International

CONTENTS

1. The Mark 1

2. The New Kid in Town: Financial Spread-betting. 11

i. How it works – just not for you! 17
ii. Come on in! The marketing of a myth 56
iii. Follow the Yellow Brick Road 69
iv. Urgent action required! 77
v. Join us! 79
vi. The end game 81

3. Old Skool Reinvented: Poker, Bingo and Casinos 91

i. Poker 93
ii. Bingo... and their fruit machines 103
iii. Casinos... and their fruit machines 107

4. The High Street: The Amusement Arcades, the Bookies and their Fruit Machines 117

i. The amusement arcades 117
ii. The bookies 119
iii. Their fruit machines 125

5. The Making of a Gambler 133

6. Why We Gamble 141

i. You don't take up fishing in order to catch fish 141
ii. Addictive tendencies 151
iii. They know you better than you know yourself 157
iv. Getting their message out 171
v. The Ace of Spades 190

7. How We Gamble 198

8. Exit Strategies 239

i. How to spot a gambler 239

ii. How to stop a gambler 242

9. Regulation 266

10. In Recovery 288

To my wife and family, I apologise.

1

THE MARK

If you look at the other people around you and you can't spot the mark – the person being targeted for whatever sales pitch or con – then that mark must be you. We know this. What we don't seem to realise is that everyone around us might all be the marks – but we are too. You think you are somehow better than the rest: more intelligent, more educated, street-wise, neither naïve nor gullible. You won't fall for marketing or subliminal sales messages and be taken in by the con. But that's what everyone else thinks too.

So, when I attended an 'information' event at TD Waterhouse with at least 50 others, I went there aware that it was no more than a marketing trick. I looked around at those there with me and could spot the naïve, the uneducated, the gullible. I'd call the event a sell-out apart from the fact it was free. I turned up and ate my complimentary sandwiches – a trick in itself so that you stay longer – believing I would just read between the lines of what they told the assembled crowd. I was better than the rest. I would be that winner. Spread-betting wasn't really gambling anyway, in my mind. I would be just like the masters of the universe with a phone in each hand, barking out buy/sell orders across the office floor at Nomura. Many people have this as a day job, employed by others to do so, and both parties do very well out of the arrangement. I could become one of them, right? So what if a reported 90% of people don't win trying to become a 'trader' through the spread-betting route. The industry needs its losers or else it couldn't exist, meaning that I couldn't profit from it – and I would profit from it, because I would naturally be in that small percentage of winners. I thought like this. So did everyone else in the room, no doubt.

Five years later, I am £130,000 down. My substantial savings have reduced to zero. I have sold the car and made a start on the capital of the house. I was that mark – just like everybody else.

*

If you somehow haven't realised it by now, this book is not about how to win. It is about how not to lose. It is a handbook for today's gambler. It is not a *Lonely Planet* guide, as they give you information about places you may actually *like* to visit. I just tell you how to escape from the place you have been suckered into visiting. A bit like an extended version of *The Beach* – may start off just great but then turns into a horror show. My E.P. lasted 5 years although I can trace its origins back thirty years before. How did it get to this? I have a degree in economics, I had time to dedicate to my new activity and the finances to back it up too. But now I realise I am no different from the overweight pensioner who has a plastic cup brimming over with shiny dollar coins as they rest their fat arse on a stool in Vegas in front of their favourite slot machine. Or an OAP doing much the same in an amusement arcade in Hastings. Or a hundred other people performing similar acts of faith in the misguided belief that their particular form of betting is going to pay off even though their own personal history of financial mismanagement within the confines of Ladbrokes or their 888.com app would suggest otherwise. But we gamblers think that fortune awaits around the corner. We do not realise that we are just going round in circles – and as my young son can tell me, circles do not have corners.

This book is for everyone who repeats destructive, unhealthy or just dumb-ass actions time and time again. You may be an addict or just have addictive tendencies. Whichever you are, it ain't good, is it?! If you recognise some or all of the behaviours that I outline then whatever you are, you have a problem. Recognise yourself for what you are, then try to change. I have made a few suggestions on how to do this. I eventually managed to give up and have stayed stopped for four years now without too much problem. I have not had those terrible relapses associated with alcohol dependence. I think I am like the majority of people, who have addictive tendencies but are not true addicts. I will help you to see the gambling industry for what it is and once you educate yourself more about it, you may never want to go there again; just like when you find out what goes into your food – you then never touch certain products again. Discover more about yourself. Discover more about the business. I don't want to title my book, 'I can change your life'. It ain't that simple. I can help change your life but you are part of the problem. I say 'part' as there are plenty of external factors working on you. I can help unfog your mind. Detoxing your head will involve some negative emotions; you will suffer from regret, guilt, remorse, hatred, jealousy… there's a long list here. We will unclutter your brain from the flotsam and jetsam of withdrawal. One day, you will feel reenergised, refocused and refreshed. Your mind will be empty and clear but your bank account won't be.

Whatever form of gambling you go for, the multibillion-pound industry that feeds off of us employ pretty much the same techniques. They tailor each product to particular audiences but the message is similar. They understand the mathematics of their business better than you or I ever could. And, more importantly, they are experts in the psychology of it all. You don't really know what you are doing even if you are convinced you do. They, on the other hand, know what you are doing even before you do it. They are the true masters of the universe and the masters of your own self-destruction. They will argue that you do what you do of your own free will, but they are more than an accessory to the crime. Think of them as supplying you with the latest Glock handgun for your own protection, together with award-winning, industry-leading training and education that they always boast about. Throw customer support into the package and you have everything you need. They do not highlight the fact that they have handed you something lethal. One day, that spread-betting account, that poker site, that online casino will cause you pain. You may walk away with only a flesh wound or you might end up with something far more severe. I have somehow managed to limp away and recover. Some never do. Some of us gamblers unknowingly sign our own death warrant when we register online to gamble. But the vast majority will not find themselves in such dire straits. We will just live with that hundreds or thousands or hundreds of thousands pound black hole. We will go through the process of denial, self-loathing, the 'what-have-I done?' sense of stupidity, the anger at oneself, the hatred at the industry and named individuals who make their fortunes out of suckers like us, the realisation that 'a sucker' is exactly what we are, the desire to punch the betting companies' bosses smack in the face for making an idiot out of us then laughing all the way to the bank... But what's done is done. Live with your dumb-ass decisions. You are a fully paid-up member of the Dumb Fuck Club. You are the same as thousands upon thousands upon hundreds of thousands of people out there. Keep your DFC membership card in your wallet as a reminder never to go there again. And if you are just setting out into what the marketing tells us is the exciting world of gambling, then take it from within the pages of this book that, yes, there will be moments of 'fun' – but the moments of despair will overwhelm you. Like the football team who wins a match or two early on in the season then proceeds to lose almost every other single game before being relegated, you too will have that sense that if you try harder, if you have a little luck, if you have better finances, then you can turn your season around. It ain't gonna happen. Your finances will be ruined, your self-esteem will be destroyed. Still want to bet?

How do you ever think you can win? Gamblers lose their houses and make others extremely wealthy. Most just donate a percentage of their income month after month; a sort of gamblers' tithe. The temples to gambling are evident in Las Vegas. The mansions of the millionaire owners and bosses of the UK's gambling industry dotted around Surrey and their holiday homes overlooking golf courses on the Algarve are there too, if you know where to look. It is clear enough, if us gamblers are forced to notice, just how much they take from us. They spend millions alone just on machines to count all that lost money. Those hoppers are emptied when almost everyone is safely tucked up in their hotel beds; they will wake up long after the casino staff have emptied these caskets into troughs that they wheel along the rows upon rows of machines. Apart from the security aspect, it is better that the punters don't witness this act; rather off-putting otherwise to see the machines they have been sitting at for the past four hours being relieved of thousands of coins. So the 5 a.m. crew perform this task, just like the farmers where I grew up; both earn their living from this early morning milking. Any chips you lose at the table get swept away and disappear down an opening in the cloth. They do a good job at hiding all that money they take off you. And for the high-rollers, the 'whales'? They feed in $100 bills, press the start button which spins those reels that come to a halt after as short a time as the casino knows they can get away with then automatically feed in another one, barely even noticing if they have actually 'won'. Time is money for the casinos so why programme the slots to spin and stop after six seconds when you can set them to stop after three seconds and double your money? The gambler doesn't care. In fact, he wants them to stop as quickly as possible as he needs to feed the beast in front of him in order to feed the beast in his own head. But you're better than that, aren't you? Only pensioners and the gullible would play 'slots' that are programmed to win. But whatever form of gambling you do is no better. I should know. I even made it easy for them to take my money. I typed in my bank card details so they never had to worry about counting loose change and bank notes. I just sent them balance transfer after balance transfer. I filled their coffers for them. If a reported 90%+ of spread-betters are losers, this means that a small percentage are spread-betting winners. This is enough incentive to give us gamblers something to go at. We will naturally be in this 10% with our guile and cunning, so who cares about the losers? Most poker players lose. So what? That won't be me.

The slots will be programmed to take $90–97 for every $100 put in. So you keep on losing up to 10% of your ever-decreasing gambling fund until the machine has beaten you and all your coins are chinking their way into the casino's coffers at the base of the machine. The slot-jockeys carry on because every now and then they win, which keeps them going. Or they get that near-win. The near-win is worse than the constant small wins. If you need four melons to get a $100 pay-out, but get three melons and a single click away from that fourth melon on that last cylinder then you think you have been unlucky and next time, next time… The near-wins are the real bastards. They are a clever little psychological trick. Those machines don't keep spinning three melons and a near fourth or else the punter may realise what the game is all about. No, just drop this near-win in occasionally. And whoever is standing in front of that machine hasn't quite twigged that any near-win is actually a loss. This is the world of the fruit machines that I grew up with in every pub I've ever been in and every amusement arcade too; small amounts of 'winnings' and the lure of that big win that you almost, almost won. But if you think yourself immune to the flashing lights and the beeps and bleeps of the fruit machine, and think yourself far too smart to fall for them as you log on to IG.com or walk into William Hill, then just remember that you win small amounts and you almost, almost had that big win. You are no different. Your skill and judgement in selecting your horses every week, or predicting whether the Dow will rise or fall each day will be about as successful a strategy as the slot-jockeys'. The fruit machines are programmed so that you lose. The bookies don't even have to install one of these to make money from their other customers, as the greatest money-making machine is that one inside their customers' head. But the bookies also love these automated money-spinners so they do install them too. They have now invented the Robocop of money-making machines to stand on their floor space. They are about as similar to the traditional pub fruitie as a musket is to a machine gun. They will have the same effect on your wallet as a blast from the latter.

The bookies have massive overheads to pay out: staff wages, rents, IT and so on. They need to take in millions just to break even. The punter has none of this and still can't break even! Doesn't this rather suggest that we have no chance? There are some millionaire, and a few billionaire, owners of these businesses. Some are listed on the stock exchange. William Hill, IG and Ladbrokes are FTSE 250 listed. The UK gambling industry's turnover runs into the billions each year – which you and I give them. Around £3 billion for 2016 – and that's just for online! Never have so few been so thankful to so many, as Churchill might have said.

What do gamblers read when they are down and want to make it back and more? The title is effectively, 'How to make money gambling', usually with some snappy title like *The Naked Trader's Guide to Spread-betting*, a book aimed at the financial spread-better that I used to be. What gamblers should be reading is, 'How you *think* you can make money gambling'. Once you understand the psychology of it, once you understand how the gambling companies understand this and use it to pick away at you to make you gamble, then to gamble more and more often, once you understand the laws of it all, once you understand the latter, then you will click 'yes' for confirm delete for that natty little gambling app icon on your phone.

I may repeat a few details from chapter to chapter. Some people just skip to the section most relevant to them and as some points are very important I have included them again. Also, the gambling world is merging, some sectors have now crossed over into another. But the gambler should be used to experiencing repeated actions. That is what we do time and time again, week in, week out.

Or it used to be what I did over and over – but now I have quit. No more sneaking away to the toilet with my lovely internet connected device; do this and you are no better than the alcoholic who hides a bottle of Asda vodka in the cistern. But the trouble with not gambling, the trouble with not doing coke at the weekend, the trouble with not doing anything you enjoy is what do you do now to fill your time, to give you a buzz, to make life more exciting and worth living? No wonder so many ex-sportsman turn to drink. When you've been living life in the fast lane, what do you do when you stop? You are back to the day-to-day grind of your job. Gambling gave me hope even though I now see this was complete bullshit. But hope it was nevertheless. And without hope, we struggle. You may well already have more than one addiction you are struggling with. Give up gambling and there is a good chance that you will replace it with another addiction. Any psychologist will tell you that. The substitute could even be a worse replacement than what you gave up. Some addictions are more destructive than others. It's not great if you give up smoking, then increase your dependence on alcohol. The trouble with addiction is that many of us associate it with drugs, with hard drugs like heroin in particular. We do not see ourselves as someone out of *Trainspotting*, so we don't recognise our own addictions. Our own drinking and cocaine use we may just regard as recreational. Visiting a pay-per-play girl for sex once a week is just something we do, like going to the gym – which is also the reason given to the wife for where we have been for the last hour. You could have completely innocent addictions – watching or playing sport, YouTube for hours on end, Facebook, online news, online games. Then there's shopping. Women often prefer fashion and home acquisitions. Their husbands might take the piss out of this then go and buy electronics and power tools, then every few years combine the two and buy an even more powerful car with loads of 'spec'. Whatever addiction you have and then quit, you will miss it. You just need to find that something that works for you that keeps you away from that desire that will always reside in you. I started replying to emails in Haiku when I first quit as some sort of challenge in the day. But I need more than this to keep me alive.

There are books glamorising gambling, and even working in a lap-dancing club or high-class prostitution (not just *Belle de Jour*). These worlds are littered with victims. A once sweet girl I've known since childhood lives one of these lives and her life sure as hell ain't glamorous! She puts on a show for her family (and a different one for her clients) but we all know it's as fake as her tits. My life as a high-roller, which I became in the end with the amounts I was gambling, wasn't glamorous. The spread-betting firms didn't exactly shower me with gifts as the casinos do with true high-rollers who get penthouses for the weekend. Nope, I didn't even get so much as a key-ring. Don't read the books you want to read, the books that tell you how rich you will become, the story you want to hear; read *this* book, the story you don't want to read, the story you'd much rather ignore.

2

THE NEW KID IN TOWN: FINANCIAL SPREAD-BETTING.

Back in the sixties you actually had to go to a racecourse to place a bet, or phone somebody there who would place the bet for you. Then this was relaxed and bookmakers such as William Hill opened up betting shops and have never looked back. In the late 80s, when I was betting on horses, you had to pay 10% tax on your stake or your winnings. You would prepay the tax unless your bet was evens or odds-on. This is seemingly the smart thing to do, although as you are more likely to lose, it actually isn't. But you pay it because otherwise you must believe that you are destined to lose and who would bet then? So the government take in more tax offering this prepay option – looks like they are doing you a favour with this arrangement but they're not. This tax was reduced to 9% which meant bookies actually printed the nine times table on the reverse of betting slips. Racecourses were made exempt from any sort of tax to encourage people to attend and to sustain the actual thing which was the lifeblood of the high-street bookie. Finally, the off-course tax was completely abolished. The government's hand was forced due to bookies moving offshore to Gibraltar where they offered their customers tax-free phone betting. The government figured they could get the punters back through the doors in the UK if they switched to taxing bookies' profits. In the end it seems the bookies have won the battle as they go from strength to strength. Just look at their profits.

Now the world has changed once more. Ladbrokes *et al.* change with the times and have expanded their portfolio to offer all sorts of ways for you to lose your money: online casinos, bingo and poker have been added to the list of punters' favourites. And as every gambler knows, it is far easier to lose money online. The bookies' door never closes. And typing in numbers on your bank card means you are far more likely to lose far more money. You would not hand over 50 £10 notes to the girl on the other side of the counter at Coral but online, it's so tempting and easy. I've typed in figures in the hundreds and in the thousands to feed my account more times than I could mention. Now you can bet on just about anything: welcome to the world of financial spread-betting.

I have to start with spread-betting (SB) as it became my own personal demon. We gamblers usually end up specialising in one form or the other: bingo, spread-betting, the fruitie, bookies. But being a specialist doesn't make you any good – it's just your delusional method of choice for parting yourself from your money. The techniques and strategies employed by the SB companies will be much the same as with any other form of gambling. The emotions, the reasons for starting, continuing then finally giving up are identical. The psychology and make-up of the gambler and those who prey on us are universal.

Now we have financial spread-betting and the related contract for difference (CFD), or as anyone who tries it finds out, Complete Fucking Disaster. Strictly speaking, it's been around for a lot longer than you'd imagine; since the 70s in some cases. But broadband and smartphones have led to an explosion in the size of the industry and the number of providers trying to get in on the act. CFD sounds slightly more sophisticated than spread-betting, so the industry is trying to rebrand the latter and remove the actual concept of gambling from its name: so we get spread-*trading*. They are finding it difficult to make it catch on even with their own staff. A customer service person I once spoke to answered the phone using the true name that they would like to banish, before stuttering to correct himself. But to call it something that makes it sound anything other than pure and simple gambling is disingenuous, or more precisely, complete bollocks. You are not an international oil trader or metals trader or commodities trader earning a million a year staring at eight screens at your desk in the City. No, you are that guy on the train home after work with his smartphone in his hand or that bloke sitting on the toilet upstairs with his iPad balanced on his knees as his wife cooks a meal downstairs. But the SB industry do not use an image of a worried guy locked in his bathroom, staring at the screen of his choice as the 'trade' of his choice moves against him (as it inevitably does). Best portray the amateur 'trader' as someone who can dip in and out of whatever market he chooses, make a quick hundred or a thousand then get back to his day job or wife or girlfriend. He will not be an overweight bloke, or have a receding hairline, or still have those annoying pimples of youth – he will look like someone out of a Gillette advert.

How did someone who has a decent degree and what I thought was a decent amount of common sense get sucked in? I can see that I was a prime target. The most common gambler is the male gambler, which I am. The business tries to attract the female gambler but they struggle with this. It's just not such a female characteristic. We men like to take a risk. It's what got us out of caves in the first place. We like a challenge, something that we will succeed at with skill and cunning. I prefer to do something that is difficult rather than do something that is easy. Who wants to play golf against someone they can always beat? We men try for the most attractive and intelligent girl. We want, we *need* to push ourselves. I am not just describing the alpha male. We almost all have this desire, this urge. We mistakenly believe that we will have a natural talent for it. Women are generally more logical in their approach to risk. Men are not.

Others express their desire for a challenge in far riskier ways. I only lost my cash. Others lose their lives. Men have an overinflated opinion of their own abilities. Many have drawn the illogical conclusion that if they are good at one thing then they are very likely to be good at many things, often unrelated. So, if you are a top accountant then by extension you can buy yourself a 1000cc Ducati and throw it around bends. Sunday motorcyclists have the highest mortality rate of all. Or you have limited mountaineering experience, but take a group expedition up Everest. Or you decide in your 50s that the Tour de France looks exciting, so why not buy yourself that turquoise Bianchi and go hill climbing. Great idea, until you have a heart attack at the side of the road. Not widely reported but I've noticed more than a few cases of this. If you're really successful, then you buy yourself that speedboat or sports car. You think you are a great driver, so a speedboat is the same thing, just on water. Great, until you swing it around, everyone falls into the sea and your super-powered speed boat keeps on going round in circles. This seems to happen with regularity, or at least it's more widely reported as it's more dramatic, often with multiple casualties. The overconfident don't seem to educate themselves about their new dangerous hobby, so they don't hook themselves up to an engine shut-off switch. No, at least I didn't kill myself or anybody else. Women have it easy. Apart from the pain of childbirth, they generally don't go in for death-defying activities almost on a whim, which men seem to crave. So they will never be gamblers either. Yes, there are exceptions – but that's all they are and will remain so.

I got taken in by the industry's marketing; old-fashioned marketing too. One of those glossy bits of paper that fell from between the sheets of the *Financial Times*; a paper I thought I might read on occasion to become more informed somehow about what to do with my money, about *real* investments. I fell for a fake one. They even had a supplement entirely devoted to spread-betting. It was one of those Trojan Horse advertising features that attaches itself to the appropriate publication to give it that air of respectability. I could so easily have thrown that SB supplement and *City Index* leaflet into the bin with the rest of the rubbish. I started to throw away my money instead. I never really regarded spread-betting as gambling, even though the clue to its very nature is plain to see in its name. This is why they are trying to rebrand themselves; they are trying to trick you into believing you are a trader by shoehorning that word into its name. I read that supplement cover to cover and decided I'd give it a go. I signed up, was sent some very glossy brochures, received a £100 bonus and I was away. Now I realise that I was away with the fairies. They gave me their courtesy call to check my financial status. Yes, they want to know if you're a homeowner and have assets. Course they do. They are not interested in your financial security for *your* benefit. They want to know for the same reason a bailiff or a burglar would. They have no interest in whether you are educated (meaningless anyway – just increases your confidence and arrogance), your experience with financial products (which SB isn't but they market it as such) or your suitability in any way. They also want to know your attitude to risk and inform you that your losses may be substantially larger than your initial stake. They tell you the last point because the regulator insists they do. They'd keep that point to themselves otherwise. But telling most men something is risky only makes it more appealing. You can freewheel down a hill on your bike applying the brakes frequently – or you can get down over the handlebars, ignore the cars behind you getting too close and try to hit 40 mph before you get to the bottom. I always choose the latter. So, risk is a financial aphrodisiac.

The fact that I was a man and have the typical male attitude to risk played right into their hands. This is no different for the poker player. Next came my single status and my financial assets and savings. I had tens of thousands of pounds doing not a lot, so why not use it to good effect and turn it into hundreds of thousands? It looked so easy. Financial spread-betting appeals to the wealthy middle class who think they are financially savvy. They have pots of cash to spare and, even after they have lost the lot, the wife might not even get wind of it. The gaping hole can be covered and filled in before she notices. Don't bank on it, though. There must be thousands of men out there whose *mea culpa* and crawling for forgiveness feels worse than the actual loss itself. But they do not post their financial stupidity on Facebook, so it remains the hidden and growing financial cancer on today's middle class. No one admits to it so it remains hidden. No one except for me, that is. But

you can gauge the massive size of this combined loss very easily. Just look at the turnover and profits of the growing number of spread-bet companies. Everyone is getting in on the act. The banks offer spread-betting, using identical trading platforms as they generally employ the services of the true spread-betting companies. They do very well out of this relationship. Having Barclays offer you this service gives gambling the illusion that this is a financial product. It is not. Putting £1000 on the 2.15 at Ascot is much the same type of financial investment. The spread-betting companies also inform you that it is tax free. Again – that illusion of financial investment. The 2.15 at Ascot is also tax free. Does anyone believe betting on this or on the dogs at Crayford is a financial product? Of course they don't. But spread-betting? We seem to fall for that one when it's no more a credible investment vehicle than betting on the winner of the Eurovision Song Contest.

i. How it works – just not for you!

Financial spread-betting seems a simple way to make money from the outside. You can even set up a dummy account and trade with fake money for some pre-entry practice. 'Dummy' account is very apt, although 'fucking idiot' account would be more accurate. It is unconnected to any reality. The psychology of betting with Monopoly money is a world away from using your own hard-earned cash. I would have no problem walking into Ladbrokes with a handful of Bank of Waddington currency and putting £10,000 worth of pink £500 notes on the favourite. True, the girl on the counter would think I was a nutter but I'd have no worries if my selection trailed in last. Your mindset is completely different with real money. You might be thousands up with your dummy account, believe that you can replicate this with a live account, then find yourself thousands down a few months later, wondering where it all went wrong. Would you play *Call of Duty* if your arse was really out there to get shot at? No, if that was for real, you'd drop your M4 rifle and peg it out of there in the opposite direction. *Grand Theft Auto*? You'd park it up safely, walk away whistling and hope nobody has noticed. Whether you have the balls to jump straight in like I did or need the 'help and support' that the SB companies are all too willing to give you – including that dumb-ass account before you make a real deposit. They have got you either way and the frequency of typing in those three security numbers on the back of your bank card will increase with an unnerving regularity.

How does spread-betting work? Simple. You give the spread-betting companies your money. You lose it gradually or sometimes suddenly. You pay in more and more. You never see your money again. The mechanics of it is almost a side issue, much like the slot-jockey has little interest in the internal mechanics of the machine they are feeding. Let's not call it 'playing'. A fruit machine is hardly a game. This would suggest it is something someone could win at, whereas no one can. Golf would not be a game if the diameter of the hole was smaller than the diameter of the ball.

Spread-betting is not a niche market. Gone are those days. It used to be rarer than a baccarat table in a small provincial UK casino. And like baccarat, it attracts big-stakes gamblers – like I became eventually. It is now thriving and growing. The biggest provider in the market boasts about how they have over 150,000 active users. The UK regulator puts the number of 'funded retail client's accounts' at 1,050,000; this includes dormant and multiple accounts. There are 125,000 UK and 400,000 overseas-based client accounts currently active. There must have been many hundreds of thousands of others too, whom have completely 'left the building' like me and so surely closed their accounts. These regulator numbers still look a little low to me. The SB firms love to inform you about how popular it is, just how many people choose their particular brand – this all legitimises it and by selecting them, you are with the best, the most reliable... remember that all these reassurances are essentially bullshit. But bullshit that convinces you, that reassures you and that you all too willingly accept.

Upon signing up, I was sent two very thick brochures all about spread-betting and CFDs; these were catalogue thick. Not Littlewoods or even just 80s Argos, but it was unnaturally thick. There are reasons for this. First, they can bullshit you with just how great a thing it is, how easy it is, how rewarding it is. It would be years until I would discover that they omitted two important words off of each of the above phrases: 'for them'. There are pictures of good-looking, successful guys running their fingers through their silky hair after successful trades, smiling away on the phone. Now, I realise that this is not Mr Client like me. No, it is more likely to be some SB company middle manager, content with the bonus he has just been awarded, and phoning an escort agency to celebrate. The second reason to send out such thick brochures is that if you have pages upon pages of terms and conditions, you need a lot of glossy printed pages of marketing and positivity to precede it or else you cannot hide it away at the back, as it would also form the middle and most of the beginning too – it's 'burying bad news'. Most clients will give the brochures only a cursory glance. It was a legal requirement to send clients the terms and conditions (T&Cs). If you want to mask the T&Cs then the regulator won't mind. Nowadays though, I imagine that all you need do is tick a box online. It all looks professional. And that's exactly what it is. They will also do a very professional job on you.

Let me describe what the trader believes. First and foremost, he believes he is a trader. He is not. He is a gambler. The spread-betting company closely resembles a bookie. You don't trade shares or commodities or whatever. Neither do they in their core business (nowadays some do have a side-line in actually buying and selling shares outright; this gives them the veneer of credibility whilst endeavouring to mask their true nature). The spread-betting gambler may regard himself as some special class of *rational* gambler. He is not that either. He is purely and simply a gambler. Throughout I use the pronoun 'he', as in all probability the gambler is male. Not exclusively, but we male dumb-asses make up the vast majority in all fields of gambling save for one or two non-skill games. Walk into any bookies at any time of the day and you'll be hard pressed to find a female customer. Unlike most shop assistants who work in any other branch of retailing, the women who work behind the counter must view their customers as essentially nuts. They have a point.

So, what do we 'traders' do then? Remember, neither side in this charade actually trade anything, yet the gambler regards himself as a 'trader' and the SB bookie presents as an online 'trading' site; only one side of this arrangement is fully aware of the truth.

We place a bet on whether a particular market will rise or fall. This could be in any sector, be it commodities, oil, stock indices, metals, foreign exchange or individual share prices. So, if you think coffee will rise in price, place a 'buy' and watch the money roll in. Simple. My personal preference was to bet on the overall stock market, mainly the Dow Jones, sometimes the FTSE. The Dow consists of 30 companies, the FTSE 100 – these generate a weighted index. The former is officially called the Dow Jones Industrial index, although this makes it sound like heavy engineering, and yet Disney is one of the 30. Spread-bet bookies often incorporate this '30' into the name of the index they offer. Here's how it works. Let's say the Dow is at 14,000, which it was back in 2008 before it nosedived. I believe it will fall, so I place a 'sell' position at this price although the SB provider charges me a spread of two points, so I actually sell at 14,002 when the market is really at 14,000. Betting at £10 a point I am instantly £20 down, but if the market falls then I can easily recoup this, so we gamblers will pretty much dismiss this transaction cost as irrelevant. In comparison to final profits and losses, this is a fairly acceptable belief to hold, although after a short while trading, it too becomes a factor. On a good day, after placing this trade, I can sit back and watch the Dow drop further so that by the close of trade, 9 p.m. UK time, the Dow might have fallen 102 points from the 14,002 starting position to finish at 13,900. You don't have to be a maths genius to see that in one day I have made 100 points multiplied by £10 per point equals £1000! So why clean toilets, work on the checkout at Tesco's, suffer abuse from customers in that call centre you work in, bust a gut working on the building site, bore yourself to death in the office or suffer constant attendance at management meetings, when you can just sit at home, have the telly on, and sip a nice cup of tea while you watch the money in your spread-bet account increasing by the minute? That's why spread-betting becomes so appealing, so addictive. I have had days like this – many days like this, and better. The most I have made in a single day was £13,000. That's a lot of money. But there are two sides to every coin. Place the same 'sell' trade then sit with your cup of tea and watch it climb and climb before it closes at 14,100. Now you are in the shit. You have now lost £1000. This is a big loss. No, making money is never easy, whatever the marketing seems to suggest.

The reality to how the market operates is usually different. Markets can continually rise or fall throughout the day but the SB bookies' best friend is volatility. Like betting on black and that little roulette ball finally settles in black, but you have still lost because it went into red first. Any particular market can swing gradually or violently back and forth over a few minutes, hours, days... decades. If you try to trade this volatility by switching your positions constantly, you will incur more spread costs and will end up stressed and in a real mess financially and emotionally. Just look at the last decade and any particular timeframe within that. Don't think 2008 was such an anomaly. There will be many days where the market will rise and fall 2%, both within the same day. Don't believe you can trade through it even when the SB bookies assure you that their trading tools will help you 'navigate' volatile markets. You will just be like that unfortunate fishing boat in *The Perfect Storm*. You can have all the navigational aids you like. It ain't gonna help. You will not realise you are making money in the calm before the storm. You do not see the storm coming and when you do, you will actually believe you can survive it, conquer it. You like a challenge. You will fight against the elements and prevail. No you won't.

Back to my example where I place the 'sell' trade at 14,000 and by the end of the day it falls to 13,900. Placing a £10 sell, I am £1000 up, right? Nope, my equity has reduced to zero. I have lost £1000. I could have lost £2000. How? Simple. Before the market fell to 13,900 it climbed its way up to 14,200. The SB bookie closed my position before this point, reducing my funds to zero. Yes, I could have funded my account to hold this position, but this is not an easy thing to do. If it rises another 100 points: another £1000 loss. There are times when it falls 50 points, which would give me a cool £500 profit so I simply click 'close' and bank the cash. Difficult to do. Why not just hang on and wait for an even bigger fall and double or triple your winnings? You kick yourself when it continues down and you missed it, but what if it reverses and goes back up a hundred? You are now sitting on a loss. Do not think that you will take this easy £500 then 'buy' just as it rises to benefit from the change in direction. You will only do this in hindsight. You will be facing in the wrong direction too many times and will suffer big losses. You will not get in and out at the right time. The system is set up for you to fail. They have a bigger advantage over you than the addition of one or two green squares on a roulette wheel.

You think you'll win, they *know* they will. The gamblers' mindset will lead to the following actions. You may have already done most of them:

DOUBLE DOWN. How you believe you can *accelerate* your winnings: when the market has fallen and I am £500 up from a £10 per point position, why not add another £10 'sell' so you now hold a £20 per point position? Blackjack players 'double down'. You do the same or just increase it in some way. Now when it falls you are £1500 up! Easy. No, not so easy. Put on an extra £10 when the market has fallen 50 points then when it rises 25 points you are not up at all but only at the break-even point. When it goes back to its starting position at 14,000 you are now £500 down plus £40 in spreads! Did you just get greedy? You bet into a winning position as the 'experts' recommend, but this is not like increasing your stake when you have a great hand in poker. The 'experts' also include those who work in some way with the SB bookies: they put forward all sorts of strategies that look convincing but they know will fail. Attempting to accelerate your winnings might just accelerate your losses. Your doubling down has left you doubled up and writhing about on the sofa.

SCALPING. There are those who try to get in and out within seconds. This is known as 'scalping'. It is in the SB bookies' terms and conditions that they can requote prices when they like, which is a great little caveat to execute in order to stop any advantage the scalper might gain. If you spot the market is falling and so place a 'sell' trade, they might well requote you as it falls further. When I wasn't requoted I often *lost* money. With the same falling market and the same 'sell' trade placed, the trade goes through. It just so happens that instantly the market reverses and I am plunged into the shit. To make matters worse you will then find it surprisingly difficult to close this losing position as the market continues to climb. You enter self-psychological warfare as you decide to hang on in there, waiting for that reverse. You feel a little cheated that you are now in this position. You eventually close at a loss. They spend a lot of money on their Java programmers. They have not become a multibillion-pound business by accident. I am sure the SB bookies understand the psychology of refusing orders; delay and destroy is their mantra. I am not playing this game any longer. 'FTSE' will now only mean what I do with my partner when we are out in a restaurant.

SHOULD I STAY OR SHOULD I GO? What do you do if your position goes against you? Hold on and hope it reverses or get out fearing the worst? I have both gotten out and held on. Sometimes my decision paid off, sometimes it didn't. I have also increased my stake, betting into a winning position and coming out thousands up. This strategy has also cost me too. I have held both losing positions and winning positions in the hope that my losing positions would reverse and my winning positions would increase. I have had losing positions give me an even bigger loss and also give me a profit, and had winning positions grow further and also reverse and give me big losses. Whatever you do, however clever and informed and level-headed and financially secure you are, the SB bookies will fuck you sooner or later. They will screw you over far more than you could ever have envisaged when you set out on this dumb-ass escapade.

'AVERAGING DOWN'. The market moves against you by fifty points. You are already betting £10 a point so you are £500 down. Do you hang in there or take your losses and run? I have no idea what others call it or what the SB industry and their psychologists refer to it as, but I thought of it as 'averaging down'. You could close your position, take a £500 hit then place a buy and hope it keeps on climbing to get your £500 back. If you close your position and reopen it the other way then you have, in effect, doubled your spread. You go another £10 sell instead, taking the bull by the horns. The gambler is generally an aggressive beast and will take the fight to them; this is another reason why the bookie in whatever arena, who has the edge in the first place, always does so well! So now, if you take the average of your two positions and their opening points, you only need it to fall 25 points (from its new higher position 50 away) to break even, then anything beyond that is a bonus (let's discount the spread for simplicity's sake). But if the position continues to go against you, then you get into a worse position. Maybe you are 100 points in the wrong direction now, so you sell again for £20. You are now holding a £40 position. You have built your stake into a losing position. I have seen profits result from this strategy but I've also put myself in trouble. Equally, I have also added into an already winning position only to see it reverse and give me an unhealthy loss.

ON THE NIGHT SHIFT. You could hold your position overnight. The SB bookies will charge you interest for this. Holding your position overnight also has other major drawbacks. Even though the adverts make it look cool to be trading into the small hours, it ain't. Most of us have to go to work in the morning. You cannot watch your positions 24 hours a day. They don't stay up late to help you but will switch to their daytime operators in Australia. The SB bookies' employees in the UK have better things to do at 3 a.m. on a Wednesday morning, like sleeping. You will not feel the advantage in the morning after having an interrupted sleep and by the end of the week you will be knackered, making your SB decisions even harder to fathom. Sooner or later you will wake up to find your position has been closed whilst you slept. The market number might be exactly where it was the night before but the volatility meant you have no position remaining. The SB bookies have a lot of scope to alter these premarket numbers. It is only when the market is open that they need to quote real numbers. My positions have been closed at night as the market number set by them fell to the level where my equity was insufficient, only to ping back up the instant it hit this point. The SB bookies employ some of the best people in their IT departments, who set the parameters. Who knows how they operate other than themselves? Can and does the regulator monitor this? I have seen some odd-looking premarket spikes. As I was running various companies' platforms at the same time I could compare them. Often there was nothing in common. It looked like two different periods. Why would one company's premarket graph remain very stable yet the other had a massive jolt in the middle? They were both 24-hour sites so it made no sense. It makes sense now. People put on those stop-losses. They get hit during the night. Or your equity is not sufficient to sustain price swings. You wake up and you are dead in the water. What's stopping your SB provider taking the premarket number to a point where it hits your stop-losses or lack of equity threshold? They may incur costs if it hits the positions where other gamblers have set levels where they automatically take profits, but any system worth its salt will be able to offset these losses against the profits. They can carry out these operations precisely. It's not a difficult operation as the number of stop-losses greatly outweigh their opposite counterpart, and the equity mentality of the gambler means that they will trade too large vis-à-vis the threshold point so these can easily be crossed too. Also, the 'take-profits' may well be set at a much more distant level than the stop-losses. People get scared more easily, another factor that plays into the SB bookies' hands in numerous scenarios. Losing a grand or five is a massive deal to many people. They won't be able to save this again for a year. They create a price not too dissimilar to competing high-street bookies offering you different odds on a horse. That stop-loss puts *them* in control, not *you* as you believe. Losing money out-of-hours feels like losing a bet before the horses have even come under starter's orders. They do their best to shoot the horse dead on the way to post, as it's going behind or when it's waiting in the stalls.

Or they get it in the stables as it sleeps. That Java programme can destroy both the shorts and longs. Volatility in the premarket numbers of closed markets can be the result of overnight Asian markets or news, but what's to stop the SB bookies artificially introducing whatever number suits them? The spread-better will turn on their iPads before their partner is awake or whilst sitting on the toilet with their smartphones to see that their horse will never be coming under starter's orders. The SB bookies' Urgent-message-fund-your-account-even-though-we-know-you-are-asleep warning has popped into your inbox. This might be your first indication that you are fucked. You get to work and see one or several sent to you at around 3 a.m. Any spread-better knows what they will do next.

Here we find another trick of the trade. The SB bookies are proud to boast about how narrow their spread is: only one or two points on major indices. But out-of-hours trading is a different ball game. Want to fund your account and get a position running again? Of course you do! You're a gambler. Sorry, *trader*. Now you find you are faced with a six-point spread! Wait a few more hours and you are offered a four-point spread before the market finally opens and you get that two-point spread again. But psychology being what it is, you can't wait until then, so have to suffer the bigger spread. Add into the equation that your initial position that was closed incurred a two-point spread at best and you have *de facto* opened a new position with an eight-point spread!

That £10 per point bet put on during actual Dow hours and costing £20 in spread has now cost £80 plus the overnight interest! Think you have big balls and can handle all these tricks and all the stress; think you are wiser and more knowledgeable than me? The bigger your bollocks, the more you will lose. The size of your balls only matters in one respect: as my dad would say, "They'll have your guts for garters." As I would say, "They'll have your balls for the driving range in the morning."

Anyway, you can't stare at a little screen all day, let alone at night. You should be concentrating on your job. If you do then you'll have a better chance of promotion and actually earning more money than you would through gambling, have more time for people and avoid having accidents because you were distracted by the FTSE suddenly jumping a hundred points. Would not want to have to sit in court and tell them how I was distracted whilst driving as my attention was fixed on my smartphone, mounted the pavement and killed a child. Or tell this to the child's mum and dad. I'm sure something like this will happen one day if it hasn't already.

LONG-STAY OVERNIGHT INTEREST. Whatever position you hold over a holiday period you will have been stung by the overnight interest. The SB bookies tell you how tight their spreads are; I only discovered this hidden charge after I had incurred it. The London market is shut, the US is open (they even open Boxing Day) but bound to be light volumes. Why did you hold a position over a holiday period where you will be stung with fees and the market won't move much anyway? Short answer: desperation. Even though the US market is open, the massive spread on FTSE still holds (with IG, I noticed when I was gambling). What risk do they actually take? What costs have they actually incurred? If you hold your position, day after day, waiting for that big fall or that big rise, it will cost you. So even when the market is flat, you lose. Chances are though, with the built-in volatility of the market your losses from this will dwarf those annoying overnight interest charges. Never had a good explanation about why they can charge overnight interest. Surely it should be *them* who pay *me* as they are holding *my* equity? How can they charge interest on both a sell and a buy? Surely they should cancel themselves out to some extent? This is not small change; the UK regulator estimates that they hold £3.5 billion of our money!

THE PLATFORM. That online 'trading platform' is no more sophisticated than an online betting slip. However, the SB bookies will highlight the sophistication of their 'trading platform'; you can set up all sorts of automatic systems to 'maximise your profit'. This technological illusion does the trick for the SB companies. There is an obvious conflict of interest here that is staring you in the face but you choose to ignore it. They might call it 'buy/sell' or sex it up a bit and call it 'call/put' to make you feel like a real trader – but remember you are not, you are a real idiot. Are they helping *you* take money off of *them* by giving you the latest trading innovations and technology? Come on! They somehow manage to trick you into *believing* that all this really will help. That's what it's there for – and to speed up the extraction process from the target client and to make him bet – and lose – larger and larger amounts. Even when it doesn't work he'll use it again, convinced that he'll know better next time. They will also tell you how their execution costs are better than their rivals'. Every spread-better gets annoyed with 'slippage', where the price quoted on the screen is not the actual one you will get, so they will market themselves as your friend who won't do that to you – watch those caveats though; there might well be substantial periods when they can. They will only market these 'benefits' so you will think the terms are 'fairer' and therefore bet more, and therefore lose more. Think of your lovely trading platform as a diving platform – you believe the pool is full of water but as your head hits the bottom you realise all but six inches has been drained, as they wanted to fill their private pool next door.

SUNDAY TRADING. I also used to stay up for the 11 p.m. premarket open on a Sunday night. I have seen the Dow premarket open instantly a hundred or more in one direction only to come back to where it started almost straight away. I have had those 'urgent' messages drop into my inbox seconds after this out-of-hours opening. The first time I noticed this I got away with it but it almost gave me a heart attack. My strategy to handle this sudden spike before the almost instant pull-back was to make a £10,000 deposit a minute or so before the premarket opened. Whether this saved me so that the SB computer system was then unable to spike sufficiently to wipe me out, I'll never know, or it just couldn't run a programme to deal with this sudden burst of funds seconds before opening. You'd never get those funds on in time after the event. You'd just be wiped out. No, I added them before – just in case. It might even have been a manual operation on their part. Only the SB bookies know exactly what goes on behind the scenes. That £10k of extra equity would require such a large spike to wipe me out it seemed a highly unlikely event – the thought still killed me though. Without this £10k they could have taken that £10k that was already supporting my position. I would be almost suicidal to see this disappear only to see the market return; I can only imagine how I'd feel if they had somehow managed to spike it to also take the £10k I had just funded. A spike can occur at any point in the night, of course. You curse and swear when you discover your positions and balance are both zero. But you don't say 'fuck it' and quit. You already have another position running!

The trouble with my strategy of adding £10k to my account premarket is that once the money is in there you then use it for the following week's collateral. You do not refund it back to your account. Sometimes you will. Often you will say to yourself that you will. But then you are too busy with real life to sort it out. Before you know it, you are dipping into this number. You may even say to yourself that when your balance returns to £10k then you'll refund it. You find yourself thinking this with whatever number you have funded your account with; it's that 'winning back your losses' mentality. We all know this sounds crazy but you will end up thinking this way, whether you play poker or spread-bet or anything else for that matter. Collateral damage will take on a whole different meaning for the gambler. Even if you succeed in winning it back you still don't refund it (Read Chapter 7, 'How We Gamble').

THE STOP-LOSS. This is there to stop you incurring any further losses. It is there as a safety mechanism. This is what the SB bookies inform you. Like they offer this to you to do you a favour. In a yo-yoing market, a stop-loss is likely to be triggered. A stop-loss still means you have lost. You might not lose any more but you have still lost. You might even feel grateful that they informed you of this miracle cure; it's just that you lost money out of the arrangement. You have been conned again and you haven't even realised it.

In normal hours, the market can very, very easily hit your stop-loss then ping back the other way. You can also set up the opposite; to take profits when it hits certain levels. Gamblers generally do this when they are unable to monitor their positions, much like the stop-loss. Where are the respective points set? Do the stop-lossers lose more than the profit-takers make? Only the SB bookies have the data on this and they're not telling – about this or anything else either! I would imagine that there are many more stop-losses set than the opposite and that the SB companies do very well out of them. I draw this conclusion from the fact that they encourage us to do it! I have set up trades to click in with a sell every time it falls 50 points. It did this four times. I still remember where I was when I set this up – from the toilet of the airport departure lounge. Yes, the gambler will bet wherever he is. Nowadays, if you hear groaning from the toilet cubicle next to you it will not be a couple having sex but someone being screwed by some gambling app. But my profits grew and grew. Paper profits, that is. Then it pinged back up 200 points. Found this out once I had reached the hotel after a nervous three-hour transit from the airport. Not a great way to start a holiday.

Don't think you can set one up to protect yourself over the weekend. If you have set a stop-loss 50 points below where the market closes and it opens Sunday night 200 below where the market closed, this is now your new effective stop-loss point. You will suffer this 200-point drop. If it then suddenly pings back up 200, then too bad! You have set up a stop-loss and you have been stopped out 200 below.

Lose big, bet small. At some point you will get that big win and also suffer that big loss. You might want to get straight back in again. Or the stress of it all, win or lose, will mean that you will decide to take a break. After a big loss, you might well tell yourself to calm down and get back in with a very low stake, say only £2 a point. A month or two later you are whacking on those £10 and £20 bets again. Before you know it you are back at the point where you were a few months before! You might play about with those £2 bets for a while and get in and out very quickly to make £8 or £10. No, not thousand, just £8 or £10!

Why would you do this? First, because you have to bet. Second, you want to convince yourself that you can make a profit – even if you lost £10k the previous week! Third, to get some level of satisfaction even if it is a pyrrhic victory. This applies equally to spread-betting, high-street bookies and to poker. Even though bingo and casinos are purely games of chance, those who find themselves attracted to these will also follow this pattern.

THE SPREAD. I noticed one SB bookie has reduced their spread on the Dow once more. It's now 1.8 points and not 2 points. They made a big fanfare about this and how they were doing it in the clients' interest, 'responding to our clients' needs'. But they are not in the business of giving money away. The gambler gets tricked into believing that they have a better deal and are being treated more fairly. The SB bookie knows that the reduced spread will mean an increase in gambling and any loss they make from the tighter spread will be greatly offset by increased profit from current and switching clients. They also do not tell you that this low spread is hardly across the board, and is only during market trading hours. There are markets with unbelievably high spreads. They know that you will want to try these other markets at some point. They know this as they know the psychology of the gambler and have seen it in practice a thousand times before. The gambler will not stick with the in-hours low spread of the Dow or the FTSE. They will convince themselves there is money to be made in less popular markets, such as the Spanish IBEX 35 or the Italian whatever-it-is. The gambler thinks they are clever moving into a lower-traded market and that even with the increased spread, it is well worth it. The SB companies do not highlight the fact that the margin is high during trading hours and outrageous outside these hours. But moving into less popular markets is about as shrewd as switching from betting on Royal Ascot to going over to an evening meeting on the all-weather at Wolverhampton.

DAYLIGHT SAVING. The SB bookies have their steady cash flows from overnight interest charged and the spread they offer. The way around this is not to hold a position overnight and only bet during market hours. But at best, you will just lose money more slowly this way. At least you will also be able to sleep safe in the knowledge that you won't wake up in the shit in the morning. Sometimes you will wake up annoyed that you didn't hold that position as now you would be sitting pretty – you believe you are missing out on easy profits. But your profits will not offset your losses and those trading costs you incur. You do not realise this until later, usually years later. So you will hold that winning position as you believe it will grow. It might – could also reverse. You will also hold that losing position in the hope it *will* reverse. You will not sleep well again.

INSIDER TRADING. A share price can easily move 20% in a single day. How can you profit from this? To put it simply, neither you nor I can. You might be lucky – or just lose a fortune. But if you have inside knowledge, then you can! Insider trading is, of course, illegal in the real world of buying/selling shares. But in spread-betting? Get a third party to do it for you and use the cloak of spread-betting and you might well get away with it. Do the spread-betting companies report this suspicious behaviour to the authorities? They could even benefit from it themselves. Those clients who regularly get it right, they can track and use for their own benefit. These individuals might have an inside source or be an inside source themselves in a government department about to release economic data on employment or manufacturing, or they might be in a ratings agency. The list is almost endless. In 2016, surveys on whether Brexit would happen could massively impact sterling. If you knew the content of these surveys before they were released, you could benefit quite easily. You could add in a layer so that you become hidden. Someone in the Cayman Islands? Or just your mate on Canvey Island would do. It will be way too late to trade on so-called 'market-sensitive information' by the time CNBC report it. The market may even then move in the opposite direction to what you expected from this good or bad news. You are too late. You were not in the loop. Bet on it now and there's a good chance you will lose. Others take their profit while you get in to take a loss. The betting companies who spot suspicious betting patterns in, say, tennis do report these things to the authorities. But then they would find it much more difficult to benefit from it themselves plus it presents them as a responsible company and this sort of positive publicity for the betting industry can only be a good thing for them.

DATES FOR YOUR DIARY. Thursdays and Fridays (and Fed days) are the real money winners and losers for the spread-better. There are others depending on the market of your choice. Can easily move up 100 points then straight down again or vice-versa. Five-hundred-point swings destroy everyone. Could move up hundreds then down hundreds within 10–20 minutes. The SB providers have a party on these nuclear days. They could sit on their hands and watch the money roll in but they are too busy taking phone calls from desperate punters. Destroys you whether you are long or short. And if you want to trade when the data comes out then you will face a bigger spread as data release happens an hour before the market opens (for the Dow). This was often the most stressful part of the week for me, as not only did I try to react to market-sensitive data but I tried to do it whilst I was supposed to be working too. Not easy when you're a teacher! Often I had a position running and just had to leave it and wait an hour until school had finished and I could check. This was even more stressful! Then there were staff meetings. I had no chance of checking anything during these. I may be able to dodge a bullet or two but why did I still believe I could dodge a WMD? Even more bizarrely, I actually believed I could bat it back to them, like some cunning cartoon character, and make a fortune. But usually it ends up in an 'Itchy and Scratchy' type bloodbath and I am not as clever as that little mouse. Data can be better than expected and the market goes down or worse than expected and the market goes up. No, I have not got that back-to-front. It could go the other way too. Or just bounce around. As the market has a distinct tendency to zigzag, any profit is only though luck and the probability that you have to be right some of the time. Your big win days will not compensate for your big loss days and ditto for your small win/small loss days and everything else in between. The wins and near-big wins are what drives the gambler. Just like a golfer who scores well on one hole and thinks they can do this again and again. In theory, they can. In practice, it's only the scratch golfer or professional who can. But the golfer keeps on trying. The spread-better keeps on gambling...

BIGGER BETS. As my losses grew I was betting £10, £20 a point, straight off. Then it got MASSIVE. Add a zero to those numbers! My trading balance started spinning by the thousand rather than by the hundred within an hour. Then came the ultimate bet. I can hardly believe I did it. £500 a point on the FTSE. With a one-point spread, this meant I was already £500 down the instant I placed the trade. The plan was to get in and out very quickly. I remember feeling sick as I actually hit the 'place trade' button. But luck was on my side. I waited for the one point to return me to zero then three points in my favour then bam! Close the position and a cool £1.5k! It was just nuts. What if the market had instantly moved 50 points against me, which it is prone to doing? I repeated this trick several times (see below). Not everyone will reach this stage. I give myself a gold DFC badge for this. The same applies for those, like me, who hold a massive position over the weekend. Anything could happen. China release economic data on a Saturday. I went through a patch of always holding a massive sell position over the weekend as I was convinced Israel would bomb Iran at the weekend. I once made several thousand when some rating agency downgraded America's credit rating. Sent the market down 200 points the second it opened. Also did well out of elections, which Europe like to have on a Sunday. Never suffered from my weekend positions but I so easily could have. Why does the gambler do it: desperation again. You do it to win back your now massive losses in chunks – these will then grow even larger. You might well not feel 'desperate'. You just think you are ratcheting it up, playing in some big league. No, you are just out of your league and out of your mind!

IG Statement FTSE: I also got out even quicker with these bets; the stress killed me. I went on to perform similar tricks with £500 on the Standard & Poor's (S&P), for instance. It didn't always work. I say 'tricks' but this was akin to a magician sawing *himself* in half! And I am no magician!

chris stringman

STATEMENT
04 OCT 2012
Account No. S****
Printed at 01:00:51
Page 1

ACCOUNT SUMMARY IN STERLING

Details	Total £
CASH BALANCE	11,232.11
RUNNING PROFIT OR LOSS	0.00
TOTAL SURPLUS OR DEFICIT	11,232.11

TRADE RECAP: INDIVIDUAL SHARES

Opening Date	Time	Deal Code	Details	Curr	Shares Buy (+) Sell (-)	Price	Open/ Close	Controlled Risk Premium	Commission
03OCT12	10:05	25P25R	DFB Wall Street		+£100	13480.20	Close		
03OCT12	10:05	25P25S	DFB Wall Street		+£50	13480.20	Close		
03OCT12	10:05	KAHYA2	DFB Wall Street		+£100	13480.20	Close		
03OCT12	09:00	HZT6AJ	DFB FTSE 100		-£50	5793.50	Open		
03OCT12	10:05	J9J8A5	DFB FTSE 100		+£50	5803.70	Close		
03OCT12	10:06	J86MAZ	DFB FTSE 100		-£500	5800.50	Open		
03OCT12	10:09	J5W5AQ	DFB FTSE 100		+£500	5799.50	Close		
03OCT12	10:10	J88XAZ	DFB FTSE 100		+£500	5797.50	Open		
03OCT12	10:13	KC2NAW	DFB FTSE 100		-£500	5798	Close		
03OCT12	11:21	K6G4A7	DFB FTSE 100		-£500	5814	Open		
03OCT12	11:38	LD6KAJ	DFB FTSE 100		+£500	5811	Close		
03OCT12	13:44	MRV4AD	DFB FTSE 100		+£500	5814.20	Open		
03OCT12	13:48	MTEFAM	DFB FTSE 100		-£500	5815.50	Close		
03OCT12	14:46	NWS3A5	DFB FTSE 100		+£50	5814.30	Open		
03OCT12	20:29	STJ6AL	DFB FTSE 100		-£50	5815.50	Close		

CLOSED POSITIONS AND LEDGER TRANSACTIONS IN STERLING

Date	Deal Code	Details	Shares Buy (+) Sell (-)	Opening Level	Closing Level	Amt Due to you or us (-)
03OCT12		BROUGHT FORWARD				23,316.11
		BET CLOSINGS				
03OCT12	25P25R	DFB Wall Street	-£100	13439	13480.20	-4,120.00
		D2V4AZ is now completely closed.				

S**** | 01:00:51 | 04 OCT 2012 | Page 2

CLOSED POSITIONS AND LEDGER TRANSACTIONS IN STERLING

Date	Deal Code	Details	Shares Buy (+) Sell (-)	Opening Level	Closing Level	Amt Due to you or us (-)
03OCT12	25P25S	DFB Wall Street	-£50	13461.50	13480.20	-935.00
		EL2AAK is now completely closed.				
03OCT12	KAHYA2	DFB Wall Street	-£100	13435.50	13480.20	-4,470.00
		D6P4AG is now completely closed.				
03OCT12	J9J8A5	DFB FTSE 100	-£50	5793.50	5803.70	-510.00
		HZT6AJ is now completely closed.				
03OCT12	J5W5AQ	DFB FTSE 100	-£500	5800.50	5799.50	500.00
		J86MAZ is now completely closed.				
03OCT12	KC2NAW	DFB FTSE 100	+£500	5797.50	5798	250.00
		J88XAZ is now completely closed.				
03OCT12	LD6KAJ	DFB FTSE 100	-£500	5814	5811	1,500.00
		K6G4A7 is now completely closed.				
03OCT12	MTEFAM	DFB FTSE 100	+£500	5814.20	5815.50	650.00
		MRV4AD is now completely closed.				
03OCT12	STJ6AL	DFB FTSE 100	+£50	5814.30	5815.50	60.00
		NWS3A5 is now completely closed.				
03OCT12		Returned to card ****2920				-5,009.00
04OCT12		CARRIED FORWARD				11,232.11

This statement was generated outside Market hours. Please note that for valuation purposes, all open positions are valued at the closing mid price. However, for the purposes of any margin call calculation, the appropriate bid or offer price for long and short positions respectively will be used. Therefore the amount due for immediate payment will differ when the market re-opens.

THE CONSTANT GAMBLER. My mind was occupied by gambling 24/5 – let's call it 24/7, as I worried/thought/planned over the weekend too. Not forgetting the actual trauma of late Sunday night – it didn't matter where I was; I needed to see those numbers constantly. You think this gives you 'control'. But you are running out of control. I had heard about 'Google Goggles' that were coming out soon, with a heads-up display inside. This could have been the next step for me; another step too far. I had already walked way over the edge and was just about to disappear down into the ravine like Wile E. Coyote; I had been walking on thin air for much longer than he ever did. Whatever new strategy I adopted or market I tried, l had as much success as Mr Coyote's new ideas with ACME's latest product – these were also 'innovative tools'! The markets can twist and turn and move at whatever pace suits them, as nimbly as the Roadrunner. But still the doomed cartoon character persists – as does the gambler who will always carry on regardless. Whether they are fucked off and depressed and desperate, or they are winning and are content or elated, it makes little difference; they will still bet big/small and frequent/infrequent. There is little correlation between the size and frequency of a gambler's bets with whether they are actually winning or losing. I could equally take a break after winning or losing. I was always going for 'the big push' for one last time; this strategy led to carnage in WW1, and had much the same effect on my bank balance. Would I put £1000 on a horse, just to get it to the stalls even before it ran then have to fork out even more once the gate popped open when it fell behind or was in front? But that's exactly what I ended up doing with spread-betting. Spread-betting is the ultimate in in-running bets. Sometimes my horse would never even make it to post. Sometimes it wouldn't even get to the racecourse but would lose consciousness on its early morning journey. Who would give the kiss of life to a horse! But that's no worse than what I tried with my efforts to revive my spread-betting positions.

The rule is to, 'Sell in May and go away'. There's no economic reason for this; none at all as far as I can see. No, it's just that betting on the market is a damn stressful pastime or occupation. It's a 24/7 beast that you can't take your eye off of. You can't relax by the poolside or be out on the golf course because you fear that any second now your positions will be wiped out. Something will happen. You can't risk this so you need to stare at a little screen all day – just in case. The only way not to worry about your positions is not to have any. The markets have statistically been flat over the summer as the real money men want a break.

FREE SPINS! I have seen my SB account numbers, made up of 15–20 bets that I have built up, rolling onwards and upwards to £41k profit. That's a lot of dough! My positions often had BIG numbers after them. I rolled my positons – like a craps' dice time and time again – because I'm a gambler. Gambling is as much an adrenaline sport as white-water rafting down the Zambezi. Could lose it all. This time I kept half of it. Other times I actually lost money from strong positions. But it's just great for the gambler to see a whole set of numbers, each in the thousands. Reminds me of the pot going up and up with every spin of the fruit machine reels when it gives you free winning spins once in a while when I was a kid. But a fruit machine always ends up the winner. So did the SB website. So will any gambling website. These big wins and near-wins trick you into believing that you will be that long-term winner; that you will get more wins and bigger wins. I tried to 'Get rich or die tryin'' as 50 Cent recommends. Some literally will – will do the latter, that is. I just beat my finances to within an inch of its life.

SECRET LOVER. When my partner goes out to meet some friends I secretly invite in my friend, my mistress. She is a fucking evil mistress, mind. She can't give me what I want but I give her what she wants, far too often. Get some sort of peace when I am alone with her and my partner won't be back for hours, much like a junkie can shoot up knowing they will not be disturbed and they can enjoy the pleasures of 'Golden Brown' alone (as an 11-year-old I took The Stranglers lyrics at face value). I got the same sort of peace and rush that a heroin addict gets. My mistress just went by another name – Miss Jones. Okay, so Dow Jones were actually two blokes but long since dead blokes who surely couldn't have envisaged people gambling on their names people gambling on his name. Do you feel ok with the fact that you are *only* cheating on your wife financially? The Dow is a mistress that comes out in the afternoon and evening but I still had to see her in the morning when she is getting ready. I am not alone in choosing the Dow over a European index so I can focus on my job during the day (this soon changes!) then focus on her in the evening. If you work nights, you may well bet on the Nikkei. Sometimes though, she gets up early or stays awake all night and cheats on me by the time I see her again. "Why did you do that?" I have asked her all too often. She can be a real bitch! But I still stuck with her for years. Friday night, Dow shuts down for the week. Market closed symbols appear. Takes me an hour to come down sufficiently as like a junkie I was: a) feeling guilty/stupid, b) thinking about how to stop, c) longing (logging-in?) for my next fix and planning how to avoid its dangerous side effects. Thought C is always the dominant one for the gambler.

A WIN, WIN! I had some concept in my head that spread-betting was like betting on the horses where you almost couldn't lose. I had this analogy that it was like backing a horse where the minute they were in front is the point at which you were allowed to cash in your betting slip for first place. Most horses are in front at some point. The Dow can bounce up and down so whether you are long or short there will be an opportunity to cash out. Easy pickings then. If you think along these lines, you will be sadly disappointed! You will take profits too early and hang on in too long with losses. When you are long and it rises 50 points you might cash out only after it has fallen back to being only up 10, or it may even fall another 100 points but you hang on in there for it to go up again where it was only an hour or two before – but it never does. Yes, there are many scenarios you could consider. You think you have a plan. Then somewhere down the line when you sit there with your massive loss you will be lost in confusion as to how you never managed to make that profit. Don't be confused any longer. You failed because the whole system, from the SB bookies to the markets themselves, is set up for you to fail.

THE VIEWING PUBLIC. If you are spread-betting you are in no way affecting the market, just like if you are betting on the weather, you have no influence on whether there will be snow at Christmas. Institutions that are actually investing real money move the market. Those investment banks with their multiple screens set out for each individual trader (*real* traders, who get paid to do their jobs) are the ones who make the Dow or FTSE move. The millisecond economic data is announced, their system trades automatically thanks to very clever guys in their IT department. Any gambler sitting at home with their laptop or on the train with their mobile device cannot possibly react at these speeds. But you believe you are reacting – that feeling of being in 'control' again. You are working with third-hand numbers, relayed to you by the SB firm who get their data from a third party. You cannot compete.

THE EQUITY REQUIREMENT. The SB bookies convince you that you now have more capital, there will be more profits for you when they lower the equity requirement. Again, you fall for another one of their tricks.

The equity requirement might mean you need to hold £100 for every £1 per point you bet on the Dow. Each market has its own requirement. So if you hold £1000 you can bet £10 per point on the Dow. The equity requirement has been reduced even within the few years I was gambling heavily. It used to require £120 per point on the Dow but with five years this was down to just £60. Why would the SB bookie offer this? 'An improvement to the service we offer for our customers', or some other such bullshit. They do this to make more money, more quickly. The spread-better has a tendency to over bet. It never starts out like this but it will end up this way. They will bet very near to the limit allowed for any given amount of held equity. In theory, they now need only fund their account with half the amount previously required so it could actually appear that this will benefit the client. But it will have the opposite effect. The client will end up funding their account more often. The client will just double their bet or just up it if the equity requirement is halved. Let's say the equity requirement dropped from £100 to £50. If you had £1500 in your account, when the position has moved against you the SB bookie will be asking for more funds when you fall below the minimum holding of £1000 when you are betting £10 a point and it drops 50+ points.

Remember you need to hold £100 for every £1 bet (£1000 for that £10 per point bet). So, when the Dow turns against you by more than 50 points, those fund requests start dropping into your inbox. With the new, lower equity requirement even if you keep the same balance of £1500 but now you are betting £20 a point, the Dow again only has to tiptoe over 25 points before those fund requests come through again. You have lost £500, the same as before but from only a 25-point move. As it moves a further 25 points against you, you lose another £500 to take your total loss to a grand, double what it would have been with that higher equity requirement, after you have funded your account, which you are now accustomed to doing. You are now playing with bigger amounts: bigger bets and bigger amounts to find when you inevitably find yourself in the shit. Now the psychology of it changes. This is no longer like that game of poker you play with your mates for small change and fun. Even if you stick with your original bet size, it just means you will let it run twice as far against you as you previously had and lose twice the amount this way too. Add in the central feature of the markets – volatility – and your big bet with a low equity requirement gets the tills ringing. It is starting to snowball. They haven't bullied you into anything. It's a very clever con on their part. You haven't even noticed what they are doing or how it works. Even when they close your positions, they don't just close them all at once and leave you that £1000 that you had required. Their Java-programmed system will close positions gradually so that they can take you all the way down to a balance of zero. I've had big positions then discovered the system has whittled me down to a £2 bet with only a couple of hundred left in my account! It felt like someone had looted my golf clubs and I now had to resort to playing a round with only a seven-iron.

HINDSIGHT. Not just what the losing jockey sees (!) but what you seem to believe could really have happened – and you still believe it will in the future, in real time. There are many third-parties out there who easily convince you that this will be possible. I could have cleaned up if I'd backed that horse at 33-1. Great if I'd shorted oil at $147 a barrel then got out at $35 a barrel, and even then gone long, out again when at $120 then short again to $35. The SB gambler can see this (from the past!) then thinks making money is easy. But it doesn't work like this. In reality, may have got on short at $100 a barrel as surely it can't go any higher, then by the time it's gone to $147 you're dead! Or, you manage to hold on to your position, keep funding it all the way to $147 then take your nice profit as it falls to $80. You have some profit – but don't forget there are other charges you have incurred whilst you held on and on. So you take a break. It falls to $70 a barrel. This is really low, you think, so you go long again. So, by the time it gets to $35 a barrel, you may have lost all your lovely profit. Maybe you listened to all those as it went up and up telling you it would soon hit $200 a barrel. So you got in at $100 then again and again and again so by $147 you have a lovely profit. But it's going to $200, right? So not only do you hold your long position but you increase it as it falls (a form of 'averaging down' – making the most out of the 'cheaper' price, in effect). By the time it hits $125 a barrel you are now at break-even. Most gamblers will keep on funding, some more than others. You will now lose somewhere between a bit and a fortune. If you hold on and hold on, by the time it hits $35 a barrel you will be sleeping on the streets. You have lost your house and have no money to bet when it starts going up again. The bailiffs have taken your possessions and your wife has taken your kids. Worst-case scenario, but it happens.

You have not been 'unlucky'. If you decide to throw *yourself* in with the lions, then don't complain that you were just 'unlucky' that the lions were hungry that day as they maul you and slash your throat.

One of Bloomberg's female presenters was always going on about the market finding a bottom. This was when the Dow was around 11,000. You only know you have hit the bottom years after the event – in hindsight. Sure, there are many who piled in long at 9000 or 8000 only to lose a fortune. Do not try to ride the bull up and ride the bear down. Bears do not all hibernate in winter, whatever the averages and statistics might trick you into believing. Just remember that both a bull or a bear seem very happy to turn around and rip you to shreds!

The Dow rises from 14,000 to 15,000. Kick yourself that it now falls back to 14,500 and you didn't get in short at 15,000? You could just as easily have gone short at 14,500 and either have been closed out at 15,000 or at best just got back to break even. You would not have made any money but you will convince yourself when you see drops and rises that you missed out on something. No way would you suddenly have ploughed in big at 14,000 and taken a massive profit at the peak of 15,000. You are far more likely to have built up your stake from say, 14,200 and kept on building to 14,800 then put some more in as it fell to 14,600 then got out at 14,500 at break-even at best. You will then regret not taking the profit at 15,000 but will somehow believe you have learned from this experience and will do better next time as if somehow next time you will know exactly where the short-term peaks and troughs are! No, you are throwing darts at a dartboard blindfolded. A lot of the time you will get in and out at the *wrong* time and face the *wrong* way too many times. Takes a disproportionately small number of holding-on-to-losing-position times to destroy your profits from your winning ones. Another scenario: you are short but can't believe why it keeps on going up. You are sure it will fall so you add to your short position to take advantage of the high number before the fall ('averaging down'). At some point, you will have built up such a large position *facing the wrong way* as it continues to climb that you are either closed out or get out at a big loss. Same applies to the long position for the reverse scenario. You will have some blinding days. But by the end of the month or year or however long you stick at it, you will be destroyed. It is almost certain that you cannot get in and out at the right time. You are destined to lose. You might be lucky sometimes (you might well think it was your skill and judgment) but don't kick yourself when you don't choose the right time; you were just lucky when you *did* choose the right times. You are far more likely to get it wrong so you cannot blame or bemoan your bad luck when it does go wrong. It is set up to go against you. It is no different from radio station hopping in the car. Sometimes you find that song you love – but it is already halfway through or almost over. Occasionally, you catch it at the start. Then when it is finished you hope something else good will come along. Could be a song you hate though.

Some reading this will think that £10 a point on the Dow is crazy. That's what I would have thought back at the beginning. I was only betting £2 a point. It soon rose to £4 then £8. We all do this. We then go nuclear sooner or later. You can never imagine even contemplating this at the beginning – but then you find yourself pushing that button.

A BIG LOSS DAY. I pushed the button. My partner cooked the meal whilst I sat on the toilet and logged on, just in time for the Fed's 'QE to infinity' decision. Shot me down in flames instantly. I tried to trade through it but as the market zigzagged around I lost big time. Firefighting really. At one point, whilst it was still zigzagging all over the place, I had to eat with my partner and just leave it and try not to worry. Food was ready so I couldn't stay any longer. Position had worsened 20 minutes later, after we had eaten. Felt fucking tense during the meal, which in effect I would soon find out cost me a grand to eat.

Made TWO card payments for £6k EACH in a couple of hours and lost around £30k in two days! More than my annual salary! Still left a £150 Dow sell to roll over until the next day – chasing my losses. I threw everything at it; like I was attacking a British army Challenger tank with a chainsaw. Started with the system closing me out for an instant almost £17k loss. Seventeen-thousand-pound-loss as I sat on the toilet! That's a big fucking loss! Felt physically sick from that. Tried to trade my way through it (!). Remember, these are not bets on say, a horse to win with me staking £150. No, this is £150 A POINT! Went through the whole range of the gambler's emotions in the space of an hour or two: panic, frustration, pain (physical and mental), desperation, (limited) relief, moments of satisfaction, betrayal (by the actual markets themselves), deceit (of my partner), grief (when I realised my loss for the night), loneliness and isolation, anger, a deep sense of my own stupidity, anguish and a touch of self-loathing. The negatives greatly outweigh the positives; much like my bank balance that I shuddered to look at when all those numbers with all those zeros would go through my account (again). But I still 'needed' to be in a position and ran over a £150 per point bet; that ain't small. But the only position I should be in after a day like this should have been the recovery position!

S**** | 01:04:00 | 14 SEP 2012 | Page 2

OPEN POSITIONS: INDIVIDUAL SHARES

Opening Date	Opening Time	Deal Code	Details	Curr	Shares Buy (+) Sell (-)	Opening Price	Current Price	Deposit Required	Running Profit/Loss
13SEP12	19:31	W9Q7A5	DFB Wall Street	£	-150	13549.50	13525	7,500.00	3,675.00
Totals for deals in £								**7,500.00**	**3,675.00**
							All currencies £ Equiv	**7,500.00**	**3,675.00**

CLOSED POSITIONS AND LEDGER TRANSACTIONS IN STERLING

Date	Deal Code	Details	Shares Buy (+) Sell (-)	Opening Level	Closing Level	Amt Due to you or us (-)
13SEP12		BROUGHT FORWARD				26,129.07
		BET CLOSINGS				
13SEP12	SV4FAQ	DFB Wall Street T6EFAQ opened 06SEP12. The size after this close is 31.	-£119	13276.40	13416	-16,612.40
13SEP12	25KPR2	DFB Wall Street TAZMAX is now completely closed.	-£100	13389.50	13395.50	-600.00
13SEP12	25KPRZ	DFB Wall Street WL44AB is now completely closed.	-£25	13320.50	13395.50	-1,875.00
13SEP12	TJ8NAD	DFB Wall Street T6EFAQ is now completely closed.	-£31	13276.40	13395.50	-3,692.10
13SEP12	TYA5AY	DFB Wall Street TTWVAH is now completely closed.	-£150	13435.50	13419	2,475.00
13SEP12	T9GFA4	DFB Wall Street TUM2A5 is now completely closed.	-£150	13421.50	13416	825.00
13SEP12	TYL7AY	DFB Wall Street T7ZUAH is now completely closed.	+£100	13416.50	13417.50	100.00
13SEP12	VHNXAQ	DFB Wall Street UAHAA2 opened 13SEP12. The size after this close is 68.	-£92	13411.50	13468.50	-5,244.00
13SEP12	V3K8A5	DFB Wall Street UAHAA2 is now completely closed.	-£68	13411.50	13489.50	-5,304.00
13SEP12		Card payment ****2920				6,000.00
13SEP12		Card payment ****2920				5,999.00
14SEP12		Short Interest for 13/09/12				-110.03
14SEP12		CARRIED FORWARD				8,090.54

This was my worst loss day. You can see the signs of desperation as I attempted to win it back quickly. I can still remember the first hour very clearly. But lose a fortune in a day or a month or a year, it doesn't make too much difference although your emotions are heightened!

You think the above is just nuts? Well, yes, you'd be right. It is hard to believe I would behave this way and with the FTSE a month later (see bet bigger) but gamblers end up doing such things. When you are on the verge of doing exactly the same, reread my book! Big bets, massive bets were becoming the norm. This is what all gamblers do eventually. Putting massive money on the table? No problem. It's only stake money, right? Then you lose it.

HANG ON IN THERE! I almost always seemed to want (or need) to risk it, right up until the final seconds of the trading day when the market was still open. For me this was nine o'clock UK time, spread-betting on the Dow before the bell rang (several times – they don't do understatement). Often I had to end up rolling it. You never planned to roll it; you wanted to avoid all those charges, widened spreads and widened stress. You thought you would only trade in regular market-open hours. But this doesn't last. You are down as the bell strikes so you roll it to recoup your losses the next day. You don't want to incur more spread costs by closing before the markets shut then reopening the next day, and you believe that it will reverse anyway overnight and you will be up before you even wake up. You also do this out of desperation, hope and – if you are up – the gambler's inability to stop when up (Read Chapter 7, 'How We Gamble'). You did the same the week before but you only rolled it then as you were up and wanted to increase your winnings overnight; it's just that by the morning nothing much had happened apart from waking up stressed and suffering those niggling little charges. Like staying right until the lights come on at a nightclub and then you cannot avoid the realisation that you haven't pulled. You knew 30 minutes before that it wasn't going to happen and you should just leave and avoid all the 2 a.m. carnage of drunks and fights. But no, you stayed. More of a pain in the arse than trying to get a taxi amongst the 2 a.m. chaos and you could well wake up with more of a hangover than from ten pints and a kebab. Painfully stressful, doubly so when you are trying to do this secretly, behind your partner's back. Even harder when they are sitting in the same room as you.

SWITCH MARKETS. Oil is, by its very nature, slippery. The price can move up and down like the tracing on a seismograph. But I still believed there was scope for me to make money. I did that classic gambler move of switching from one game to another in the belief that this would somehow be different. This strategy comes to you usually later on in your failing spread-betting career. You might mess around a little at the beginning then have your 'favourite' for a while then you reach this stage. Oil: when the price keeps going up and up all the bullshit talk is about how high it can go then a few years later, how low it will go. There's OPEC, the value of the dollar itself and a hundred other factors to consider. What does the outside – that would be 99.99% of us – really know? I'd given it a brief try before; I used to try and trade when the oil and gas reserve numbers were released and announced by some female reporter with suspiciously large lips on Bloomberg, reporting from the Nymex. I asked myself what I know about oil but then what did I really know about the Dow?

*

So there we are. Recognise yourself? I am not too interested in constantly reading others' 'happy' news as it gives such a false impression of someone's life when I often know far more than they publish on Facebook. Facebook is like the person in the street's own version of *Heat* magazine. I have not posted my gambling losses online. And neither has anyone else published theirs. Millions could have. But you do find the odd celebrity who reveals all or at least the courts reveal all for them. Dietmar Hamman, once of Liverpool F.C. says he lost £200k in one night spread-betting. Now that's a lot but it's all relative to one's assets. I think he started to wonder what the fuck he was doing at that point.

I thought one day – no, I *believed* one day – that I would actually visit New York out of my massive trading profits and have my picture taken with the Charging Bull in Manhattan and then wander past the New York Stock Exchange, the scene of my greatest victories. All this for sitting around in my pyjamas or sitting on the loo or walking around Sainsbury's with my mobile or… yes, this is the way us gambler think we will make millions. The cool and calculated businessmen in the SB marketing material (models, let's not forget) in their pressed suits, waiting in the executive departure lounge, smartphone in hand or relaxing in their brand-new pad with their brand-new iPad with their smiling brand-new girlfriend, making thousands and not having to worry about a day job… Well, this isn't how it happens. These are adverts. This is not reality. Try to picture yourself on the toilet or on the cramped commuter train or driving down the motorway or furtively doing what you shouldn't be doing at work or sitting downstairs when you should be upstairs seeing the kids to bed, or having sex with your wife, or putting off going to the gym, or cleaning the house or yourself… if you are already gambling then you don't so much have to picture these scenarios. You just need to *remember* them. You may have other *favourite* scenarios that you keep repeating. You can play poker or bingo or spread-bet whenever and almost wherever you like. May well be able to do this on planes soon too – and if you are travelling with your wife, you may even have to invent your own version of the mile-high club. You will go to the tiny toilet and bet from in there!

The true measure of stupidity is repeating the same thing time and time again and expecting different results. I tried to vary my strategies sometimes but the thing I missed, the thing I missed even though it was staring me in the face, was that I *was* repeating and repeating the same thing time and time again. It wasn't what I was betting on – that's irrelevant. It was the fact that I was betting – that's what I kept repeating and somehow expecting different results.

Best comedy on the radio in recent years? *The Bob Servant Emails*. Worst comedy on TV in recent years? *The Bob Servant Emails* (under a different title). Shame really that the writers can't transfer the comedy of the 'talking lion' to TV. Killed myself laughing over that one. Tried my own Bob Servant email when I received an email entitled 'Terribly' from a name on my email contact list, claiming that they had been robbed at gunpoint in Madrid. I replied by asking what I could do, then got the Western Union money transfer response. Tried to string him along by saying that I was really worried and I would fly out that night with cash and a small hand-gun (plastic composite to get it through security; respond to bullshit with bullshit). The guy sitting at his computer in Lagos or wherever never got back to me. So why do they send out these emails, even with poor English? Because they obviously work with a few people. Now I think those who actually send money are the real legends of DFC. Millions of pounds leave the UK every year through these 419 scams; this is, however, a small fraction of what the SB bookies rake in. I am not much better – I fell for that supplement in the *FT* about spread-betting. I believed it would bring me riches just like the suckers who really do believe there is a prince in Africa who needs your help to get his $40 million out of the country and he'll give you 25% of it, but first he needs £2k for the paperwork (Western Union please). I kept getting the encouragement from someone sitting at a distant desk. Didn't even have to use Western Union, just use my bank card and type in those three digits. As likely to receive thousands paid to me out of my spread-betting account as I am to be met by a talking lion on my doorstep sent from Africa!

I don't think I will relapse like so many alcoholics do, but the SB companies try to tempt me back in. I will resist the bastards. I will not get suckered back in like the alcoholic who can't resist walking down the alcohol aisle in Tesco's. They are always sending me questionnaires, emailing me about a new improved service, telling me what their new shinier logo represents, some named individual who is keen to help – they want to draw me back in, no different from your neighbourhood drug supplier who wants you back as a customer and is oh so nice to you when he sees you in the street. Don't forget The Stone Roses' late 80's classic – a song about betrayal; not unlike gambling, then! The title, as all of us of a certain generation know: 'Fools Gold'.

Watch Germany 2014 or Spain 2010 World Cup winning teams: they pass the ball around precisely. Easy for any local league team to do the same. But they can't. If they were up against these sides, it's only 11 v. 11, so why couldn't they beat them? They can't because these teams are world class and the other side have day jobs because they are miles away from making a living out of it. If you think you can beat IG with its 1000 employees, or poker players who do it for a living – versus you, there can only be one result.

Spread-betting is like they are playing poker against you – but they can see all your cards. Difficult to win at poker when you are holding your cards to actually face the guy opposite you! If you are worried about execution costs and problems when spread-betting, then just remember that the SB bookie isn't. They know that the one thing that is for sure, is one day it will be *your* execution!

ii. Come on in! The marketing of a myth

Over or under the radar, the SB industry have done a great job at getting their message out.

LIVE FROM THE TRADING FLOOR! The SB bookies get some 'economic expert' to present from their company HQ so that their company logo can be visible behind them and the trading floor, which actually isn't a trading floor at all, can also be displayed. There are lots of people behind him wearing suits and talking on phones. Lots of screens too. They're an investment bank, right? Free advertising on licence-fee funded TV or on commercial TV. They actually present themselves as no different from a bank; respectable and valued, someone you can trust.

THE TROJAN HORSE. The *Telegraph* did promotions with SB providers; then I notice later there are some pieces that highlight SB big-time winners. The SB bookies also get minor celebrities to be involved with their products. Are people encouraged to try by reading such thing? That SB supplement from the *FT* back in 2007 suckered me right in. The supplements on SB are not journalistic; they are no better than 'advertising features'. Any journo working with them to produce this seems to rely on them extensively for their information. It costs money to produce these so-called 'supplements' which the SB industry will gladly pay for – plus a bit more, a lot more, for their Trojan Horse to tag along with a respectable publication. Stick this stealth advert in a respected newspaper and you turn it into journalism at a stroke, something the public are more likely to believe than an advert.

I'D LIKE TO THANK... Some investment magazines even give them awards! The readership laps it up because they want to hear that their gambling habit is really an award-winning investment decision! Sure, these investment mags have a lot of useful and valid information, but the readers need to separate this from the crap – from the misleading and the hidden adverts. Children often regard anything printed as pure fact; are adults any different? I read how one girl said she would stop if she lost £2000 spread-betting. But I know it doesn't work like this. The SB bookie who had a hand in this article knows it doesn't work like that either. I'd like to create my own awards: I'd give out 'Trojies' for the worst (best?) Trojan Horse advertising. There would be many candidates.

OLD-SKOOL TV ADS. SaxoTraderGO on TV advertise their CFDs as an 'investment', pure and simple. The actual warning that the SB bookies are obliged to add to their ads is so small and often appears as if it has been written in a 'distressed' font, so that unless you have an HD TV the size of *Guernica*, it's practically impossible to read, especially in the few seconds you are allowed. If you didn't already know what it was, you wouldn't know what it was.

Cool-looking guy places a trade on his mobile; you get a glimpse of some green-lit, winning trade on his smartphone. Just place a trade, forget about it then come back to it hours later, whenever you want really, and wheel in the cash in a big wheelbarrow, imply those TV ads. His five digits make *him* five digits as he swipes and presses. Real businessmen and real success stories don't waste their time in a virtual world that is real enough in which to lose your very real money.

But it appeals to just about anybody, although mostly men in their arrogance or desperation, depending on how they feel in their job, in their relationship, within society and within their own skin. I am sure a fair few pensioners with a little retirement cash and a lot of retirement time get heavily involved, after all they advertise in magazines aimed at pensioners. The pensioners think their 60 or 70 years make them worldly wise. They might have been successful in their profession. But they will be conned as easily as the Alzheimer's sufferer who forks out £20k on an unnecessary new roof. The pensioner may think that the poor dementia sufferer was naïve or taken advantage of, but they are no different. The biggest players will be those in their 20s, 30s and 40s who want to be that man in the Savile Row suit in the ads. A few probably already have that made-to-measure suit and think that as they have made a success in one area of their life then by extension they will naturally be that successful spread-better or poker player too. Most will be frustrated men in suits believing that gambling is the answer. This target male, aged 20–40, also has a lot of disposable cash – which they will soon dispose of. The 'game of skill' gambler treats it professionally. We study, we strategise, we put in the hours – we believe the harder we try, the more successful we will be. I did all this. I lost £130k.

There is also an ad for FxPro running with an East European Kasparov-type character who studies the charts, even writes on a blackboard like someone out of Bletchley Park – yes, he too is a code-breaker. He will work out some formula to make himself money – like you could too if you have the right tools. Log in and you'll find them! But you are not Kasparov. In fact, you are up against Kasparov characters in whatever game you are playing. And Garry Kasparov does not try to beat his opponents whilst sitting on the toilet. You will.

VERY OLD-SKOOL: One of the SB bookies put you into a raffle to win a car if you place *x* number of trades; another offered you an iPod if you got a friend signed up who then starts trading; the SB bookie has 30 pieces of silver iPods to give out. Another tempted you with yet another 'improvement' to its trading site. You can 'test-drive' it. This benefits the SB bookie in two ways: First, they can see if it works from a software point of view, and whether they make more money with their new 'improved' system (always remember that 'improved' means for them!). Second, it sounds like something special and something that is a privilege to use. Just like test-driving an actual car; the car dealerships know that people who actually get behind the wheel are then more likely to buy. Unlike with test-driving a car, you will not drive away a happy customer and have years of happy times with your new purchase. The 'test-drive' will encourage you to trade and therefore lose; you think that you are using something new, something that will give you that edge. Even when it doesn't you will try again, convinced that it will.

SEMINARS. In seminars, they reinforce your belief that you are a trader, that the SB site is an investment vehicle, that it is a financial product; where they are coaching *you* how to make money out of *them*. They are coaching *you* how to make money out of *them*. Written it twice just in case you didn't get how nuts that statement is on first reading. I am struggling to think of something in life more bullshit than this idea. They're as good at acting as any Oscar winner. The SB business is not an illegal backstreet gambling den. Nope, the SB business is legal and corporate. Just because it has the veneer of respectability, doesn't mean it is. The SB bookies know that their clients will bet and then lose more after any seminar. We clients now have the skills, we've read that *Naked Trader* book; we come away from these seminars, logging on before we're even out the door, keener than ever to implement some new strategy we've just conjured up.

In any other sphere of education, if the student actually became worse after being taught something, the teacher would be in the shit. But with SB, the teacher will get praised and get a bonus for this increased business through bullshit education. They will highlight the sophistication of their trading tools. They are overwhelming you – you will switch from graph to graph looking for the answer. When it doesn't work, you will return to these graphs, believing that you need to work harder, educate yourself better and go to another seminar. They will keep on overloading you. They will supply 'breaking news' on the platform as you trade. This is the next trick: distract. You now have to factor this in to the equation. The fruitie makes all sorts of beeps and whistles; you look around for what it all means. The trading platform does the same. Distract and overwhelm. You will struggle to concentrate. Like a military assault. You don't realise it at the time but it works on you. It makes your decisions worse. They will tell you it informs your decisions and makes them better. Whatever they tell you, the opposite is likely to be true.

I went to a seminar at a company HQ but the SB firms also go out into the community. They hold events in many other places, such as at universities. This gives their business the respectability they need and the impression that there really is something educational about what they present. One event was held at the University of Reading, which – coincidence or not – is the alma mater of Tim Howkins, who was IG CEO until December 2015. These 'lectures' will draw in many students, who one day will earn good salaries and will then end up losing them, as well as people who have never been students but will be inspired by the setting and its implied educational nature. These investment (tax free!) information events are no better than a health information lecture which stresses the importance of smoking for health then sells you cigarettes after the event. Sounds unlikely? Cigarettes were actually marketed for people with lung problems in the 50s. Sounds crazy now, but evidently not then. Spread-bet your way to riches with guidance from the people who you need to take the money off. Apparently, this doesn't appear just as nuts as the 'smoke your way to health' idea to the thousands who attend the 'SB your way to wealth' seminars! Would a high-street bookies turn up at a university and explain how to read the form of a horse or the different sorts of bets the punter can chose, when to take your winnings (profits), the different markets you can bet in (indices, commodities) and even what to do if things don't go your way (the stop-loss)? They will invite you to these seminars, they will email you information about areas of the website which give you all the insight you need. At least at the high-street bookies educational seminar you would understand that it is all about betting – gambling pure and simple and not a tax-efficient investment vehicle.

The SB bookies have now ramped it up a gear and not only offer you an evening seminar but will invite you to spend the whole Saturday with them! You will be well and truly encouraged by Monday morning to place a 'trade'. A bit like trying out a cult for a day. You would never join a cult. But you will act in a similar way to a cult member before you know it: you will spend all your waking hours thinking about it, you will donate all or a large part of your money to them, you will neglect those around you and your job, your eating patterns will change and sometimes you just won't eat at all, then finally you will realise what you have done and ask yourself how in the hell you got suckered in once you have left. And just like in a cult, the recruiters will give you all the assistance you need; that's their main job. There may even be some Messiah figure that you aspire to be more like: the sharp-dressed guy leading the seminar or the Gillette guy from their ad. Motivate, encourage, support. Just like a cult. If a parent has been doing this with their no-hoper singer offspring for years and then they audition on *The X Factor*, Simon Cowell would say they are delusional and unfair to the child. Some would call the gambling industry con artists. If you are selling a product which claims to bring the client benefits but is almost guaranteed not to bring any whatsoever, isn't that the definition of a confidence trickster? And if you wonder what the letters IG actually stand for, then try to imagine that they have named themselves after their thousands of clients: 'Insanely Gullible' or 'Invariably Greedy' or maybe just 'Idiotic Gambler' or 'Impulsive Gambler' then at some point further down the line 'Inevitably Gob-smacked'. You are one or more of these, maybe *all* of these. And don't ever, ever forget what DFC stands for. And by the way, IG actually stands for 'Investors' Gold'. Which one do you think is the most apt?

TRADER TALK. The bingo sites run chatrooms for their predominantly female users. For the spread-better, it's all about the cash. We have no interest in having a natter. For those that do you can go to trade2win.com if you like. All of us spread-betters have massive wins as well as losses so which ones are we more likely to recount? And when the website is sponsored by FxPro, what sort of impression about spread-betting are you likely to come away with? The choice of website name already sets up that trading illusion.

'TRADING TOOLS', 'innovation'. These are bullshit terms coined by the industry to con you into believing that you have the edge over others and the markets themselves by using them. The key word here is 'believing'. You are not that difficult to convince. One of the biggest fears for the pseudo-trader is volatility – this is not unfounded! For this reason in their marketing they always emphasis that they give you the edge in volatile markets. This is what you want to hear and you actually believe it; you believe it because you *need* to believe it as you have suffered big losses because of it – of course you have. That's what markets are like! You cannot complain about the mud if you play rugby. The only edge they give you is the edge of the blade with which they will cut you to shreds.

Just look at the golfer who wants and needs to believe in that wider sweet spot on his driver to cure his slice. Golf is full of innovations and new, improved this-and-that. The male golfer loves this technical mumbo-jumbo, like *Coefficient of Restitution*. The golfer will still have his problem. The spread-better will find he now has a bigger one.

TECHNOLOGICAL ILLUSION. The SB bookies will even offer you an algorithm package if you want. You have heard about algorithms; it's what the big boys use. So it will work for you too, then. Better still, it will do the job for you, without mistakes. The Kasparov character offers it to all those losing 'traders' out there as their salvation and adds that you don't have to share your profits with computers. No, and they won't pay your losses for you either (they don't mention these)! Just use the 'algo package' and it will do all the work for you! Even when something like this doesn't work, you still believe in it. Maybe you didn't apply it right, you think. These tricks keep you believing, keep you losing. Algorithms and computers have to run the market; they need to react to data in milliseconds. No human could do this. There are automated systems in almost every area of life so it's fair enough to use them in the markets. Real algos react and re-react to other algos' reactions. This repeats and repeats. Even if the SB client is using some algo package or another, they will always be behind the curve. And if the SB company is offering this to you, then just like that stop-loss, it surely must be shit.

TRADE BIGGER! I have phoned the SB company before to place a £1 bet, which they say back to me as 'the minimum'. This is not just a throwaway line by that SB employee. This is a calculated phrase. It works on you on many levels yet it's so simple. 'The minimum' means, "Why are you trading so low? You'll get nowhere with this. No one bets this low. If you are a serious trader then you need to bet more. This is so low why are you even bothering..." They embarrass you, they soft-bully you. When I pick up my hire car, they always try to sell me an extra policy to avoid the excess if I have an accident. I always decline. They always come back with the same line: "OK, so you're going to risk it then." They know what they are doing. Must work on many who then change their minds.

THE INFORMATION ILLUSION. Walk into a bookies and you walk into a working-class world; men who have come straight from work, their clothes splattered in paint or oil. The middle class think they are better than this. They are not going to stick a few quid on a horse they know little about. In step the SB bookies and the poker sites; here we think of ourselves as 'traders' or 'players'. We do not read form guides pinned to the bookies' walls but study market strategy and economics or read books written by multiple World Series of Poker bracelet winners. The middle class are no different to the working class even though they think they are wiser and smarter. In fact, the middle class will lose more money. As a proportion of their income it will probably be the same but some will let it get out of hand. Do not look down on the plumber who sticks a fiver on some horse he has just decided on ten seconds before the off at Sandown. Many a spread-better will decide in much the same timeframe whether to bet up or down. Some punters will decide on a horse that morning or days before just like the spread-better has a clear plan in his head. Very few put any sort of bet on before doing some bullshit research. The internet now offers this information illusion for everyone. You might previously have read the finance pages of the newspaper but now you are more likely to look at a dozen online sites. The betting shop punter still likes to read the *Racing Post* pinned up between the betting slip holders and those little pen dispensers but there is also plenty of information online. You might as well not bother. The information is not there to help you win. No, it is there simply to *encourage* you to bet. We have moved largely from paper to digital or more precisely from a paper information illusion to a digital one.

SUCKER LITERATURE. Why do people read books like *The Big Short*? So that they can learn from them and spot the signs in the future in order to make money, obviously. But after reading books like these, they are desperately looking and think they see the signs when they are not there, so they end up losing money. They will lose much more than they ever did before by reading that book. The real signs will be there one day but that day may not come for another 50 or

80 years. These desperate shorters often got burned in the past when they were facing in the wrong direction and are now trying to profit from their past naivety. They missed the first big short and will make sure they don't miss that second one. 'I Won't Get Fooled Again', as The Who say. You will only not be fooled again if you stay well away. The section in Waterstone's on spread-betting and layman-speak economic guidance books grows month after month. Stands to reason as hundreds of thousands believe they can make money out of it – then reach for these books for a little help and guidance. Write a book justifying the next big climb, give it a snappy title like, 'A Quicker Rise Than a Virgin in a Brothel' and you'll get plenty of takers. You will also be right at some point in time – like what actually happened after the big 2008 fall. You will actually believe you are better equipped after reading market literature. You are just keener to try. You cannot believe you will fail. That's why SB bookies recommend it. The more you believe you are educated, the keener you are to trade and the more you will lose. You go back to the research again. Then you go back to funding your account again. The pattern is easy enough to see. But only if you stop and think – and only after you've quit. Most gamblers who stop and think, decide completely the opposite. There are many who write books after making a mint out of share dealing; so you can too! But they are always industry insiders; former traders, financial journalists etc. They used to do this as a job, they have information not accessible to you. The next big winners will be those with 'beautiful minds' just as before; it will not be you who have read a few books who think this will lead to fortune and being surrounded by beautiful bodies. If all we needed do to become an expert 'trader' or poker player was buy a book or follow a system, then we'd all be millionaires.

At the 'seminar', we were recommended to read, *Reminiscences of a Stock Operator*, a book written 70 years ago. So I did – and learnt nothing from it although I thought I had. It does the job for them; it encourages you to 'trade' and therefore to lose. It's good for them to suggest such a book as it is necessarily vague so no one could sue them for following any advice contained within. Like a dating site recommending you to read *Wuthering Heights*.

The difference between golf and spread-betting instructional books is that the former might help a few whereas the latter will help no one at all. In fact, the latter will do the opposite. If you want to read *This Time is Different*, then just read it as something of historical interest. But don't for the life of you think you are now worldly wise from the knowledge gleaned from its pages and that you can profit from your new-found wisdom. You won't. Just as surely as reading all the Star Wars books and watching all the films won't make you any more of a Jedi Knight.

YOUTUBE. You still think you can win? I am sure I could chart my trading strategy over one day or several hours, explain how I spotted the support and resistance points, got in here and out there and made a nice tidy profit. Follow my strategies and it'll work for you. What I don't show you are the times when it all went tits up! I tried many different strategies and traded different markets – I lost £130k. Maybe if I had traded forex or pair-traded or traded coffee futures or zinc then I would have done better. Bit like saying if I had bet on the greyhounds rather than the horses I'd be up.

SUBSCRIPTION SERVICES. Subscription services, often advertised through those YouTube uploads, offer advice after a payment of a one-off or monthly fee. You will be supplied with a full range of colour charts that give you guidance about your 'trading'; they won't tell you exactly what to do – as they really don't know and don't want to get sued. This 'attached' industry feeds you ultimately useless information which you pay them for – you then feed the core industry that they feed off and help grow. There are three participants in this cycle. Only two of them benefit.

YOUR TRUSTED PROVIDER. Those suited professionals on the SB websites give the appearance of the trustworthy advisors or bank managers. They talk about their market analysis for *your* benefit, they talk about their traders and the trading room. But ask yourself this: do they really buy and sell shares? Do they really have traders as you understand the term 'trader'? Once you are out you will realise that this is no more real than the dragons and holes in the floor that the acid tripper sees. They will supply you with whatever you need, much like a drug dealer. They can supply you with a 'portfolio' as they call it, of 'trading tools'. This is like offering you a choice of weaponry for you to blow your own brains out; you just don't realise it at the time. Pull the trigger and the bullet doesn't come out in the direction you thought it would. The only *tool* is you. They will make everything sound a bit cooler than it really is: Foreign Exchange sounds a bit dull – let's call it FX. Then let's use some lovely sounding acronyms too like the FTSE or the DAX or the Nasdaq or the Nymex. You may know what some of them stand for. Essentially, they all stand for your destruction at the hands of the SB industry. They have a dealing room where they take your money and give you the impression that you'll get something greater back. Your neighbourhood drug dealer also has much the same place and promises much the same too.

There seems to be an explosion of SB companies out there. This can only mean one thing; they have the middle class enthralled, a massive stratum of individuals – mostly men – who have the financial means (and cunning to mask their losses) whose delusional gambling continues as their self-confidence, university education, belief in spread-betting itself, sense of adventure and acceptance of a challenge are all actually conspiring against their future prosperity unbeknownst to them. Even though the ever-growing SB industry reap in billions in revenue the problem remains hidden and unreported as their clients cover their tracks for them in order to protect their own skin. As I have stated, financial spread-betting is the self-inflicted financial cancer for today's middle class – but it is both preventable and curable if you understand the causes and the symptoms – and don't choose to ignore them.

iii. Follow the Yellow Brick Road

We all base our gambling decisions on some sort of information; the man in the bookies reads the *Racing Post* pinned to the display boards or the form guide in *The Sun*. The spread-better studies graphs, economic data and whatever else he deems important. For both, what they believe in is largely irrelevant.

GOVERNMENT AGENCIES' DATA RELEASE. My life was dominated by dailyfx.com/calendar that listed all the times and importance of every release out there so I could plan my week. I would think through how I could make myself free to 'trade' on key days. Sometimes this was impossible. Sometimes I just made it possible by adjusting my teaching so that even though I was in class, I could set them off with a task before the data hit when I'd need that five minutes free to trade – then I would follow it until the school bell rang. It is an embarrassing thing to admit. Is what you are doing any better, really? You are like that aspirational voter or shopper. You are that aspirational gambler – you think you will move into the big leagues and do it as a profession even – that would be its logical direction in your mind. No, you are not aspirational – you are just perspirational, sweating as your positions move against you, your greens turn into reds, your hundreds of pounds of losses click over into thousands…

You can get on after economic data is released; you can see it is clearly moving in a certain direction – until it reverses and you are in the shit. Wait ten minutes or an hour or two so that the volatility has settled down – but it can reverse at any point. May go continuously down 100 points in an hour then reverse and go up 200 over the rest of the day. The Dow has a habit of going one way all day only to go back the other way in the last 30 minutes of trading – but don't bank on it. Spotting any short-term trends is a nightmare. Spotting medium- and long-term trends isn't any better. Even if you are right some or even most of the time, you will still lose as the entrance and exit points the spread-better takes are almost impossible to get right. They are only easy to spot in hindsight.

You can try to trade on data when it is released. But good employment data could even send the market down as a really good number was already factored in and if the data isn't anything other than great, then down it goes. Or good/bad numbers moving the market could be linked to the future Fed rate moves. Even if some number is great or terrible it can still move in an unexpected direction after a degree of volatility that could last for minutes or hours or days. How do you know how much is factored into the market before rate decisions and data? You don't. There are many factors at play and it is hard for you to second-guess. These extra dimensions cause added volatility – which will kill you. You might see it rising and rising so get on only to see it immediately plummet again. Or vice-versa. If you hold on and hold on it might never come back again. If you are still holding on in 2016 for a fall since 2009 or 2012 or even just 2015, you are now in deep shit. If you held on in early 2008 for a rise after being long for 2007, you also put yourself in the wrong place. Hold on facing the wrong way for too long and you could be declared bankrupt. Who would take this risk? That's why we have to get out at a loss. This is just one of many reasons why the SB industry always come out with a profit.

One bit of economic data that will never be a true measure even though it could be one of the easiest to compile is the Retail Price Index (RPI). The Office for National Statistics are always very smug in telling us how they update it every year, including things like the cost of sending a red rose from London to Glasgow, but they don't include the costs that millions incur in real life. How about adding in the decreasing cost of drugs and prostitutes? But as we are wasting so much of our money gambling, it hardly matters that the cost of a pint of milk has gone up 1%. Or that the girls on that A-road on your way back from work haven't increased their prices for the last five years.

There is only one law that real traders adhere to, the one law that they can never break: don't get *caught* price fixing. One or two do end up in jail. Who knows exactly what goes on in the world of wheat futures or yen/dollar or a thousand-and-one other markets? Who regulates them all? The major players in the markets themselves? That would be self-regulation. Let's regulate just how much money each of us can make, shall we? Markets are by their very nature international and complicated so any regulator has a tough job. So do not think you have any chance sitting there trading away in the minutes after economic data is announced on 'Bloomberg breaking news'. You are not a shipping magnate who already can make a good estimate at those trade numbers. You are not in any privileged position. You will never be part of the jet-set, just the DFC.

COMPANY DATA RELEASE. 'Earnings season', company results, bellwether companies – are you going to trade the market based on an indication from one of these? Trade an individual share, perhaps. I shorted Apple after the results came out and the market fell – placed the bet whilst on the underground to add to my list of 'trading places'. Bet into my winning position. Never really understand how numbers can look so bad then nothing much changes it seems and by the next day (or even a few hours later) the market has said, wait a minute, these numbers look good. Does the 'conference call' really change people's perceptions that dramatically? Needless to say, I was in the shit again.

PATTERNS. Always had some belief in Fibonacci but either the theory is a nightmare to apply, or I am just not good enough at maths.

TREND LINES. According to some, the Dow should be below 10,000. January 2017, it hit double this number.

SUPPORT AND RESISTANCE LEVELS. There are points at which a higher price is unable to break through (i.e. resistance) or where it cannot push its way back down below a given price (the support level). You can find many different 'trough' and 'peak 'numbers in the past; there are sets of both of them. Which do you rely on? Which are pertinent at the moment? Even if you think you know the current price support or resistance level, you never know how many times the market will test these before the breakthrough. When it hits a previous peak, then sell, or a previous trough, then buy. It's just that there are more troughs than a pig farm, so which one to choose? Markets have a habit of dropping through these troughs from time to time. Just sell then, if it goes through the trough. Problem though, could just be a fake trough-breaker and it might just ping back up again. Same applies to the buy at the peak approach. There are more peaks than in the Alps so be careful. And just like the mountain climber you are just as likely to be killed going down as when you are going up.

The market is set up to make you lose. This is the norm; if you like, being what you think of as 'unlucky' is the norm. It's a similar picture in whatever form of gambling. Or running across the motorway; are you really just 'unlucky' if you are hurled 20 feet into the air and smashed to bits?

ECONOMIC REPORTS. UK loses its AAA status from Moody's so FTSE falls? The Dow fell heavily when US lost its AAA rating from S&P. FTSE ends the day up! Eurozone recession 'to persist' says European Commission. That sounds negative. European markets end positive, DAX up 1%, CAC up 2.25%! Dow finishes on an up too. Throw in some volatility and another great week for the SB companies! When the market fell at least 150 points on these reports the 'longs' were wiped out. And those that were short were laughing and bet into it as the 'experts' recommend. So when it reversed and went back up to its original starting point all those shorts were now sitting on big losses. Do you hold it over the weekend? The SB companies have made money out of those both long and short.

WHAT'S IN THE NEWS. Geopolitics: North Korea, Israel/Iran. 'Lehman on steroids' got people licking their lips ahead of the EU/Greece crash. Didn't happen.

EXPERT OPINION. Some people made a name and money for themselves as they predicted the financial crisis of 2008 *before* it happened, unlike those who think themselves clever for giving the reasons for the crash after the event. Many could do this with the horses too! Lost count of the number of people predicting a Euro meltdown and Grexit in 2012 – seemed like shooting fish in a barrel. The BBC's *Working Lunch* programme implicitly recommended buying into Northern Rock after it got hit early on. The reason being that it had fallen far more than others in the sector (!). There were experts back in 2008 saying the market would pick up soon. And the market did rise 1000 from 10,000 to 11,000 at one point and had many rallies of differing magnitudes. The business news channels then invited these experts onto their shows. Never saw them again as the market headed toward 6500.

The media. We go along with oft repeated phrases we hear in the media, even though they are completely inaccurate or misleading: 'Little Johnny defied the odds and survived' such and such illness. If the chances of survival were 10,000-1, then obviously there is one child who survives. That would be 'Little Johnny' then. They don't report on the other 10,000 who didn't survive. (10,000-1 would be a highly accurate set of odds unlike those completely made-up ones that you get at the bookies.) America looks rich on paper and on aggregate – but averages hide the true picture. Take a random four people: one earns \$3 million, one earns \$2 million, one earns \$1 million and the fourth earns nothing. But on aggregate the guy on nothing actually 'earns' \$1.5 million. Statistics have a lot to answer for. Try telling the fourth guy, who lives under the bridge, how rich he is! Often, we view facts in as skewed and illogical a way as possible all by ourselves without outside assistance from the media. We *will* be that poker star or spread-bet rich guy even though there is no evidence that we have the skills required to be a poker hustler and there is no evidence that I have seen that the spread-betting millionaire even exists. We all think that we don't believe what the media tells us and we make up our own minds. We listen to experts; experts are experts because they know more than us, right? Like doctors are experts and we trust them, we trust the investment expert too, even when he or she is from a spread-betting firm. We listen to what the IMF have said regarding the economy and reported on the BBC as if this prediction will happen. Be careful what you rely on, what you believe in.

INFORMATION ASYMMETRY. Here's an economics term that describes the difference between what the experts know and what the likes of you and I know. The internet has closed this gap. We all now know how to get cheaper car insurance. The experts don't have the advantage over us now. But your belief in the new era of information symmetry is only information illusion. Just because you can comparethemarket.com that doesn't mean this concept carries over into every aspect of your life. You are not an expert in markets unless you work in them, are employed by them and earn an actual wage, and not that one in your head. There's enough dubious information on the internet that people rely on far more than they used to rely on in pre-internet days. Just look at dating sites. Pre-internet you could ask a girl out face-to-face and have an exact idea of what she looks like at that precise moment and hazard a fairly good guess at what she weighs and her age. A dating 'sight' was far more reliable than a modern-day dating site. Nowadays, log on and it is likely she has understated her weight and age and chosen a flattering picture that might not even be that recent. I know. The latter is what I used to do. Men also lie of course. So, you rely on dating site profiles and market information and you still believe that information asymmetry is dead!

TIMING. Some people realised there was a problem with Bradford & Bingley, the US housing market, credit. When all the world agreed, we had a problem. If you happened to listen to their advice in 2006 then you'd have lost if you'd shorted. Timing is everything. You were too early. Whether you're a financial Doomsday seer or an everything-looks-rosy economist, you are bound to be correct at some point. Recessions happen every ten years or so with boom times in between. Even the horse-racing tipster will sometimes be right with his 33-1 selection. Does that mean you follow his advice in the next race? Even though the credit-rating agencies have missed so much over recent years, people still listen to them, professional people too. Some said we were heading towards a great depression number of 4500 on the Dow. There's only one true indicator of how you should bet and that is sent directly to your inbox:

iv. Urgent action required!

You will find, however you trade, that those important and urgent messages will appear in your inbox; the 'margin call'. How to avoid these? Delete your SB account will be the ultimate answer but you will delay and delay this decision – because you are a gambler. Because you think you can still win. The first thing you will do when you get those 'important' – you need to fund your account – messages, and those 'urgent' – you *really* need to fund your account – messages is you will do what they say. You will log on like some dog on heat and type in those three security numbers on your bank card. These messages are a psychological trick to get you to do something in a hurry, almost without thinking – so you don't really have time to comprehend exactly what you are doing, or whether it is really worth doing (of course it isn't!). Ten minutes later you might be doing the same thing again. You send them money forgetting its true value. You can have a great time with £1000 – you can buy something you really want, you can go on holiday. You stop yourself doing this but somehow willingly send it across to the SB bookie. You think it is only your stake so you will get it back. You will never see it again.

The next stage before you call it a day is when you assign those 'Important' and 'Urgent' messages to spam so you never have to see them. Your spam filter will sort out your problems. Most of the time though, even before your best friend, the spam filter, hid them for you, you would never see them – well, not in time anyway. You will either be asleep or be doing something else, like working for a living and then you would log-in, in a panic, to see your balance severely reduced and your positions slashed. Your positions look pathetic – which is how you feel. Think about how hard you work to earn that money that you then give away. You may think those 'love-bombed' middle-aged women who fall in love with a US Marine to whom they then send money, only for the new love of their life to disappear as they were in fact, someone typing away to hundreds of women from internet scam rooms, are just naive and gullible. Are you any better? Their dream of love is no more a fantasy than your dream of wealth. The difference between the 419 scammers and the SB industry, that really riles me still, is that the latter is completely legal! Time to delete your app.

You have already spent hours upon hours by yourself, watching and 'reacting' to market numbers. You might have sat all day, barely eating as you attempted to 'trade'. It might even have worked on occasion so you start believing that if you could be focused on this day in, day out without the problem of actually having to go to your day job then you would become that professional trader. You will have achieved your dream job – you make easy money, you are your own boss, you work from home. But when your 'trading' has your undying attention, you still can't make it work. Next comes the 'avoidance' and 'ignoring' stage. You just go shopping, play golf and try to forget about it. You might check on your phone but sooner or later you don't even do that. You take the 'fuck it' approach and just check what happens in a few hours' time or even at the end of the day – you can escape the numbers for a few hours but not the worry. This is, after all, what you have been doing through the night for years anyway. You may repeat the cycle a few more times before you stop – either you run out of money, run out of patience or your wife runs out on *you!* The urgent action required is actually that you stop.

v. Join us!

Come and join the party! No, not as a gambler but as one of us where the actual money is! They employ the brightest and pay well. You need a 2:1 degree just to get an interview at IG. The fact that they can be selective and pay top money just shows how well the industry must be doing. I am sure these interviewees have to convince the interviewing panel how 'customer focused' they are. The soon-to-be employees actually believe their own bullshit that they are helpful and informative. At least the hangman, who is undoubtedly professional in his job and helpfully guides his victim up the steps, is not going to pretend to be anything else. He is not inviting the condemned up onto the platform he has built overlooking the city to enjoy the view. No, he slips on the noose and it's game over. But the SB punter doesn't realise he is the condemned man. Even when he can feel the rope around his neck, he thinks it's just an itch. No, he will admire the view. He will feel the hangman's hand on his shoulder and think it that of a friend. Only when he is twisting and spinning on the end of the rope will he turn to see what the truth is. But he will only see the hangman's back as he is already moving on to his next victim. If you are already involved in gambling that will be you. Get that rope from off around your neck. There will be no Clint Eastwood to snap the rope with one shot to save you. You need to run a fucking mile before you too are left dangling.

The board members all have excellent credentials and excellent salaries. Makes me sick that I funded the gym membership and free fruit for employees! They have thousands upon thousands of active users making them millions! Both figures are growing.

So how much do they take off you? The truth lies on their separate investor site (2015–16 accounts). The market leader, IG, has over 150,000 active clients who have allowed them to make £207 million profit in one year alone. That's PROFIT, not just what they make out of punters. What they actually make is not just the profit but the operating costs too. This more than doubles the figure to £456 million! That would be almost half a billion pounds, then! They pay their employees some good salaries! That we fund! And this is just one company. They have a market capitalisation of £2.9 billion and hold hundreds of millions in cash reserves! They can't hide these numbers as they must declare them as a publicly listed company – although I'm sure they'd like to. But you won't find these numbers on their spread-betting website!

There are other big players too. You can also infer how they are doing when Stewart Wheeler can afford to donate £5 million to the Conservative party in one go! Old Etonian Mr Wheeler made his fortune founding IG. But it is hardly confined to spread-betting and just one political party. Peter Coates, director of *Bet365* has made large donations to the Labour party. The ban on TV ads was lifted in 2007 under a Labour government. Mr. Coates says he is a lifelong labour supporter. And you still think that YOU have the edge? I could have just stuck to betting on the horses; takes less time and I would have had to bet fucking big to lose £130k! Imagine that, whacking down a grand or five on the bookies' counter. I could never have done that. But it's so easy to do online with a bank card. No, I shouldn't have stuck with the horses. With the amount I lost, I should have just *bought* a racehorse!

IG can afford, amongst other things, to make a 10% contribution to their (1000!) employees' pension schemes, tickets to polo (!), top-of-the-line-Aeron chairs (sure they're good!) and give them a bloody good ('Sensational', they describe it) Christmas party! Life at a SB bookies is sweet! Life as an SB client is not! The losing client pays for this. An Aeron chair will probably cost upwards of £500. If you've been spread-betting for a while now, then you've already paid for a few.

If you realise what you are doing, then you must see that one day you will be in real, deep shit. Take a deep breath and you can already smell it in the breeze… one day you will go 'all-in' as the poker players call it. Sometimes it works, often it ends in disaster. A risky strategy when you feel you have no other option or when you are supremely confident. But how can you bluff your opponent when they can already see your hand? They will always take your bet. This must clearly tell you something.

vi. The end game

I have been up Shit Creek with the sponge paddle that the SB bookies assured me was an 'essential tool' on too many occasions. I always thought I could navigate my way out. Now I realise that no one can. The canoe you are in is also made of sponge and everyone will sooner or later be dragged down into the aforementioned creek.

With my last bet, I tried to switch from the Dow to oil. Yes, exactly like switching from the horses to the greyhounds. I realise that now – I may even have sensed it at the time. Did my research. Yes, the information illusion suckered me in too. Even though Brent Crude means more to me as some comment on a Ricky Gervais character than anything else, I was prepared to stake thousands on it. The only good thing I can say was that it ended up being the final straw. That Brent Crude trade was my final bet. I was actually at least £20k up at one point with it; lost it all and £5k of my own money too. I finally closed the position, the same as I had tried the night before but was denied by the system, when I was massively up, £100 a point on Brent Crude. Then when I'm facing a loss no longer a problem for the SB bookie to close it when I clicked what was to be my final action. It seemed unfair. I took this up with the SB company; they batted me away – all those caveats again. Then it was Goodnight Vienna! I refunded the remaining few thousand to my account. I had done this on numerous occasions before when I tried to quit or was just pissed off. Sometimes the figure was in the thousands. Often after a big loss it was only into the hundreds. Once I refunded about £40 from a balance that was into five figures the week before. Now, four years later, after my final closing balance turned into six figures – into the red – I haven't been back since.

I probably lost £20k on overnight interest, dividend adjustments and the spread alone. These costs are just like the skimmers on the coin-pusher arcade machines, those little gaps at the sides that make the arcade the profits; the crack cocaine of the betting world for the primary school child. I tried to 'live the dream' but ended up living the nightmare. You have lost the second you log on. Watch the guy who loses at the start of *Lock, Stock and Two Smoking Barrels*, how physically sick he feels, how he feels dazed, like he's been in a car crash. The soundtrack is Iggy Pop singing, 'I Wanna Be Your Dog'. That's exactly what you'll be! The gambling companies' dog.

So that's it. The past. The 'end game' where I finally tipped over my king. I didn't have too many pieces left on the board but my opponent somehow managed to have more pieces than they had started with. The spread-bet bookies killed me just as surely and inevitably as Death kills Antonius Block in *The Seventh Seal*. 'Nothing escapes me. No one escapes me,' he tells the knight, 'and no one'. So too the high-street bookies, the bingo sites, the poker tables, the casinos.... Your fate is sealed early on. Death walks by your side for as long as it takes. For the unfortunate, death is not just some sort of metaphor; it becomes very real. Think it won't happen to you? Men are four times more likely to top themselves and far, far more likely to gamble. Men kill themselves for a whole host of reasons. Gambling losses cause financial hardship, embarrassment, breakdowns in relationships, shame, guilt... Gambling is sure as hell a reason for suicide. Why risk it, however stable you think you are? If you're still doubtful, dwell on this. What is the biggest killer of men under 50? Car accidents? Cancer? Hard to believe but it's suicide; takes around a hundred men a WEEK in the UK. Death walks by our side but many of us end up doing the job for him. Gambling really could be 'the end game'.

(Footnote: The Seventh Seal (Ingmar Bergman, 1957). Knight plays chess, not *Twister*. That was *Bill and Ted's Bogus Journey*.)

So goodbye to gambling. Goodbye to those important and urgent messages that plop into your inbox like a turd when you are at work or with the family. You see them on your phone or on your work computer. It doesn't matter where. It will distract you from your job or your family. It will stress you. Your gambling will cause you to rush your work or be tetchy with your colleagues or family. You will be late for meetings or the train home. You will rush conversations, desperate to cut it short so you can check your positions again. You will spend your whole lunch hour with a sandwich in one hand and the mobile, with its market numbers flicking around, in the other. You will drive the car with the phone in view, you will stare at it a second or two too long and slam on the brakes. You will go to bed late ('Why aren't you coming to bed, darling?') and get up early. You will even check your positions in the middle of the night. The only position you should think about in bed should be with your wife! However the marketing bullshit goes, staring at a screen at 2 a.m. is no fun at all. This is why the professionals who do this for a living have switched off after the markets have closed and have spent a worry-free evening at some high-class restaurant with their high-class girlfriend and are now sound asleep as you should be.

You will try to ignore the messages of impending doom like the pilot who turns off that annoying beeping warning system when they have a problem. You will think, 'If only: 1) I had stayed long/short, 2) I had got out there and gone long/short'. Before eventually you will think '3) I wish I had never got involved in spread-betting in the first place!' For everyone thinking about getting into spread-betting, please refer to reflection 3 straight away! Unfortunately for the gambler, option 3 never even enters their head for many years.

I caught up with an old friend when I was back in England a few years ago; my ex-golfing buddy tells me how he got a £300 bonus for the year – and he is quite happy about this. Seems he busted a gut all year for this and to receive £6 per week is, to me, a kick in the bollocks. But the real killer, not that I told him, is that this amount wouldn't even cover the 'buy-in' for many of my bets. I would have to tell him several times for him to actually understand what I'd been doing as the scale of my gambling was so unbelievable, he wouldn't get it the first time. Or the fifth time. How can anyone get their head around it?

Five hundred pounds on the FTSE with a £500 buy-in? I still struggle to comprehend it. Remember that I started out with £2 bets. This is one reason why a gambler doesn't tell anyone, especially to a non-gambler. They can't comprehend why anyone would gamble, especially these big bets. You can't explain it to them – you can't really explain it to yourself. No one can listen to Metallica at low volume, you need it louder to get some buzz out of it. But you shouldn't turn it up to 11, so that it destroys your ear-drums!

Kweku Adoboli was sentenced for fucking up with other people's money (convicted November 2012, he lost UBS $2 billion!) although, fair play to him, he also lost £123k spread-betting with his own money. Even a so-called professional got it really wrong. As usual, it's the small fry who don't cover their tracks that get hung out to dry. Mr Adoboli follows a long line of rogue traders. I read Nick Leeson's book, *Rogue Trader* (good) and watched the film (poor) and tried to learn from it. But, just like him I made back my losses then actually made money (very dangerous) then got cocky and tried to make more money with bigger bets. I was even worried that if I actually started making money I may well make bigger and bigger bets then one day I might lose it all and be declared bankrupt. I dodged the bullet holding those massive positions over the weekend, positions that require £12,500 in equity alone (with a reduced equity requirement – a few years before I would have needed double), £250 a point on the Dow! Nick Leeson made back his loss then managed to lose £800 million. Wasn't his money – although he ended up in jail. That £130k I lost was mine.

If 99.99%+ of us cannot run out for a premiership side and expect to even touch the ball, why do you think you would be able to compete with the true professionals in poker or spread-betting? The laptop jock cannot trade their way through volatility; it's about as easy as juggling spaghetti. These pro traders really do make enough to get that high-performance Porsche or high-performance prostitute. These men and the DFC operate in different worlds. A DFC member cannot trade his way out and up to where these men inhabit. Don't even try. Remember that you are not trading. You are betting. You are not buying into any real stock or currency or commodity. You do not go into Ladbrokes and place a 'buy' trade on a horse when you back it for a fiver. You do not own £5 worth of racehorse. You are just gambling on it, just like you are gambling on some index or commodity to go your way. Better if you *did* just stick a fiver on a horse. Just forget in-running and wait until the first-past-the-post bet is over and you are done. You do not have to roll it over until the next day. The winning jockey is getting a pat on the back from the other jocks. Take your winnings or your losses and just feel safe in the knowledge that it's finished. Get on with your day and relax; a £5 loss doesn't really get you membership in the DFC.

I once watched a mother in a hotel restaurant store her ciggies in her baby's pram next to the baby's feet one evening, whilst she sat and ate. Baby did the same with the ciggies. She eventually noticed after almost a minute. I would have told her if it had lasted any longer although it seemed kind of pointless; if you're so stupid as to store your *smokes* next to your baby, what's the point in saying anything? So what does she do when she notices her baby munching on her ciggies? Tells the child off who then starts to cry! But my gambling was as dumb as the mother who feeds her baby tobacco. I was putting my hard-earned cash into a SB account and somehow not expecting those who stared at my funds with wide eyes not to take it.

Oil destroyed me in the end but it could have been anything. The Dow lost me the most over the years, but whether it be a commodity or an index or foreign exchange that you decide is best suited for you to make a killing, it won't. I may have been up at some point betting on crude but I didn't realise that I was now covered in oil and it wouldn't take too much to set myself alight. I guess I can be a beacon for others now. Anyone who reads about my burning corpse of a bank balance should be warned sufficiently, although far too many believe that they know better, that they won't make the same mistakes. Self-immolation would be stretching it a bit too far as even though I am now making a point, I never meant to do it. I thought I would be up there with the professional players, those oil futures traders who make a million for themselves year after year. I just succeeded in making others richer in a completely different industry. I know I am not alone in my accidental financial suicide. Just avoid becoming the next. The SB bookies' ultimate aim is to turn your bank balance into a series of noughts. They almost succeeded with me. And whilst the SB client is left with only noughts, the SB bookies add even more noughts to their bank balance. Just that they have a few alternative digits in front of them.

In theory, it seems very possible to make money from spread-betting. Communism looks good in theory, a football team having the same form home and away makes sense in theory – it's just a patch of grass wherever you play, after all – easy to get a birdie in golf and shoot 65 in theory, easy to plan a route around the world by plane, train and ship in theory. Why would spread-betting or poker be any different?

Give me the money! After my first big loss where the SB bookie let my position run and run, I ended up with a negative balance of £13k! Forget equity requirement.

Nope, City Index were happy to grow my loss. Then come the letters and constant phone calls. They leave messages DAILY on my answer machine asking me to pay up – so I switched it off. I avoid answering the phone at all. Had numerous messages left from some hard-nosed woman. I'm sure she's only doing her job but who would want a job like that? Answer: someone hard-nosed. Then she phones me at work! This would be embarrassing if anyone at work knew what the company did. Still, it gave me palpitations when the secretary told me there's someone on the phone from City Index in the staffroom in front of everyone. Sure, there are many in the same position as me. Unlike me, they have to hide it from their wives or admit to it. The SB bookie will be oh so helpful and give you all the help and support you need until you owe them money; then they will be on to you every day until you pay up. Every day, without fail. Some will be unable to pay. Some will lose their cars or their homes. And their girlfriends and wives. Why did they not close my positions but let me run up a massive debt? Answer: if they had closed my positions I wouldn't have run up a massive debt! They know what they're doing. I didn't. I paid up. Paid monthly, every month for a year. Actually posted them off a cheque each month. You could call it a 'reality cheque' – just that it wasn't. I was back gambling again within a month.

Then Brexit came along. The SB companies put on extra staff on the Friday 'to assist their customers'. I felt gutted that this book was not published sooner, gutted that I was not able to warn many tens of thousands of that personal financial iceberg that they were headed towards. The spread-better piles in short as the market falls after the Brexit vote. You have put in those stop-losses, just in case it reverses as you make your way to work. You get to the office and check. Your stops have kicked in or the SB bookie has kicked you into touch and closed your positions for you. You have lost all your paper profits – and all your equity too. But you will make it all back with the US election, won't you? The Dow was 800 points down premarket then by the following Monday the Dow hits an all-time record high! Many spread-betters are now betting massive and imagining their losses from Trump and Brexit being wiped out in a week and thinking of how many tens of thousands will be coming to them within a few months. At this point they click onto the Porsche website and flick through the optional extras. Yes, someone who is actually making money out of spread-betting is doing the exact same thing.

Volatility will get you over whatever period. Swings of 1000 points over a day or two happen all too often, as happened in US election week 2016. If I spell 'volatility' incorrectly I often get my spell-checker offering me 'virility'. They are not as unconnected as it seems. Any male believes volatility is a challenge. Spread-betting is not a challenge unless you think playing tennis with a frying pan is a challenge. Your opponent has a lovely racket, remember, and they play tennis for a living too. Find a challenge that is actually achievable.

You may think you are different, you may think I made easy mistakes, amateur mistakes. You have a better plan. If you really believe this then your own DFC membership is only a matter of time. My autobiography will become yours. The SB bookies will tell you that it carries a degree of risk. There is no degree of risk unless you define risk as total. Like someone telling you jumping out of an aeroplane without a parachute is risky. But they will tell you that you make the decisions and there are safety mechanisms in place for you, just like a parachute and that they are always 'here to help'. They've also given you all the 'tools you need' too, remember. Yeah, but when you pull that rip-cord and it comes off in your hand, you realise that you are seconds away from hitting the ground hard. But it wouldn't have mattered if the rip-cord *had* worked as *they* packed your parachute anyway and replaced it with old seat covers from their Aeron chairs.

3

OLD SKOOL REINVENTED: POKER, BINGO AND CASINOS

Prostitution is said to be the oldest profession. Gambling must be the second oldest. And playing cards for money was thought of soon after. Everyone has had a game of late-night poker round a table at their mate's house or at some university hall of residence. And playing for loose change with friends isn't a bad thing. But now that we have high-speed internet at home and in our hands, the rules have changed. Poker has come a long way since the fourth Earl of Sandwich came up with his novel way to sustain himself at the card table, as the popular belief holds. We now play with complete strangers and with our bank cards. Would I have turned up and played with five complete strangers when I was at university and brought along with me £500 in crisp bank notes? No, I bloody would not have. But that's pretty much what the nation is happy to do nowadays.

Texas hold 'em is now the game of choice as it's simple and as such, gives the illusion that you don't have to do much to win at it. Unlike spread-betting, there are actually players out there who *have* made a fortune by gambling online. The website owners are doing very well out of it too without having to worry one jot what the 'flop' will reveal. But there are only a handful of individuals who can make a living out of it. These have become well-known in the poker world and the industry is happy to highlight its winners. There will always be lottery millionaires and these get wheeled out for the cameras every week. The big winners get reported nationally. The massive winners get reported internationally. Having winners in any gambling sector is the best marketing money can buy – especially as it is effectively free. Never seen a spread-bet millionaire though! Even the bingo halls make sure there's a national bingo winner and stick her in front of the cameras. Gets more people playing, increases the prize pot, increases the size of the next big win and there you have it. More profits for the industry that they are less keen on publicising – right up until they have grown so big that they want to enter the stock exchange in an Initial Public Offering (IPO in the trade). Unfortunately, for the vast majority of its clients who have made these companies so profitable, the IPO passes them by and they do not see the statistics. They just carry on pumping the companies' coffers full of their hard-earned cash and sometimes their wife's inheritance.

For the millions who gamble, they think they will be the next millionaire, the next success story or in the case of bingo and the lottery, the next lucky winner. Those poker players think they have the skill and dedication. They have less chance than the eight-year-old boy who thinks he will become a professional footballer. The true poker stars will milk everyone else until they are dry. They all have one thing in common, too. They are, to some degree, geniuses at maths. Chances are, you are not. Liv Boeree, who has career winnings of $3 million achieved a first in physics with astrophysics, for instance. Female players are rare. Those with a background

in maths are not. If you cannot work out the probability of pulling an ace from a pack of cards, then poker is probably not for you. And this is at its most basic level. Probabilities at the most complex level can only be understood by a tiny minority. These players know the odds. They do not hope time after time that such-and-such a card will come up. They bet appropriately and rationally. You are not going to be the next Liv Boeree nor get together with her either. As I know that my maths may be good but not that good, I have never registered. I know my limitations. Do you know yours?

i. Poker

Pubs and clubs now run their own Texas hold 'em tournaments to try to win back some custom after the smoking ban. At least here you get to meet people, albeit people who think wearing shades and a baseball cap will turn them into poker experts. You are less likely to get carried away here than online, just like walking into a bookies to place a bet on a horse with a tenner is not likely to turn into a bet for £500. If you think poker is for you, then just turn up here. If you win consistently and have a strategy that works time after time, then maybe you are not like the rest of the 99.99%+ of the population who are no good. Remember a *good* gambler is someone who actually wins week after week and not someone who just learns how to lose more slowly. So, if you are no good at maths, cannot beat even your friends or strangers in a pub for low stakes, do not have that X-factor that you need to succeed, then do not log on, even if they offer you that £50 sign-up bribe – I mean incentive.

The online sites will employ actual professional poker players to endorse their brand. ('That could be me!' you think. No, you believe subconsciously that it *will* be you!)

Then they have those celebrity players. Boris Becker pops up a lot; he enters the tournaments. Yes, the sponsors are happy to allocate free spots to famous faces. And now he has established himself as the face of poker he is widening his gambling portfolio – and wallet – to advertise spread-betting too. Other celeb players are now grinning away on poker ads – like the original Ronaldo playing online against Rafael Nadal. They use them as you associate them with winning in sport, so poker becomes a sport by association – so you too will be that winner and as poker has magically been transformed into a sport, you can now become that sporting icon that you once longed to become; maybe you haven't missed your chance after all. This is all essentially bullshit – but bullshit that you absorb. Now I see Cristiano's face with some CGI tiger superimposed on top plugging Pokerstars.com – yes, you too can become that poker beast. I wish they wouldn't endorse such bullshit. I mean, they hardly need the money.

In order for the snooker club I frequent to survive it now offers poker nights. People generally prefer to play cards face-to-face but playing in clubs will further increase their interest in playing online too. It can also be the reverse; Ronaldo and Rafa sparked an interest, punters logged on and learnt the rules and some bullshit strategies and now they show up to play across the room from me – who is only interested in potting balls – as they take quick swigs from that half-bottle of vodka they are hiding between their knees – better than an ace or two I suppose although the manager is none too pleased as he discovers their empties the next morning. The internet sites have developed a minority interest into something the media would describe as 'gripping the nation'. For many of them it's gripping them by the balls, much as spread-betting used to do with my bollocks.

You will make some dumb decisions early on in your online poker career and lose stupidly. You may learn from your early mistakes but you will just go on to make new ones; you will play differently, win slightly more often but overall you may just lose more slowly. Then when you are on a streak, or becoming more desperate or whatever emotion courses through your veins, you will bet bigger and bigger and lose more and faster… until the day you just go 'all in': this will be your shittiest day and you will vow never to bet again. It will last a week or a month and then there you are, back at the table, new shiny chips in hand. You will start off cautiously but before long will reach the same point once again. Eventually, after repeating this cycle several times you will give up.

A gambler has the mentality that just one more time, you could get that big win you've been waiting for – no, the big win that you *deserve*. Difficult for the unskilled poker player to fold (that would be 99.99%+ of all players. I define 'unskilled' as those who lose, as how can anyone who loses say they have skill?), after they've fed the pot to any extent. Throwing good money after bad is any gambler's preferred option although they do not realise it at the time. The skilled poker player knows when to fold, when and how much to up the pot; he knows the maths, the probabilities, just like Kasparov can calculate the possibilities and options that his opponent will come back with. Both the grandmaster and the pro poker player can foresee future scenarios and eventualities far better than you will ever be able to. You will build up a list of players to avoid and even some not to. You will think you are learning all the time whether to hold or fold or raise (yes, you *love* raising!). You will *think* you played the odds but sadly you don't realise that you don't play like a pro. You get in big at the wrong time and get out at the wrong time too. You will have some blinding wins. And some crushing losses. This is not some rite of passage you need to take. Take the advice of the kids' programme I used to watch as a child: 'Why don't you go out and do something less boring instead?'

You are not as skilled as other poker players and will only win small money with good hands where others know how to build the pot, to draw you in before sweeping all those chips in their direction. You will also find you lose far too often with what appears to be a reasonable hand – this is because you don't understand the maths which means ultimately that you just don't understand the game. The unskilled can't bluff effectively. Everyone sitting around that table thinks they know what they are doing. Everyone thinks they will come out as a winner. You will come out a loser. How much will you lose? If you read the previous chapter on spread-betting, then you will know how much you will lose from poker. And it won't be that amount you set yourself, saying 'if I lose this much, then I will quit'. Why not? Make sure you read Chapter 7, 'How We Gamble'.

Texas hold 'em is such an appealing little game. It's so simple and so easy to win, right? Draws in millions of players with their cool little online player handles sitting around the table all thinking the same. Just remember that there is only one pot. There are one or two real sharks out there who actually know what they're doing and will take your money off you whether you bet lots of little amounts or one or two large ones. It doesn't matter much to them. Would you prefer to be shot or suffer death by a thousand cuts? Texas hold 'em is undoubtedly popular, as is bingo and many, many other forms of gambling. Just because many people do it, doesn't mean it's good. Eventually, one day you will look back and think, 'What the fuck was I doing?' You followed the crowd, you believed the marketing. Just try to think for yourself. Something is popular? My parents along with millions of others watched *Dallas* in the 80s. What a pile of shit. Joe Dolce got to number one with 'Shaddap You Face' as the British public deemed it worthy of keeping Ultravox's 'Vienna' at number 2. Your losing hands will annoy you, will frustrate you, will drive you as crazy as if you were forced to listen to Joe Dolce over and over again.

I watched a documentary about gambling. It will remain nameless – due in no small part to the fact I can't remember what it was called. For me they spent too long with the winners. Drove around in some online poker star's Bentley – he started off losing but guess what, he won it back and barrow loads more too. Just like you – well, the first half only. And now you believe even more than before, that you will also be down the car showroom within a year or two. This is no more or no less than an advert for the bookies. Any gambler or potential gambler watching will always think that this could be or is in fact *likely* to be them at some point in the future. Nope, just tell it how it is for the 99.99%+. Fair enough though, they did show some losers too. I do not want to hear about the guy who lost all his student loan gambling only to win it all back and become a millionaire. If you lose your student loan playing poker or whatever then you ain't going to see that money again. If you chase it, you'll lose whatever else you have too and some you don't – maxing out credit cards and building up student debt that you can hardly explain to your parents was incurred purchasing textbooks. You do not learn how to win by playing more. You only learn how to lose in a variety of ways. The only variable amongst gamblers is how much and how fast they lose. And how fast you lose your friends and family too.

There are a few who know they almost always win, from experience. The majority, bizarrely also think they will come out as winners even though, from experience, they know they almost always lose – they ignore this fact. Gamblers know that casinos have the edge but they believe it to be only marginal – they believe there is enough room for them to make a profit. It's just everyone else whom are the losers, not you. This mentality runs throughout gambling in whatever form. This 'marginal' advantage that casinos or the bookies have is not as marginal as you think. It's actually quite large and only the short-term lucky can come away winners. Those professional poker players too can exploit your false belief. They chip away at your chip stack until you are down to your last half or third – then they take it in larger chunks as you become increasingly desperate and bet larger amounts. Applies to all forms of gambling. You might stick with the same slot machine or you might decide to switch to a higher stakes machine for your last $100. The casinos make it even easier for you though; you don't have to switch machines. You can stay put, just press a button to up your stake and away you go. There is even a machine that switches between $1000 and $5000 a spin! You might well go 'all in' on that last poker hand. You will probably do the equivalent on the roulette table. But do you know what? You will be back the next day or the next week. You will find some money from somewhere.

Pop up to Waterstone's and buy a book then. You won't find too many books simply titled *How to Play Poker*, but a fair few called *How to* Win *at Poker*, which reads to you as 'How to earn a living playing poker' written by someone who actually does. But there's a simple test with books like these. If you really intend on buying one, then you should NEVER play poker. If you think the answers are in a book then you do not have the knowledge or ability to do anything other than lose money. About as useful as me buying *How to Become Britain's Next Top Model*.

The online sites will 'reward' loyalty in some way – some casinos also do this. They will rebrand poker as a world championship title fight, making it out to be a sport, man against man, which is what you crave as that competitive male. There will be that word 'million' splashed all over the place; yes, this is your chance! The bingo sites list the names of those who have previously won thousands. They will market to that kid inside you; the one who loved those sew-on badges and little silver cups that you received at school. We like to win and get those accolades and adulation. So the poker site might award you a badge of honour for your 'achievements'. This keeps you on this particular site and keeps you wanting more; it might be the only possibility in your life for you to win, to receive praise. But it is false praise. It is a marketing gimmick that you all too easily fall for. The only badge you can wear comes from the DFC.

Watched a Matt Damon film called *Rounders*. He loses $30k at the poker table. Then, guess what? He wins it all back at the end! How many thousands online think they will also win it back? You won't. Maybe you can be that poker winner, the professional poker player like on late-night TV. It's a game of skill, not chance, after all, isn't it? You'd be crazy to just 'gamble'. For the 99.99%+ it is almost identical to a game of chance. You need to be great at maths and have a few more attributes too. Most don't. You don't. Would you play golf against any golf pro and expect to win? Would you line up in the Olympic 100-metre sprint final and think you can come away with a medal? Would you play chess against any grandmaster and expect them to offer you their handshake? So why do you think you can win at gambling in any of its forms? Games of skill or games of 100% chance are almost identical, but the marketing tries to convince you otherwise. The poker player and the spread-bet 'investor' are not players or investors. They are gamblers and members of the DFC. As you watch the FTSE or watch the cards, do not think yourself in any way superior to those who watch for that next bingo number. You are just the same. Whether you drink gin and tonic excessively or gulp down super strength lager, you are just the same. Whatever game you play, whatever drink you consume, however different you feel from those around you playing the same or a different game, whatever class you feel you are, all makes not a jot of difference; you are still a gambler just as the alcoholic is still an alcoholic whatever their brand of choice. Both are destroying themselves. Just as you are.

The poker and spread-bet gamblers have much in common; they are both suckered in by similar marketing, both think that they somehow have the edge, both convinced it is a matter of education and experience, both think it is more skill than chance, both have devised winning strategies and both will lose and lose heavily in the end. The strategies themselves and the game have similarities too. Both accept the cost of playing (the spread-better has the cost of the spread and the poker player pays the 'blind' or the ante in other card games, so once you are 'in' you are induced to carry on – you are already 'down' so you want to make it back and more; there are also those events with an entrance fee); both have to decide when to up the bet (even go 'all in', which I did at the end); when to get out completely when winning or losing (on a 'hand' or individual trade, or to leave the table or 'trading platform' entirely, or that spread-bet 'stop-loss' like folding after feeding the pot); when to fund a difficult position; how to work out all those signs

from the other players (Draghi, Bernanke, Prodi, whoever is running Greece at any particular moment etc. for the spread-better, and for the poker player, how to read other players who are only character icons with bullshit monikers, God only knows); whether the winning hand you have is really a winning hand; whether something will be revealed which destroys your position and so on. The poker sites will advertise a massive prize for one winner. And you think that's going to be you (if only subconsciously) or why else enter? If there are 50,000 people in an online tournament and the money-fund only pays the top 20, then that's 49,980 losers. Do you think you can make the top 20? Just like me you will lose most or all of your money waiting for this big payday to come. It never will.

Gamblers usually think, to some extent, that they suffer 'bad luck', that it will somehow pass, like bad weather. The only bad luck they have had is the misfortune to be born with a brain pre-programmed to want to gamble and to be born into a society that encourages gambling with virtually no checks and balances. The actual bets are irrelevant. You are destined to lose and this is not luck. This is how the system works. A minuscule percentage have that skill to win at gambling but they are really the lucky 0.001%, just like those 0.001% who are good enough to be able to become a professional footballer. Many give up a lot trying to get that professional contract. The gambler does the same. There are some really hopeless kids who believe that one day they will turn pro. There are also some very good ones who believe the same. Neither will achieve this. It's only for the truly gifted. Why would poker be any different? Don't curse your luck when betting. Curse your luck that you weren't born with the skills needed. Curse your luck you can't bend it like Beckham if you like. Curse your luck you have not been given that God-given talent in whatever field. Few have. You are in the massive majority who haven't.

There are a fair few losers who haven't hidden it as well as I have. No way could they hide it, like the 25-year-old who won £90k using his parents' credit cards late one night. He carried on and lost it all and another £158k maxing out loads of credit cards. His dad had to report them stolen to the police or else he would have been liable for the massive bill. Losing more than I did in five years in one night? He gets platinum membership in the DFC, platinum to match his parents' credit cards by the sounds of it.

There was also some young guy who made £16k a year as a company's book-keeper. He lost over £1m of the company's money betting online on all sorts of things. Company went into administration. Yes, he was nuts and however much I fucked up I never lost more than I had although some of those massive weekend positions I held could have really destroyed me. This case highlights that gambling affects not just only the gambler. He can be sent to jail but the company and its directors have to go to the bankruptcy court and its employees to the job centre – then the kids get no summer holiday, and even might lose their home. So, however many active gamblers there are out there, the number affected by gambling is a large multiple of this. It causes financial hardship, divorce, even suicide. Gambling is a free choice by the individual – but not by those unknowing proxy gamblers that it affects.

We are all in search of something. We think we can find it in our 20s then still hope we can find it in our 30s. By the time we get to our 40s, we think we probably missed it somewhere along the line. We took the wrong turn and now what do we have. Even if we are a successful accountant, it is hardly rock and roll, is it? But the truth is worse than that hard-held belief. We were never that talented artist or musician or footballer or whatever other bullshit idea we cling to. If we were that person then we probably would have been spotted as a child, running rings around those other kids on the football pitch. But that wasn't you. Forget the idea that you missed out on that handshake with Sir Alex and a teenage apprenticeship at the Cliff. I would never have been that pro golfer. But I do not really enjoy being that person in the crowd looking on at others who are great, that man jumping up and down on crisp packets and broken glass as someone else performs on stage. It can occasionally be enjoyable but often it is frustrating. If you have no talent then you have no choice. But there is always something you can be good at, something that is sold to you as the way to be that superstar: yes, you can be that superstar poker player, that millionaire stock-market hustler. I know this is bullshit. Do you?

ii. Bingo... and their fruit machines

Bingo is the one area of gambling that appeals to women more than any other form. In America, there are a fair few slot-jockeys too. You see one or two grannies in UK amusement arcades and all ages in bingo hall foyers but the UK game of choice is bingo. Over the last decade, all sorts of other non-skill online casino games have also become popular amongst women. How popular? Hard to tell and the websites ain't keen on telling too many people! And unlike the rare case of the poker millionaire, there is no one who can regularly win at bingo. True, you can have that national massive win akin to winning the lottery and the bingo companies are all too keen to publicise this, but virtually everybody else is onto a loser. TV adverts clearly target the female market: they make it look fun and exciting – the exact opposite to the life of a bored housewife stuck at home with the toddler. Now, when the baby is asleep she logs on, meets her online friends… and loses money. Soon she will be logging on while the baby is awake. There are now all those online casino games, many linked to popular culture featured on that bingo site too. Some are simple, some seem a little too complicated. But the designers know what they are doing. Present gamblers with something with many variables and buttons to press and they will try to master the damn thing! This is one of the reasons why games of skill are also attractive. Whatever buttons you press have no real effect – the 'control' you feel, that empowerment is only in your mind.

Arguably (very arguably) one of the benefits of gambling is its social aspect. A bit like the social aspect of getting wasted on alcohol or meeting some nice people in rehab, so not that great then. But people do socialise at the races, make friends in casinos, bookies, bingo halls. But online? The bingo sites understand this social aspect and run a chat room on the same page as the bingo cards themselves. When players find friends from anywhere in the country and chat with them whilst playing, they are far more likely to go back to the same bingo website as before, as that's where their new friends are. They will also spend longer (and therefore lose more) as that is where their chat site is. The webpage is skilfully set up to display many cards so that if you just buy one it looks like you are not playing the game properly. Before long, the bingo gambler is playing multiple cards. The website operators know their game. The bingo sites will say that you can use their members' chat service and not need to play at all. Yes, chat away as all those flashing lights and bingo cards nudge up against the chat site. Of course it will entice you to gamble. The bingo sites try to replicate as much as they can of the bingo hall. With poker, as you are playing real people you are bound to want to talk to them, just like most people would playing cards around a real table. But are you that desperate or unimaginative that you have to log onto a gambling site in order to have a chat?

The lottery, which is after all a form of bingo, can make you a millionaire but probably won't. Whenever I put a couple of quid on it I always choose different numbers every time. It makes it easier to quit or play less regularly when you take random numbers, as if you stick with the same numbers week in, week out you are compelled through fear of missing out to keep on buying that ticket. You hadn't realised this before so now when you quit you hope that your 'winning' numbers *don't* come up – of course you still check the results just like you used to. This habit will die after a few months. The lottery companies want and encourage you to keep the same numbers as they know those that do will play regularly; so you get 'guidance' on choosing them – the dates of birth of you, your spouse and kids, your house number etc. They might offer a credit-card-sized lottery number card to write down your numbers for you to hand over in the newsagent's each week. It sits there in your wallet, reminding you to bet. They sell it to you as 'convenience'. The man in the bookies or reading his *Sun* form guide that morning gets fixated on a horse; he now has no alternative but to back it or he might well kick himself. And if he doesn't back it and it wins then the next time he has this 'feeling' he will *run* to the bookies (or so much more conveniently, log on). Yes, when you decide on some course of action with a bet it is almost impossible not to follow through with it. So it's best not to start contemplating lottery numbers at all, choose random ones when you are at the newsagents instead and don't go near any race card in the paper. It's far safer that way.

For some reason the regulator only allows someone over the age of 18 to bet in Ladbrokes but allows a 16-year-old to 'play' the national lottery or buy a scratch card. Some of these games have been clearly aimed at the young. Just look at their names: Monopoly, Pigs Might Fly, Cock-A-Doodle Dough! Either the young or just the naïve. But this discrepancy in the legal age to gamble seems odd especially when in other European countries you must be 18. Lotto consumers are never referred to as gamblers but as players. They are as much players as the guy who sells burgers outside the stadium on match day is a professional footballer. Players exert some influence on the game they play. With the exception of poker players, the rest of us gamblers – spread-betters, casino betters, lotto and bingo gamblers, fruitie slot-jocks – have little or zero influence on the outcome. Zero. Which is also the final destination of our bank balance if we continue.

Bingo is ever popular online but in those bingo halls, less so nowadays. So, what do the bingo companies do to fill this hole in their bottom line? Easy. The same as the high-street bookie. Enter the Vegas-style video slot machine, known in the trade as a 'B3'. And just like in Vegas or in the bookies, gamblers lose thousands on these in a morning or in an afternoon or in an evening; yes, you can play seven days a week in some places until the early hours. Less a B3 and more like a B52 for the effect it will have on your finances. Again, as in so many areas of gambling the rules have been relaxed within the last decade. From 2011, bingo halls were allowed to have a higher number of these machines in their venues – which they site near the

entrance because they know their business. And unlike at the bookies, there will probably be an ATM right next to them. Just like the high-street bookies, they are regulated by the Gambling Commission, which predicted that the number of these machines would rise by 690 from the 2011 figure of 6,226. It has now in 2016 risen to 10,014! Where did they get their prediction from? I suggest they consulted the industry itself. This is usually what happens. And then took this figure as their prediction. They obviously didn't consult any independent expert on addiction and have no idea or chose to ignore how successful these machines have been in Vegas. It seems, once again, the government are more concerned with protecting the industry rather than the vulnerable. The industry state that they are only giving their customers what they want. This is also what the drug dealer says. It is up to government to protect us from both the legal and illegal businesses who prey on us and our addictive nature.

iii. Casinos... and their fruit machines

I once visited the public casino in Monte Carlo. It didn't impress me. I never even bothered betting. For many of us their only experience will be on a cross-channel ferry. There is nothing chic and sophisticated about most casinos. If you want to mix with people who might actually dress for the occasion, then there are plenty of exclusive clubs around the country. The games haven't changed for a hundred years or more: roulette, blackjack and craps are still the favourites. There's also that massive wheel of fortune you are often confronted with when you first walk in; that's because this has the highest chance of you losing, yet that little flexible rod that slowly flicks across those last few segments gives you the impression that you nearly won – so you bet again. If you're a high-roller there's always baccarat. But the big money makers nowadays are the rows upon rows of slot machines. You don't even have to employ a croupier for these. A fully-automated, industrialised way to lose your money. For some a visit to the casino might just be a social event. Your company might even pay for a few chips for you. But unless you can get away with card-counting, you will lose. James Bond may look cool as he sits there smoking his Gitanes, surrounded by cleavages.

But this is not how it is. Why bother even dressing for a casino when you can sit at home in your underpants and play? Welcome to the world inhabited by 90%+ of all players (I must hazard a guess as it's only the providers who really know anything). Sign up to ten different sites and get ten lots of 'free' spins and credits. Why watch and join in with late-night TV or online casinos? If you are excited by this then get yourself a free app and play with imaginary money – but just remember never to switch, as you will have the mathematical certainty of losing actual money. I checked out an online casino that offered you imaginary credit. Played some random one-armed bandit game for 20 minutes – for no other reason than research for this book. Has no entertainment or excitement value to me. And what do you know, with this fake account my winnings kept going up and up! This also happened with my 'free-credits' bingo account. Either I was just a lucky guy or they do this with all these pretend accounts. It's all too easy to sucker the client in. Do these companies have to apply the same odds to the dummy accounts as they do with the real-money accounts? Thousands upon thousands of mostly low-income gamblers suffer if there is a scam here going on – those players who don't even know what a regulator actually is. Both the players and the regulators often seem mutually ignorant of each other but it is the role of the latter to be the former's protector, or else why have one?

You fell for the marketing, you liked the look of those girls flashing those playing cards at you and flashing their teeth and tits. You got your 'free credits' to get you started – after you funded your account (they are not completely free – in more ways than one) – and sat down at that poker table or roulette wheel. Casinos provide 'free' drinks all night long to their clients who must somehow ignore the obvious fact that an inebriated brain does not make good decisions. Your 'free credits' didn't last too long, did they? You felt like that poker shark, sitting around the virtual table in your cap and shades as you sat in front of your actual kitchen table in your underpants and glasses at 2 a.m. Now you've managed to lose more than you imagined and you haven't even formed any friendships, had any sort of social event. And those inviting-looking girls are still nowhere to be seen.

WHAT HAPPENS – TO YOUR CASH – IN VEGAS? IT STAYS IN VEGAS.

Maybe you have played some themed fruit machine down the pub. Could have an Egyptian theme with flashing coloured glass lighting up the Sphinx and the Great Pyramid. If you want to play the ultimate fruit machine and actually *get inside* one, like *Tron* rather unsuccessfully demonstrated with video games (twice!), then visit Las Vegas. Here you walk past full-size replicas of the Sphinx and the Great Pyramid. Or the Eiffel Tower. Or Venice, complete with canal and gondolas. These temples to temptation overwhelm you in the same way the medieval peasant was overawed by the cathedral. Now capitalism and the expression of it – the skyscraper – overshadow religion, which has been pushed to the side-lines in Britain. Read any survey on the nation's pastimes and gambling won't figure. Monitor their actual behaviour and the true picture emerges. Now gambling is many places ahead of church attendance. Whatever reservations I may have about religion I have many more about gambling! Every few years a new football stadium opens which draws in the masses in the way the church used to. We all seem drawn to something that tantalises us with the promise of something wonderful. In Vegas, you think you are playing the machine from the inside. No, they are playing YOU! You experience the ultimate in immersion gambling; *West World* for the gambler (now *there's* a better film!). Want to play a retro-pop music fruitie down your local? Come to Vegas and you can actually see Britney or Lionel Richie or Elton John.

Yes, here you get total gambling – those beeps and flashing lights are not just confined to the fruit machine. Here it's the city itself. It will overwhelm you. All those lights and showgirls will distract you. That's the idea. They hold many sci-fi conventions in Vegas. People dress up as Han Solo or Lieutenant Uhura. But *everyone* who stays in Vegas comes as a fantasy character. You will be overwhelmed in this fantasy world so that you don't know what you're doing. Vegas causes you to lose a grip on reality. All that fake gold and those plush carpets and attentive waitresses dispensing free drinks, make you feel like a rock-star. You are conned into believing that you have entered the land of luxury. No, you have entered the land of laxity. You are not carefree but care*less*. Your own money becomes unreal. You throw it around almost without thinking. You might have $5k of winnings in your pocket, a nice wad of $100 bills rolled up and squeezed in. It won't stay there long though.

Have you ever walked around with $5k in your pocket back in your home town? You forget just how hard it is to make this in your day job. So you lose it – then $5k more. You get caught up in it all. All that noise, all those visuals. Only takes one winner at the roulette table to have a win and they are often only too keen to holler and hoot about it. Does the same trick as the clunking fruit machine – it draws attention to the winners, it advertises gambling as the fun way to make easy money. The casinos even employ their own cheerleaders. No, not girls in short skirts with pompoms – although that would draw in a male crowd. No, they employ men in suits to high-five the winners, to get the crowd going. These men are normally attached to the high-rollers and big spenders, who often come alone and therefore need this pseudo-friend to celebrate with. Without them the winning is little fun and they would either slow their gambling down or subconsciously limit the number of visits they make to Vegas.

As each US state has its own gambling laws and online is also restricted, many fly in to Vegas for the weekend. The elderly seem the largest contingent in these places. They gamble away their retirement funds and waste the decreasing amount of precious time left for them. They are joined by the weekend punter who rather bizarrely has saved for the trip. It's more than likely not their first trip, so they know they will lose – they return because they have some level of addiction. America is not against online per se. They are against *foreign-owned* online gambling businesses, so they put up barriers to stop them, the most successful barriers being not allowing US bank accounts to fund these online sites. The Vegas casinos are not only in Vegas. They are franchising and spreading out all over the country and abroad; there is Wynn Casinos Macau, for instance. They want to protect their business. I used to think that Vegas was the lesser of two evils. But now Vegas is no longer confined to Vegas and run-down Atlantic City, this is becoming less true. The gambling businesses' profits will grow and grow and stay within US borders. State tax revenues will also increase – that's the only reason why individual states allow it. If a neighbouring state allows it then this causes a domino effect as its citizens just drive across the border, so they lose all that potential tax revenue, and a few years down the line they allow it too. They are desperate for the tax as much as the UK government. On both sides of the Atlantic, those who grow this tax base are you and I and all those millions of other DFC members that governments de facto encourage. We try to replicate Vegas - with Blackpool. It's hardly the same but when it's so easy to play online, who would want to bother with the hassle of getting to the north of England when you don't need to, whatever they offered?

Casinos look after the big losers very well. They don't want them to blow loads straight away. No, this would frighten off the gambler. The casinos know they can milk more from the long-term gambler. They prefer to tap into this constant stream of cash – much like the high-street bookie, the bingo hall, the SB bookie… Just look at how they treated the old lady doctor on the Louis Theroux documentary. Even paid for her husband's lavish funeral. Why? Because she had managed to lose $4 million in seven years playing the slot machines. Four million! Treated it like a job; but with this job the money flows the other way. Anyone check on her mental health? No gambling site ever does. Four million dollars says in-itself she has issues. The casinos look after their clients in any way they can. So do customer services of the online sites. There are only two

aspects in which the gambling companies have any interest in their clients: their ability to pay, and their address so they can enforce the first point. It surprises me, though, that they didn't try a bit harder to keep me as I lost at least £50k in that last year alone. Some SB bookies have an elite club; don't know why I wasn't offered membership to keep me sweet. The only time they ever contacted me directly rather than by some standard email was when they were demanding money. The only membership I earned was that of the DFC.

'I SPENT HALF MY MONEY ON GAMBLING, ALCOHOL AND WILD WOMEN. THE OTHER HALF I WASTED.'

The world's most famous casino gambler and consequently the world's most famous casino loser is John Daly, who paraphrased that quote attributed to W.C. Fields, referring to the $50 million he gambled away. Winner of both the US PGA and The Open a few years later, he has managed to squander his millions away, sometimes before he even had them. In 1995 he won the second of his two majors at St. Andrews but was already in debt to the casinos to the tune of around $4 million. Through sponsorships and appearances, he managed to work this debt off. So, what does he do? Two years later he owes them millions again. This time, in steps Mr Callaway and pays it off for him. Paying off debts or acquiring more stake money is not the answer for the gambler although we always think it is. Stopping gambling is the only answer. You need to sort out your problem first or it all goes straight to the bookies. Never give a gambler a loan. You will never see your money again. If you have decided to give them a $5k loan for a car and have transferred some money to his account rather than to the car dealer direct, then he may never buy that car. He might just use $500 for stake money. It's only stake money, his gambler's mind reasons. When he loses this, that car still costs the same and now he is $500 short. He then tries to win that $500 back. He'll be going to work on the bus.

John Daly seems to have his Jack Daniels addiction under control and some other addictions impacting on his health. The hardest addiction to kick and one he still hasn't managed to is casino gambling. Can't see the appeal of this myself as you are up against machines that are programmed to win and the mathematical impossibility of winning long-term at blackjack; as a kid I played this as pontoon, the high-rollers play it as vingt-et-un. Call it what you like, the casino has the edge on you. John claims in his autobiography that the two places he truly loves are the golf course and the casino. He also loves driving his motor home all over the country. He feels he is in control when he is sitting behind that steering wheel. This also carries over to the casino. He actually believes he is in control when he is sitting in front of the slots. In control! The machine is completely in control – the fact that the gambler presses a few buttons here and there is almost irrelevant. The machine tricks him into believing he is in control by offering him buttons to press and 'decisions' to make. You believe you are coaxing and cajoling that machine into paying you out. No, the computer programme within is coaxing and cajoling money out of you. Whatever you do has basically no effect, just that you believe it does. Those flashing lights and beeps give you the impression that you are getting there, that the big win is around the corner. It teases you like a lap-dancer who gives you the eye. She'll get your money too. You'll get a paid-for personal dance, that little win, but you won't get any big win out of her either. Both will leave you sadly disappointed.

John is one of those few who actually use that $5000 slot at the Wynn casino (a less apt name for a casino I couldn't imagine – at least not for the customers anyway). Just in case you are confused, $5000 is not the maximum win pay-out – no, it is the cost of a single spin! He says he lost $1.65 million dollars in five hours, mostly playing this. And he maintains that *he* is in control! But I know what he means – it is more like he is in a place of tranquillity. You feel relaxed and 'at home'. You are either in a Zen-like state or a zombie-like trance. But a place of tranquillity is not a place of safety. It is the exact opposite; like having a lovely summertime picnic in the countryside – just that you are sitting in an M.O.D. firing range. John could quite easily have put a dozen slots into his house and played there. But out of convenience as he is on the road for most of the year, and the fact that he seems to love the atmosphere, the ambience and environment of the casino, he comes back time and time again. Thankfully, this doesn't appeal to me. It appeals to millions of others. But playing against the SB firms is no different to what John repeats with those slots. They also seem to be programmed to win, just like the casino slots. And unless you are a household name in the poker world – then you are no better off than us SB gamblers or slot jockeys.

But you can't separate John Daly's passion for golf and winning from his desire to gamble. Or the Canadian magnate who feeds $100 bills into the 'slots' and gambles tens of thousands on the spin of a roulette wheel at his private table, from the passion and personality that made him the multi-millions in the first place (*Gambling in Las Vegas*, BBC, Louis Theroux). Unfortunately, for most punters, this spirit is only channelled in the wrong direction. We will not make money in any way from our inherent nature but only lose through gambling.

John Daly was at the top of his game not so long ago. We are told as kids that it's not the winning but the taking part that counts. This can be true. But if gambling becomes that sport replacement then, 'Winning isn't everything. It's the *only* thing'. When you are gambling, it's the winning, not the taking part that counts. You only take part.

4

THE HIGH STREET: THE AMUSEMENT ARCADES, THE BOOKIES AND THEIR FRUIT MACHINES

i. The amusement arcades

Visit a seaside town out of season and you see pensioners spinning those fruit machine wheels, one hand inserting the coins, the other hand holding their walking stick. Pensioners often play as they are bored; they are unable to do anything more constructive with their time and are often shunned and ridiculed by society. The casinos and amusement arcades will never ignore them. But little do they seem to realise, those machines and friendly staff are effectively ridiculing them even though they believe that they are in control. They may not even be fully in control of their bladders so they come to the amusement arcade or bingo hall foyer where they can experience perceived domination, control and application of their own skill although it is the reverse. They have been deceived. They park their mobility scooter outside then find a nice comfortable stool inside, the stool in front of their 'favourite' machine. Those bar stools allow gamblers to get comfortable, slows down the fatiguing process that especially affects the pensioner target, and since they're comfortable they lose more. Even when they are tired it's still possible to gamble as they are sitting down. And when the place is busy, someone is bound to win a large amount sooner or later. This is announced loudly by the machine which clunks out the coins. Those around are now conned into believing that if they continue gambling that they too will win.

Works well for the pub fruitie too; here you often get a large, captive audience who are not even gambling whom are now drawn to the allure of easy riches. These amusement arcades are not just for the eight-year-old who wants to win a Minion from the limp-wristed claw. A parent should never allow their child to enter one of these all-singing all-dancing open-fronted gamblers' boudoirs; they should not be presented with the something-for-nothing allure of gambling in any of its forms. Seems the low internet-connected take-up rate of the poorly educated pensioners who frequent these places keep these businesses ticking over through the cold, winter months until the tourists return, trying to win a SpongeBob whilst holding a stick of candy-floss in the other hand, whilst the internet generation and those whose first computer was a ZX81 log on and on and on to all those online betting businesses, filling the businesses' coffers with cash a million times faster than any seaside fruit machine ever could. They will also conveniently site an ATM machine in there for you; and to rub sea salt into the wounds, this little money-spouting machine may also extract a small fee from you for using it. You can't actually charge them up with credits from the counter where some middle-aged woman sits surrounded by stacks of ten pence coins like you can in the bookies (maybe you can in some places?). But those cash-dispensers shouldn't really be sited in there, should they? As pensioners with limited mobility frequent these places, then don't make it easy for them. This is the job of the regulator. Get them to have to leave the building and walk or scoot or struggle down the road. Then they might think twice about it – or just be physically unable to return.

Amusement arcades used to amuse – now they just abuse. The slot machines have elbowed out the space invaders machines and their more sophisticated upgrades. You might still find them but you'll have to walk past the slot machines to do it; this is not an accident. Kids who see the flashing lights and spinning reels will all one day find themselves standing in front of them and in later life might even find themselves sitting in front of the damn things. Over the years, the machines that make the most money push out those that don't do so well. But these Pac-Man descendants get the kids through the door; they have become a kind of gateway drug. Alcohol is perfectly legal and many say this was what led them on to further drugs such as cocaine. Didn't take me long to progress from Pac-Man to the real money-spinners for these places. Used to feed in those 10p coins one after another after another like my life depended on it. Which for any gambler, it does. And those machines gulped down everything I fed them like Homer does with doughnuts. But in today's internet age, many will only get sucked into gambling once they become 18, have a bank card and a job and can bet whenever they like on their unlimited internet access not-so-smartphone.

ii. The bookies

I am now offered a loyalty card when I place a bet. There is always an incentive attached to them but they are not offering them to you from the kindness of their hearts. Sign up online and they can track your every move.

The high street does not get this privilege with their customers. The loyalty card is an attempt to do just that. The more data they get, the better they can market to you and to their customer base as a whole. They also try to rebrand themselves, to whitewash themselves without any mention of gambling or betting in their names at all. Now we have names like 888sport. Makes it sound healthy, like a visit to the sports centre for a swim. You subconsciously then believe you are competing in a sport. You might feel young again through this delusion, reminded of the time when you really did participate in actual sports. But just like the spread-better with his strategies, you are stuck in some fantasy world no better than Dorothy, full of blind optimism as you unknowingly set off to see the Wizard of Loss.

Whatever game you play, it is always heavily weighted in the bookies' favour. The odds they give cannot really be 'fair' odds. They have all those overheads to cover and shareholders to pay. The true chance of any event that you bet on happening is more likely to be twice the odds that they offer or why else do you make a loss every year from gambling when you have no costs to cover other than the bet itself? Think the premiership club you bet on have a good chance of winning and the odds look favourable? The bookies have calculated the statistics and they know better than you that the odds they offer are shockingly bad. They understand that football results can go three ways, not two. Most people do not bet on a draw. Think Ronnie O'Sullivan looks good for a 147? Chances are he won't. He's made 13 maximums in 24 years as a pro so even if the odds look enticing, just remember that he makes on average one maximum roughly every two years. But he's *nearly* made lots more. Nearly? You lose. Think your cunning plan of switching to the speciality bets is better than sticking with the mainstream? No, the odds will always favour the bookie whatever you go for. Any form of bingo can easily be set up to favour the bingo hall online or otherwise, with whatever margin they can get away with, with respect to the regulator and the patience of their own customers. The SB bookie can't predict as precisely what their profits will be but they have a pretty good idea for every market condition. If the bookies could market a coin-toss game where you could bet evens on either heads or tails, they would engineer it so it could also land on its edge.

Leicester City win the Premier League in 2016. Good for them. Good for the bookies too. Yes, there were the odd few people who put a tenner or maybe £20 on them to win – at 5,000-1! To quote that prisoner hanging upside-down in the *Life of Brian*, 'You lucky bastard.' Bookies love it – for two reasons. First, they have made millions on those bets on the favourites that didn't pay-out. But bigger still will be the long-term effects of this. That free advertising that all news channels afforded them, including the BBC putting up that guy who was due to win £50,000 from a £10 stake is priceless (he cashed in early for £28,000). Far better than employing Boris Becker for 30 second adverts – more effective and free! So in subsequent seasons everybody in whatever league is going to put a tenner on their no-hopers to win. This will amount to millions more in increased revenue almost out of nowhere. No ad agency could have devised a more effective marketing strategy than this. James Vardy *et al.* are celebrated all over Leicester and in every betting company HQ all over England (and little England, i.e. Gibraltar).

You will suffer losses. It will not be bad luck. There are too many near-wins and 'if onlys…' in betting. Remember that these are losses. There are the matches where a player gets sent off for the team you are backing, the horse that loses by a short-head, the tennis player who gets injured during the match… the list is almost endless. These things happen; it can't really be described as 'luck' but more like 'life'. You can also spread-bet on a variety of events with the bookies but it is unlikely to cause you so much pain as its financial equivalent although you can still lose far more than you could have imagined.

How do professional sports-betters make money? By betting on a narrow range of sports or maybe just one. They know exactly how to do it and undoubtedly have a network to support them. They know where to get the inside information they need. They know how to place bets and the exact second to place them through multiple agents to ensure the best odds before the bookies can react. They may even place smaller bets on the team they don't expect to win in order for the bookies to up the odds on the team they do expect to win then slam, their agents strike in unison and more often than not these sorts of organisations come out on top.

Then there's the man reading his *Racing Post* that now covers a multitude of sports, not just the horses and the dogs. Or the guy reading the *Times* or watching Sky Sports' Saturday morning football show that actually *invites on* the bookies – one party get to advertise, the other gets pseudo-journalism from their guest whose company is paying for this slot in some way. This latter group of punters usually lose. You are no expert. You do not know what you are doing even though you believe you do; you shop around for the best odds, you research this and that before you place your bet. Why bother? The average punter may well bet on a whole range of sports unlike the professional; they suddenly become a golfing expert during the Masters then an expert on tennis during Wimbledon fortnight. The bookies plug these events and the wonderful odds and the speciality bets they offer a week or month before the first ball is struck. And then continue in the same vein during the event itself. Then it's the darts and before you know what you're doing, you're betting on the winner of the Eurovision Song Contest. (Ok, not a sport. But for the punter, it doesn't need to be. Financial spread-betting is not a sport either.) The punter almost feels they are participating in the sport itself by betting on them. But you are not running out for Man United. Your connection to them is not even tangential, it is completely separated from you – much like the money you have staked on them.

Do the bookies care about pro betters and pro winners? Not much. There aren't many of them. They can even track the consistent winners and use their placed bets to influence the odds and give the bookies themselves some guidance. How do the pros make money? Do they have some inside knowledge? Maybe a journo who gets info first on player injures and so on feeds them for a fee, who knows? But you? What do you base your selection on? Information that is known to everyone. Do not think when you win it is anything to do with your skill as a researcher? It is more likely to be down to the law of averages. And at the end of the week or year, you are almost certain to be down too.

Nowadays you can bet in-running on just about everything. So you can increase a position just like with spread-betting, although there is an end point at least, when the ref blows the final whistle. This is a wonderful little side-line for the bookies that is only made possible by technology; your '*smart*phone'. I once went on an internet date where my perfect match decided she'd make it an in-running date by chatting up some bloke at the bar when she went to get *me* a drink! I could tell she wasn't impressed when she met me. As everyone does these days, I uploaded flattering pictures. We have moved from an era of the blind date to the visually-impaired date, I guess.

Another bullshit phase you will go through, in whatever arena of gambling: I have placed a £2 or just a £1 position on the Dow then closed for a profit of £6 and £9! What was the point? I *need* to do something, make some kind of bet. With spread-betting I also wanted to prove to myself that I could win – even when I had just lost £10k! Nuts, I know – I knew it at the time too. I used to see people doing this in betting shops all the time; most seem to rush and place their bet at the very last minute. Nothing to do with changing odds. No, they are unsure what to do but as the horses are 'going behind' and loading up in the stalls, they have to be quick and bet on *something*. So they scribble down quickly an almost random selection and get it on as they come under starter's orders and sometimes even after the gates are open – the bookie will willingly take a late bet in their shops – they know they are onto a winner and the customers aren't. The punter ends up just guessing – this is largely what they do anyway – but the gambler *has* to bet. You must be in, even if it's a small bet. The trouble is, betting small can snowball into nightmare massive bets.

Is there anything actually improved for the customer in betting shops since I used to pop in almost daily in late 80s? The bookies will list about 100 'improvements' for their customers. If you tell a lie a thousand times, then people believe it – maybe at only a subconscious level but nevertheless it comes to be believed. So they stress the word 'improvement' and the customer gets taken in. Longer opening hours just means that you have a greater time span in which to lose. A wider choice of sports and bets

just means that you have a greater variety of ways to lose. Improved odds too, whatever that means. There is only one real improvement which they will also remind you of even though they fought hard against it for many years; you can now bet in a non-smoking environment. And in some dusty corner those GambleAware leaflets sit ignored.

iii. Their fruit machines

Walking into a bookies nowadays is fundamentally the same as back in the 80s when this was my betting venue of choice. The same people still frequent the place. It is still a working-class establishment where men wander in wearing overalls flecked with paint. And the constant attendance of the male pensioner, whatever time of day. The middle class bet, that's for sure. They never really used to – but that was before the internet age. Yes, the internet. That great engine for democracy, to disseminate knowledge or just to make shopping easier. But what did I use it for? Gambling. Not a noble use of such a wonderful invention. There *are* some changes within the walls of today's bookies. The most notable being what used to be called the fruit machine. It is no longer such a simple device. You can play a variety of games on them. From my observations, computer generated roulette seems the most popular; a game where you have the mathematical certainly of losing due to that green segment that exists. At least there are no ATMs actually in a bookies. But there doesn't have to be! When you have exhausted your notes and coins, wander over to the girl at the counter, slip your bit of plastic into their portable machine, type in those four digits which are designed to be a security feature although you seem happy to just give your money away, then back to the computerised terminal which now has

£20 of credit. This avoids the possibility that on your way to the cashpoint you either get distracted or come to your senses and don't return.

There always seems to be someone on these machines. Pop in to place a bet then stay another 20 minutes on this damn thing losing more than the bet that you actually came in to put on in the first place. And even if that bet you placed wins, you will still be down because of your computerised roulette losses. But many come in simply to play these machines. Gamblers are known for chasing their losses. If you lost playing the fruit machine twenty years ago, then you could plug away, feeding in one 10p after another. This takes time. The bookie wants to take as much money off of you as quickly as possible. So nowadays if you have lost, you try to win your losses back quicker. Now it is possible to up your stake on each spin. If you've been spinning at 50p a shot why not increase it to £1 or £2? Before you know it, you are coming into that shop and *starting* with £1 and £2. A year later it is £10 or £20. Sounds unlikely? This is along the lines of what I did spread-betting although it was more like I was spinning each time with £100 or £200! I started off with £2 'spins'. These machines can take thousands off a single individual in an hour or two. Each shop is restricted by law to four machines per shop. How do Ladbrokes and the others get round this? Easy. In my home town Ladbrokes have three small shops within easy walking distance of each other. They generate massive amounts for them. They have been referred to as the crack cocaine of gambling. For me, the crack cocaine of gambling is now online but I take their point. Let's call online the crystal meth of gambling then. Ninety percent of casino style gambling is probably online nowadays, but out of the remaining 10% a large percentage of that is in the bookies and the bingo hall foyer. The actual casino is now probably bottom of the list. I'm guessing at these numbers but you get the point. Where would you get accurate statistics from anyway? Who's going to own up to that in some survey? The gambling companies would reveal nothing if they could get away with it. But there are enough plc's out there who have to publish their reports so you get a fairly good picture. It seems these machines are their saviour. And if you cannot wait for the next horserace to start, you can even bet on computerised horseracing in between. This might seem nuts as the bookies have set up this system themselves but does the average punter fare any better with real races and events?

Now the bookies make half their profits from these gamblers' crack machines – known in the trade as Fixed Odd Betting Terminals (FOBTs). These resemble a casino more than an old-fashioned fruit machine. Whereas in the amusement arcade you might find a jackpot of £100 and in the pub maybe £500, the bookie is permitted to entice people in with a maximum pay-out of £10,000! Bookies are a bit coy about supplying information about these machines but there are some facts out there; the main players (not the customers, I mean!) make over a billion pounds in profit from them each year and this figure is growing. They are no longer just a bookies; it's more like having several high-street casinos in your town without them having to go through the inconvenience of those annoying public meetings before being granted a special licence.

Fruit machines are exactly the same as any other form of gambling; they trick you in exactly the same way. Sometimes you get a win and occasionally a big win and often that near-win. Some machines will let you spin ten times or so for guaranteed wins each time so that your little digital pot of money ticks up and up; this is a great feeling, just like when my SB balance kept on climbing. Same applies to poker. Easy to see it climb but then painful to see it come down again, sometimes little by little but all too often in big chunks too. Then there are those nudge buttons to allow you to use your 'skill' to nudge those wheels around to a win. You can make adjustments here and there with many forms of gambling but it won't help you a jot in the end.

What other machine would you feed where you get less out (eventually nothing) than you put in? Is there a more pointless exercise? Standing in front of a machine for hours (nowadays you can sit), feeding in your hard-earned cash (or DSS money, as is often the case) before walking out potless a few hours later, is a bizarre way to spend a lovely sunny afternoon. I had a teenage addiction to these but I grew out of it like teenagers grow out of buying *Men Only*. For many adults, their addiction to these actually grows. Gamblers have their favourite machine, one they basically get fixated on and forsake all others; but this is like sticking with a girlfriend who cheats on you every day. In the bookies one machine gives you the option of many games – yes, you have many varied ways to lose. You are trying to outsmart a machine and mathematical probability.

This desire for success comes from millennia of pitting our wits against the animals we are hunting, the weather that tries to make us ill and kill us and other males who vie for the attention of the girl that we really want. We need to remember that although the last instinct is with us as much today as it has ever been, times have changed. Those slithers of silicon have been harnessed to work against us and however much cajoling, practice (!) and time spent with these machines, there will only be one winner. It is not like revising for your French exam; you will not improve your knowledge or skills in any way. You will waste your afternoon, you will waste your money, you will get more and more frustrated... and then you will come back the next day with a pocket full of cash thinking that a solid block of funds at your disposal is the key to winning. Again, you are confusing this with other aspects of life where having a bulging wallet will help you or make life more enjoyable.

These all-singing, all-dancing machines attract a constant clientele in any bookies. The punter doesn't even have to accept the inconvenience of having to wait for the gate to open on the televised horse race. Now they can plough on without any interruption. The bookie just needs to install a few of these machines for a constant income stream and they only require minimal staff, whose duties fall into two categories: 1) hand the PIN terminal to the client to send their funds to the machine and 2) handle the occasional client who is astonished that the machine has taken all his money and tries to topple the thing over onto the carpet or at least tries to punch or karate kick the crap out of it. Using your credit card to gamble really opens up the floodgates. Once you hand over that, it really starts to get out of control. Your flexible friend doesn't look and feel and smell like the thick wad of readies you would otherwise have to hand over and more than likely think twice about. If the bookies where these machines are now also sited could also double up as a pawn-broker's they'd take the watch off your wrist too. But find an area where there are a half a dozen or so bookies and you will likely find those three spheres suspended from a bar somewhere nearby.

*

I still think of them as fruit machines with their mechanical reels. But nowadays those reels might well be computer generated, although your local pub usually sticks with the traditional. It has more ways to overwhelm and distract you. The images are more detailed and sophisticated. The video slot machine has enabled the process of taking your money off you to speed up yet again with all those tricks it employs; you can play multiple lines (the online bingo sites also do this), they keep you playing by bumping up that cash-pot that you almost win (the 'almost wins' give you a 'rush' too)... finally, you walk away, cursing your 'luck' that that final reel didn't click around one more time to give you that jackpot – and you vow to return the next day as you almost won. You are confusing this with how you almost managed to run 100 metres at school in a better time and with a little more effort you could have – those physical and mental challenges that are actually achievable. Beating a pre-programmed machine that cannot lose? Your mind is still programmed as a hunter-gatherer. This does not cross over to gambling (card games are the exception – for the skilled). You must try to understand that human nature is being taken advantage of by others who obviously understand it better than you do. Spread-betting and bookie bets are similar to that machine. They are set up to win just like a computerised roulette wheel. Our ancestors used to battle against invaders for supremacy. This instinct to overcome is ingrained within us. I'll say it again: this does not cross over to gambling! Back to the machines themselves, the push button replaced that slow process of actually pulling the lever on a one-armed bandit, and what pensioner has the strength to yank that thing a hundred or a thousand times? Whether you play a 'puggy' in Glasgow or a 'pokie' in Australia the result will be the same. We are now in an age of industrialised gambling whether you want to leave your house or not.

Those flashing lights and beeps and short-burst tunes keeps you aroused. Yes, gambling *arouses* you. It's not the same as sex – let's not get carried away – but it's still up there somewhere. They don't add these features to entertain you; they add them to *overwhelm* you. Overwhelm the senses and you lose track of time, space and your money, as you are mesmerised and almost hypnotised into staying at that damned machine. Those traditional pub fruities and now the new generation of 'cash-converters' are oversized a) so the frustrated punter finds it hard to pull over, and b) to confront the gambler – with his pint in his other hand – with a range of distracting, hypnotising visual and audible tools. Gambling websites from casinos to spread-betting employ similar techniques. Overwhelm with 'information and education' is the updated version of being simply overwhelmed with sound and vision. Each gambling sector tries to adopt as much as it can from all four and can sneak in a few other individualised tricks too. They prey on your desires; your greed, your need for success, to prove to others that you are in fact a success, to be challenged... there is a long list.

If I put £20 on a horse and it loses, it would have taken me say, 20 minutes to lose this; I will chose a race, read a bit of form, place the bet at the till, wait around a bit for the off, then wait for the race to run and finish. But if I let the FOBT suck in my £20 I can lose it literally in 20 seconds. Most betters spin out their £20 loss over a slightly longer time but often still only a matter of minutes, then back to the counter and that 'pay-with-card' option. The industry is regulated as to how quickly punters can lose their money but barely. With regular fruit machines, may gamblers play two machines at once! The two-machine player is all too common. You often see the Vegas gambler playing three. Some gamblers like to sit in a corner as they find it easier to play two at a time this way, performing like a prog-rock keyboard player.

How to make money gambling? Have inside knowledge; this could be legal or illegal. OR there is another way! Buy a half-decent racehorse, name it 'Non-runner', then, as no one else will realise it's a horse you can bet on, you can clean up! Think this sounds nuts? If you still believe you can make money from gambling, it's not even 1% as nuts as the strategies and ideas *you* believe in!

5

THE MAKING OF A GAMBLER

Maybe I was just born a gambler. I've always liked to take risks and I've always been addicted to something or other, mostly sport. Unfortunately, I was no better than the next guy at football or golf or whatever, so ultimately it didn't really get me very far.

When did my gambling really reveal itself? When did it become so appealing? I know exactly where and when: the Costa del Sol, 1981. I started in the same way that thousands of others do; a coin pusher machine as they're known in the trade. For me, it was a five peseta machine. You know, insert your coin at the top, let it bounce its way down between and off those little pegs, onto a moving step which hopefully will force another five peseta piece or two to fall off and onto the lower level then with a bit more luck will push a few coins hanging over the lip to topple into the collection tray below for the primary school child to eagerly scoop up. I loved that machine. I loved the mechanics of it, the hushed noise of it, even the smell of the place it was in. Yes, I know what John Daly means. I also felt somewhat in control as I tried to spin those coins into that slot. Even as an 11-year-old, you start inventing gambling strategies! I can still picture it now, pushed up against a pillar with me standing there with my back to the bar where I bought daily one of those little glass bottles of shake-before-drinking Oranginas.

A few years later I discovered an amusement arcade packed with fruit machines in my home town. The place is closed now which gives me no satisfaction as the owner is probably sunning himself on the terrace of their new home in Barbados, paid for by many thousands of kids like me feeding in millions of ten-pence pieces. And the lack of satisfaction is compounded by the fact that the venue for my years of teenage self-destruction has been replaced by a third branch of Ladbrokes. To make matters worse, 2018 will see the opening of a 145-bed casino hotel only a couple of hundred yards away!

I am sure if I looked around online I could find that coin-drop machine. And I'm sure that as is the case with most online games I could choose exactly what coin to drop. I could switch to £2 coins if I want. And in the virtual amusement arcade where, don't forget, you play with real money, I could be dropping £10 coins. Some would even play for sentimental reasons. Online your win will be accompanied by the sound of chinking coins, just as you remember from when you were a child. The gambling companies and games designers play on that child still within, they pick at our memories and feed off our nostalgia. Find an alternative trip down memory lane.

I can clearly remember one time on a school trip when we ventured into a seaside amusement arcade; the others were happy to play video games but what did I do? I played on a video game too, but mine was one of the earliest forms of video gambling: an '80s FOBT, in effect . A Bruce Forsyth's *Play Your Cards Right* type machine. It simply involved predicting whether the next card would be higher or lower than the card before. Still popular today amongst adults. Do this correctly five times and you win. Easy! Yes, I fell for those wins and near-wins. If it's in between, say an eight and you hit lower and you get a nine you believe you were unlucky, as a nine is only just higher! The system often allows you to get through to that final card only for you to lose. It's that 'near-win' trick. None of my other friends seemed drawn to these machines. Twenty-five years later I was welcomed into the world of spread-betting where once again I was betting on higher or lower numbers. Kids as young as 12 today can play on a machine where the maximum prize is £5. That's a lot for a young boy as a boy it inevitably is. He is already in training – the Gambling Commission deem this acceptable. I was clearly a gambler back then. I would bet all I had, believed I could win, fell for the tricks of the trade and probably preferred to devote more of my time and attention to that machine than I did to my friends. I can clearly remember missing out on a girl I actually really liked when I was too busy playing some damned fruitie! Childhood should be a time of new experiences and learning from our mistakes. Many of us just compound the problem and develop it into something unimaginably big that dominates our lives in adulthood.

The natural progression as I got older was then to walk through the doors of my high-street bookies. I was in there when I was 17. No one ever asked my age. Could spend all afternoon in there. I studied and analysed the *Racing Post* like I was trying to understand the double helix. Now that I was well into my teens and my 'A' levels I had switched to a game of skill, one that required study, analysis and discipline, I believed. I had those almost really big wins but was not aware at the time of the almost win trick. I had

Yankees that *almost* paid out several hundred when one of my selections came home second after already having had two winners. My £80 wins could have been so much more. But that's how it works. You go again thinking that your big win will be much bigger next time, now you are experienced and all that bullshit. Then for years I rarely bet. The occasional fiver here on golf or tennis and the Saturday double or treble on the football.

When I hit my thirties, that's when it really took off again. I had almost a decade of being the dormant gambler; the occasional minor bit of activity but next to nothing. Then just like a volcano I became much more active for a few years before I exploded! This transition from dormancy to activity was brought about by the internet. This didn't really exist in my 20s. Today's twentysomethings will be drawn into the world of gambling far easier. Some you read about in the paper when they end up in court. But for most, they remain hidden. In my 30s, I had the time and the money and was obviously looking for something to fill a void in my life. We like to be risk-takers and more than that we like to be successful risk-takers. We never became that professional golfer that we wanted to be. We want some means of escape; to escape for a while from that humdrum job, that relationship, our life! We turn to all sorts of things. It is all too easy to submit to gambling's false promises. Now I can become that professional trader that I at one time in my life, actually wanted to become. For the uneducated, they can bypass university and the stress of the 'milk round' and just instantly become a successful and wealthy trader. I gave up those fruities of my youth when I eventually realised it wasn't a game of skill at all. I switched to being the form-studying punter then spread-better – again, I fell for something that I thought required intelligence, analysis and discipline. Today that milk round has changed – the bookies are now doing so well they can pay well and actively recruit through it.

Who do I blame for my demise? My parents? who do I blame for my demise? My parents? They actually instilled in me the true value of money. Not enough guidance about the perils of gambling? I don't blame them at all. I had a stable upbringing, both parents and security. My dad did what all dads do in April. They ask their child who they want to have a pound on in the Grand National and nip off down the betting shop. I could hardly class this as sowing the seed of gambling in my young psyche. I wouldn't recommend any father to do this though but 30 years ago this was accepted as completely normal. It still is! I never won a penny anyway so it should really have shown me what a bullshit way it was to spend a pound. Maybe at the time I would have preferred if he'd bought me an ice cream anyway.

I simply blame my own gullible self and the way I was skilfully manipulated by the industry and those sub-contracted ad agencies. Democratic governments could do better at regulating the industry and seem to be behind the curve for today's online world. Those lobbyists do a great job for their paymasters. We have a rather blasé approach to the whole thing. Successive governments do not want to harm the industry in any way. Quite the reverse in fact; they go out of their way to promote and assist its growth.

I can still remember as that 11-year-old going back to the hotel swimming pool, with my little swimming trunks' pockets weighted down with silver five peseta pieces I had won on that coin-drop machine in the bar. Next was in my teens with jean pockets full of 10p coins, then came the golf club which paid out in 50p coins as £1 coins had only recently been invented. Used to ride home with the 50p coins rubbing against each other in my pockets; yeah, used to saunter into the member-only country club where I was neither a member nor old enough to enter a bar nor to stick coins into a machine. Then moved on to pubs and the snooker club. Even had a few £100 and £150 pay-outs from the snooker club fruitie. By this stage, I was bypassing my pockets and cashing it straight in at the bar for nice, crisp notes. As I remember, these big wins didn't excite me. This is the typical behaviour for the true gambler. You would think after hitting the jackpot you'd be ecstatic. But you're not. Those who are, are not really gamblers. After a big win we often walk away and will play another machine if available – this is another reason why pubs deem it wise to have more than one. I would walk away too but it would be fed back into this machine or another at some point. Or at this stage, more likely be handed over to the girl at the counter at Ladbrokes. I have seen people come into a pub, spend a half an hour on these damned machines, then leave having not even had a drink or met anyone. I did this myself a few times before I was 18. I even made the occasional trip to the racecourse alone. And now we have the internet, we go completely cash-free. Trouble with now living in a cashless society, betting this way you soon end up with a cashless bank account. The spread-bet and especially the gambling industry have been with us for a long time. Before they were in every high street you had to go to the racecourse itself to place a bet. A few decades later the internet arrived. Then came the arrival of broadband... And if 24-hour gambling in your own home wasn't bad enough, the bookies are now in hysterics on the way to the bank as you can now gamble when you are on the train coming home from work or on the golf course (I should know – I've done both) or in your car (done that too) or at your kid's school show or out for a meal with the girlfriend – when she's in the toilet or you are (that was a low point, oft repeated) or at work… Feel liberated by your smartphone?

You are attracted to those flashing lights and beeps of the fruitie in your teens then poker's competitive nature and late-night hustling when you are in your 20s. You then take a more measured view and switch to spread-betting in your 30s before eventually resorting to the slots in retirement when you are just too old and tired to think any more. This seems to be the general pattern for the gambler. The gambling companies know this and market to these target groups. You are not too difficult to seduce.

GamCare give out 'awards' in the shape of 'Certification' to various gambling companies. For instance, the National Lottery, operated by Camelot, have one. And this is the dominant national gambling business where it is deemed perfectly acceptable for a 16-year-old to gamble! (The Health Lottery too, different operator.) But walk into Ladbrokes or play fruit machines – you must be 18. I was never asked my age; I wonder how well this is regulated nowadays in the age of 'proof of age' IDs? The alcohol industry say they are doing this and that to protect people, like taking hundreds of products off the market, irresponsible products. We only have their word for that. Could very easily be products that were not selling very well. How responsible is it to sell super-strength lager, which is the drink of choice for many an alcoholic? Or those little shots drunk by themselves or added to other drinks to make them stronger, favoured by many a binge drinker. These products are nice little earners so even though these drinks seem to be as irresponsible as you could get, they remain on the shelves and by the bed of many an alcoholic to be there when they wake up in the morning and need a swig. It now seems even easier to develop a teenager into a drinker these days. And to make a gambler too.

Camelot offer a wide variety of national lotteries and an even greater variety of scratch cards that a 16-year-old can buy. They say that they withdraw the licence of those traders who sell to under-16s. But only after they have been caught twice and warned (i.e. put on their guard)! Any seller would have to be nuts to carry on in the same way as they know they'd be checked again. I wonder how many lose their licence each year? Retailers generally lose their lovely terminal because they are not selling enough! They have their certificate from the industry-funded GamCare; do they look after the interests of us gamblers or their paymasters? The government do well out of it too. Buying a ticket is a form of voluntary taxation as the tax authorities claim 12%. 50% goes to the prize fund, 5% to the retailer, 5% to Camelot and their shareholders whilst the good causes only receive 28%, but this gets a big fanfare. This reassures the gambler that what they are doing is charitable. Camelot's ad agency play on this. It is said that people give to charity to make *themselves* feel better rather than for the sake of those receiving it. You know damn well that you are 'in it to win it' when you buy that ticket; it is a selfish act made palatable by this self-delusional belief that you are a friend of charity. If you really think this way, then donate 100% direct to whatever charity appeals to you.

You can rise through the ranks if you work hard enough and have the talent; that is the American dream and the British one too. It cannot happen with gambling. Never. You have a marginal chance with poker but that's it. You are worse than the intern at the ad agency who works for no money. With your apprenticeship you give *them* money!

So that's my gambling CV. If you need references, then just read the statements from IG in Chapter 2 and online; I can't publish them all here as it would double the thickness of the book.

6

WHY WE GAMBLE

i. You don't take up fishing in order to catch fish

Why do men have affairs, visit pay-per-play girls above shops or wait for that discreet tap-tap on their hotel room door, gamble heavily, even commit suicide? Could be for a whole host of reasons, especially the last point. But for me it basically boils down to one thing: boredom. We men, in our 40s especially, get that 'well, is that it?' feeling. There is no more chase; our careers might well have settled down as have we – we are in that stable relationship with kids. But this can be damn dull, even if you *do* love your wife. Men want to carry on the chase, carry on taking risks – no, we *need* to. So that's what many of us end up doing. The consequences of the wife finding out are dire – but that won't stop us. In fact, it makes taking the risk even more exciting. Gambling won't hurt anyone, after all – until it gets out of hand – which it won't. That's what the gambler thinks anyway. Of course they do. But then, at the very least, it starts taking up too much of your time when you should really be doing something else, regardless of the financial loss. This loss will be noticed by the wife, one day.

Some will add in the illicit sex too – even if this isn't discovered, your own relationship with your wife will forever suffer. Even if you don't feel guilt, you will start to feel bored by the mundanity of sex with her – which is not good for either of you. Yes, some men think of their wives when they are with their bash-for-cash girl – they may imagine they are in fact screwing their wife and think of her entirely or think of how she was when they were both younger – so he is not really cheating at all then in his mind. No problem with your conscience then when you're with your 20-minute imaginary wife. It makes him feel young again, like the sex magnet he wanted to be but never was. Trouble is, later on they will more likely be screwing their wives and be thinking about that fit, 25-year-old they were doing the same to the night before.

But as a man, you need something to get that 'forever 18' feeling back again. Some choose drugs or spend far too long down the pub to just escape reality for a while. For those with personal demons of sexual abuse when young, feelings of rejection, financial problems, past trauma or just an intense feeling that your life is somehow over now you are married with kids and a mortgage and zero excitement in your life, then suicide becomes an option for far too many. The 'is that it?' feeling is replaced by the 'that's it!' ending. But this is only for a minority.

For most men if not all, sex used to be something exciting, something frequent, her breasts used to be something exotic. Now sex is mundane, sporadic and those breasts often have a baby attached. You want that nubile 20-year-old that your wife once was. You could have an affair but that's far too complicated with a good chance of being caught out as the conquest of choice is usually someone close: a colleague, a friend, a neighbour, the wife's sister. No, you stay safe, relatively safe which is exactly what you don't get with a relative. Many choose gambling as a substitute for sex – and it's a poor one. They are stuck because they don't want to cheat on their wives. They will never be 20 again when they could have sex with a choice of women. Now they are 40, no one who is 20 is interested in them and they are married anyway so there are big problems with this one. So us men try to find alternative releases – gambling is just one of them.

Even for the younger man this appeals. He feels he has already missed out on something. He still wants that *Nuts* magazine girl. So he thinks if he becomes that online success then that's what he'll get. He can't see his career going anywhere, so this is his chance. He may be disappointed in his personal life. That sporting career just never materialised. Gambling can be a replacement for something that you once had or a substitute for something you never did. Often sex. But there are other candidates, such as bereavement or abuse. Maybe you have always been that underling. With gambling you believe that you call the shots, you are in control. Nope, you've got this wrong. Gambling is often that crutch for you to lean on. Just remember that it's a crutch made out of balsa wood. If you believe yourself to be a failure in some way, gambling will not turn you into a success – that's what you believe, that's what the marketing conveys.

But I have kicked the gambling habit, I have a new life in my 40s and I have never had any suicidal thoughts – and I don't visit girls with camisoles either. Like most men I am not sure if I could really be classed as an addict at all – I just gambled for the escape, for the buzz and simply because I'm a man and as such we enjoy taking things to excess. I also gambled out of a sense that I had missed out on certain things, missed out on certain women. I gambled to get that life now that I thought I deserved. I gambled out of boredom with my stagnating career and life. You believe you can find that sense of achievement through gambling; achievement through your own efforts without being blocked like you are at work by your line manager. The mid-life crisis is often a sex-life crisis – and it builds up inside for many years before, which you try to ignore. It is also an identity crisis; you are not happy with how things have turned out, what you have become; it just isn't you – this is not what you wanted all those years ago.

Most don't go as far down the route of excess as I did which prompts me to ask myself about whether I am an addict or not. I certainly presented many of the signs. But it doesn't matter too much if you have 'addict' stamped onto your personal case file. If you are anything like me, then you clearly have a problem. You might have just sleepwalked into this mess. You may well not have understood how the odds really were stacked against you, especially if you were spread-betting: you might really have believed that you were 'investing' and 'trading' and not gambling. You might not even gamble on anything else but fell for this one as it's not gambling, is it? Oh, yes it is! For you, you might not even have other addictions unlike many gambling addicts. My past is not traumatic – possibly a little dull – but nothing to get upset about even though my losses run to six figures, from a man whose monthly salary barely made it much past four. Better to understand the male psyche in the first place so you can try to avoid my mistakes. Even though I risk sounding up my own arse, let's hope my *de facto* diary not only saves people a few quid but also saves a few people's lives too. But you don't even need to be 40 to get that 'is that it?' sensation. I began to feel it in my late 20s. In my

30s, I just tried to live with it and used golf as a release. This was never going to work. Then gambling subconsciously exploded in my mind as a means of escape. If I thought golf was a dumb-ass attempt at fulfilment, I could never have imagined what a tortuous alternative I had now chosen.

Men especially always want to take a chance, to 'go for it'; our thrill-seeking nature means we often don't explore and just ignore the risks and the real chance of success. We are too keen to dive right in. But this is often as wise an approach as the bloke who dives right in off the end of a pier into six inches of water. If we thought about it logically, which is more of a feminine quality, we wouldn't do it. So when I saw that successful looking 'Just For Men' model who was suggesting I become a 'trader' I agreed. Men are the hunters who go all out for the kill while women are the mothers who need to think about the needs of their children so do not take such rash decisions. Far from universally true but by the demographic of the gambling community from the male preserve of the high-street betting shop to the poker tables of the pubs and clubs, it is pretty much true although there are a fair few women on machines and online.

Telling you that spread-betting or poker may not suit everyone, only those who are prepared to take a risk actually seems more of a challenge, which can make men want to do it even more. Men enjoy taking risks, even stupid ones. It's often the case that the riskier it is, the more appealing it is as you get more of a buzz out of it. Why else would men try to scale Everest with little experience, or drive at 100 mph down the dual carriageway (or even a 'B' road), visit girls for 20 minutes for £60 or have a quick fling with a colleague, invest in businesses or shares that are classed as 'high risk'... the list is endless. But spread-betting or playing poker online? Yes, it can be as exciting as base-jumping; just that halfway down as you see the bodies twisted and torn beneath you, you realise the guy who sold the base-jumping experience to someone who has never even done a parachute jump before, has ended up killing all his clients and wouldn't be stupid enough to go base-jumping himself. In my case, spread-betting but really with all forms of gambling the aim of whichever provider is to perform a slow, drawn-out torture; death brings an end to profit, but the torture victim just keeps on yelling out those three digit security numbers. Financial loss will be something that you cannot avoid. Financial meltdown will also result if you do not wake up to your behaviour before it's too late.

Gambling is just like certain other areas of life which pretend to offer massive rewards but don't. Can you really meet a classy woman in a nightclub with whom you can have a meaningful relationship, do you find the best jobs at a job centre, do you find the perfect partner at datetheperfectpartner.com or even worse, datetheperfectpartnerinapoorcountry.com? The answer for 99% of people is no, never, not going to happen however hard you try, whatever they tell you. You believe it because you *want* to believe it, because you *have* to believe it, you have no alternative *but* to believe it, it is easier to believe it than take the harder options. You have tried other options in the past but they haven't worked. You are almost *forced* to go for the unlikely and impossible. There are always those rare cases for whom it actually *does* work out. These will be used as examples and marketed to the needy and desperate or just to the hopeful.

The gambling companies understand the psychology of gambling just as much as they understand the numbers. Maybe gambling *is* more accurately described as 'gaming' as they prefer to brand it. They know the game. Gambling is all about psychology, from the 'poker-face' across the card table to the enthusiasm portrayed by Barbara Windsor in a bingo advert. We are often told to question everything these days. This rule doesn't apply when we need to believe in something. Religion doesn't seem to have a monopoly on blind faith. Trust in God if you want, but don't trust in gambling.

Gambling attracts both the confident and the desperate. It is easy to be both at various points in your life. Can be dangerously attractive when you are in either state. This applies as equally to drugs as it does to gambling. You can be that charismatic, ladies' man millionaire City guy who does a few lines at the weekend, or some lowlife *Trainspotting* druggie. Colin Hendry, ex-Scotland international and Premiership winner with Blackburn Rovers, lost his wife through botched cosmetic surgery. Ended up going bankrupt with an SB bookie as one of the creditors (for the record it was SpreadEx). If you're down then gambling could well be magnified in its intensity for destruction. If you're up, then you will still lose but other aspects of your life compensate – until it spirals out of control and you join the first category. This is how we get to hear about those with gambling debts and problems; when it reaches some court or another – the divorce court, bankruptcy court or small claims, when the bookie is chasing someone or other. Otherwise this is hidden and will remain so. If you have a drug or alcohol problem, it often becomes obvious physically. Not so with the gambler. The only sign that the nation as a whole has a problem is when the bookies publish their profits. Inwardly, for many of us, it makes us feel physically sick when we hear or read about this. But we can't tell anyone – because our problem is secret and we need it to stay that way. We gamblers suffer in silence. The industry feeds off our emotions side – 'addiction services' if you will.

All the 'online loser' industries present themselves as the opposite. They are in the same business; the business of presenting hope. Hope will sooner or later lead to despair then you are either back to where you started albeit a bit poorer, or worse – sometimes much worse. Many people who are happy with their lives, happy with their job and their level of income, happy with their relationship, will not go near these industries. But many others will out of greed or adventure. They hope it won't destroy all that they had before. For a few, it will. Some seek out the pleasures of the flesh with girls who ask no questions. Others desire the pleasures of the *flash* – a flash car, a flash lifestyle and a flash girlfriend-by-the-hour until all that flashness attracts a permanent one. Those who live in hope must stay away from those offering a way out of their problems online and for a fee – often a bigger fee than you could ever imagine. In the end, making money and making a lasting relationship are down to good old-fashioned hard work; change your lifestyle, change your job, change your future.

Our ancestors used to get a rush from hunting wild animals. What does the man get who sits in traffic for three hours a day? Mid-life crisis kicks in. It grows and grows all through your 30s and 40s as you do not reach anywhere near the heights that you see others achieve: Premier League footballers, world champion bracelet-wearers, million-pound-a-year earning oil traders... Some find God. Or Prozac. Or gambling. There are a fair few other distracting options too. Your susceptibility to advertising, your personality and personal circumstances, your susceptibility to stimulants, your 'fuck it, let's just do it' mentality, your perception of risk and reward are amongst those that will dictate your choice. 'What the fuck was I thinking?' will eventually hit you, possibly after your wife has hit you and demanded, 'What the fuck were you thinking?' when she finds out you have squandered your joint savings.

Many of us, all of us maybe, think we deserve an easier life. After you've worked for ten, twenty years, it's easy to get all too sick of it all: the early starts, the long hours, the workload, irritating bosses... Fuck this, I want to exit stage left and find a route that leads to riches, a better life, a happier life. Gambling will give you all of this. Just play whatever game you choose and you will be the next millionaire trader, poker star, whatever your deranged mind thinks, sorry *knows*, you will become. Some people have more realistic expectations; they are not greedy. They just believe they can achieve an additional income through gambling. Realistic? As bullshit as those who believe they will be driving that Porsche Carrera S within a few years. There will be no great income, just one disastrous outcome. If you are thinking about gambling giving you an income, then to paraphrase every report since some Home Secretary a few years back made the phrase famous, any online poker or spread-betting site for you really is 'Shit for purpose'.

You will lose time and money, probably a great deal of both. You can very easily lose lots more: friends, marriage, career and even if you don't lose them, they will suffer. The only winners will be on the other side of the equation. Some of them *will* be taking a regular salary off of it and off of you. And some of them will be driving that Porsche Carrera S – that *you* have paid for.

We go into that match with a winning mentality; that team we lost to last season we are determined to beat this season. This is in our DNA. It is in our competitive nature to act this way. The gambling companies exploit this desire – we think and act the same way in an area where we cannot possibly succeed. We try to win back our losses – when you are 2-0 down you try to bring it back to 2-2 and then go ahead. Might work in football – will never work in gambling. Your maleness works against you. Realise just how you tick and be on your guard about how others exploit this.

You will not get together with that girl who goes underneath that waterfall in the *Flake* advert – although as it's from the 80s she's admittedly past her best. There are plenty who do well out of peddling the deceit of the gambling industry, in getting the average guy to believe he can achieve the unobtainable. If someone told me when I was a kid that I could play for England, I would have believed them. What kid wouldn't? But I was no footballer, just like all those gullible adults are no traders or poker stars or whatever other kind of hustler they believe themselves to be. You should grow out of this naivety of youth when you believed any old crap – but many of us don't. We have learnt nothing in those intervening years. Yes, we look back and find it laughable how we once thought we would be the next Tiger or Beckham, but at the same time we still believe that we will be just as successful with the cards or the markets. We are as gullible in our 30s or 50s or whenever as we were when we were eight years old. But once you stop gambling you will look back at your delusional behaviour in much the same way as you view your eight-year-old self, dreaming about the international career ahead of him. You are no better than those *X Factor* hopefuls. They have a dream, you have a dream and you both waste time and money pursuing it. Yes, there will be a handful who get to the finals. But there will be tens of thousands who get shown the door, tens of thousands who never reached the stage of actually performing in front of Simon *et al.*

And half of those who do are walking into a set-up. They believe they have the talent but they walk into that audition room for ridicule and not for reward. I am sure the producers string them along just like those customer service guys and girls string along the DFC market traders and poker stars. They know they are market muppets and poker puppets but they ain't gonna let on. The hardest thing for them is to try to keep a straight face on the end of the line, just in case you hear them snigger. I am sure sometimes they must be doubled up on the other end whilst they try to maintain the conversations with their faces six inches from the floor.

ii. Addictive tendencies

We are addicts for several reasons. Firstly, to get that adrenaline rush that you can't find through anything else or that you used to be able to find when you were young through sex, sport, chasing girls or whatever, but those avenues are now closed to you. So you end up an addict to something: a weekly visit to some bang-for-bucks place, gambling every day (not the weekend as that's for the wife and kids), drugs, speed… Who doesn't want to find that rush in life, the 'I'm not dead yet' feeling? You have an affair not so much for the sex itself, although that is also a great incentive, but to prove to yourself that you've still got it in you by getting it in someone else. We are programmed by our own DNA. We are thrill-seekers. It is self-imposed.

The next reason is imposed upon us. We end up as addicts to forget; to try to blot out some bad experience, some horrendous experience in our lives. Making money is not as important a motive as you think. For many, such as myself, it is a combination of factors. I have had no horrendous experience but we all have hang-ups and some troublesome times in our pasts. Many of us feel cheated or deceived over something or just that we missed out somehow. Gambling was that chance to win back that lifestyle that I should have by now but by some quirk of fate, some perceived unfairness or unfortunate circumstance didn't happen. We use gambling to try to forge a new identity and break away from the one we have; one that is ignored by others, that is shaped by parents and others, one that we believe does not actually truly represent us.

Alcoholics are said to drink to forget. A gambler also gambles to forget but often in a simpler way. When he's at the tables or on the laptop he forgets everything else. This is one reason why he continues – if he stops he'll have to remember again. We want to stay in this fantasy world for as long as we can. We do not want to leave our second life; the concept of escapism runs through much of human endeavour and experience: we go to the cinema or read a book to escape. Addiction ratchets this up. Many of us believe we can inhabit this world forever after we've mastered reading forms, spread-betting, poker... no, you will leave and re-join the real world, just like 'Mr Benn'. He always finds a pleasant reminder of his adventures soon after. This is not what you will find when you log in to your bank account or open your email or worst of all, open your post.

Don't believe I am much more susceptible to addiction than most. Have no interest in drugs, drink or tobacco, yet was drawn to gambling. I would class my gambling as an obsession rather than a true addiction. And if I am some sort of addict, it's not too much of an addictive tendency, yet I was sucked into it; so if I can be then anyone could be, or at least, almost any *man* could be. I give 100%+ in some areas of life, such as playing sport, which is similar to an addiction. But drugs? No chance. But drug addiction or gambling have much in common. A drug addict never started out with the intention of becoming one, just as I had no intention of becoming a gambling addict. You start with one line of coke then before you know it you are doing ten lines. Some are not so much addicted – it's just that they end up doing it all the time! If you only do it at weekends, does that make you an addict? Not sure but it makes you an idiot. I actually started betting £2 a point on the Dow which eventually grew to £250 a point. £500 a point on the FTSE. Fucking nuts! No different from the drug addict. Have to bet bigger to get the same feeling. A line of coke soon becomes five grams. Betting occasionally in the evening becomes betting every day, all day. Coke on a Friday night becomes all weekend, then during the week too; might even do a line off of the toilet seat in the staff loos. When your wife is looking through the clothes' hangers in M&S, you wander around staring at that little screen in the palm of your hand. You might even pick up a few things from shelves or rails – but always in such a way that the view of that little screen is never obscured. If you need a little longer, a little more privacy to fund your account to reinstate your positions then it's that old favourite; the security and privacy of the toilet once more. The man in the cubicle next door might be doing a line of coke off the lid. You are both the same. Everything else takes a back seat. Gambling always comes first. Just like the drug addict uses up so much of their time buying it, using it, coming down from it the gambler does much the same. With spread-betting, I spent so much time researching around it too. With poker, you will do the same.

Gambling can also take in anyone from any walk of life; there's a game for everyone! The coke addict might use up all their savings or even have a big income to constantly pay for it. Or could be someone on JSA who then goes on to rob and run up big debts with even bigger people. With gambling it will be with even bigger companies. There are many, many middle-class successful professionals who would never ever get into debt from their hundreds-of-pounds weekly coke addiction. These same class of people will also not get into the negative by sending thousands per week to some poker site or SB site or whatever. This is why it is hidden. Yes, we hear about the tiny percentage who lose it all or who end up in court. But we don't hear about the 99.99%+ who lose a lot or a hell of a lot, like me. There are a lot of us out there.

My story was not so much the product of addiction but one of circumstance. If you're feeling bored or frustrated in any way then you always have the internet. Then you end up running down in the morning to check your positions or to win back your poker losses from the previous night, before your partner comes down – or your parents come down or burst into your room with that cup of tea. They'll probably assume you are watching porn – the embarrassment from this addiction might even be more bearable. And it most likely hasn't cost you anything. Think of how a child feels when they come down Christmas morning to see what Santa has left for them. For the gambler, the feeling when running to check the markets will be the opposite. It will gradually grow from uneasiness to feeling shit-scared. You will never get that Santa feeling as it can always be bad. And sometimes it is. Sometimes Santa will not have left you anything, only the reindeer will have left something for you.

A BBC documentary about Amy Winehouse claimed that drug addicts are amongst that 10% of the population whose brains are actually programmed that way. They will become addicted whereas others won't. Could well be the same with gambling, I think. We all make mistakes or our darker side gets the better of us. 'The disease model' is how many in the trade account for this phenomenon. It is clearly a disorder, a functional abnormality that can be classed as a disease. But for me 'disease' is a result of a virus or bacteria, something acquired. For the gambler, this 'illness' remains dormant until it is triggered by some event which I find hard to put down to something biological per se. For me, we are born to gamble, some more than others and some use this 'gambling' urge in the way it is supposed to be harnessed, e.g. in business, sport, finding a girlfriend. The 'cure' for this 10% can only be abstinence – this again seems to be an unlikely cure for something known as a 'disease'. It is as if you are supplying no treatment at all. Some diseases kill you, others come and go with no lasting effects at all, like chicken pox. But for the 10% gambler and the alcoholic, it will always be there and will re-emerge if you cannot control it, if you cannot manage your 'illness', as GA refer to it. I prefer to call it a psychological condition rather than a disease. We have our own urges and weaknesses and indeed skills. If someone is extremely gifted in maths or languages you wouldn't refer to them as having a 'disease'. Even for something regarded as physical, such as playing football, if two anatomically identical individuals have vastly divergent skills, you wouldn't say the superior player was diseased. But it seems you can use this term for a clearly negative behaviour although I have never heard this term being applied to arsonists, 'hobby' shoplifters, dangerous drivers and much, much worse. There is enough neurological evidence to prove that a gambler's mind actually does behave differently, but this just proves that gamblers are somehow wired differently. I don't think we should be classed as 'diseased' and be eligible for a blue badge for our cars.

How many people have addictive tendencies or a true addiction problem? I would guess amongst men, 10% are the true addicts, and 10% have no inclination towards gambling in the slightest. Of those in the first category, many might even have avoided gambling. They have better things to do with their lives. Their addictive tendencies might be used beneficially in some other aspect of their life. They might just be too busy to get involved in gambling – but with the easy access internet, this group will all too easily be sucked in. I do not believe that I would be classified in this 10% and not even uncomfortably close either. Yes, I have addictive tendencies but I can also exercise self-control – just that I somehow didn't at all for a five-year period. That leaves a massive 80% of us in the middle to be manipulated and seemingly encouraged by the industry. Puts most of the male adult population in their hands. For females I would think the addictive end would be less than 1% and those with no inclination at all at least 50% – maybe more like 80%. That middle section is fairly small so it doesn't give the industry much to play with. Women can be encouraged to gamble but the industry find this very hard work; women just can't see the point really, and are not so stupid as us men. But the industry keep on trying. And in some areas they are doing very well. Take a look at the twenty-first century bingo hall – or more precisely, its foyer. Then there's the secret world of online; the industry seem to be expanding that middle section. Women will have a 'flutter' at the races but won't feel the urge to put £50 on the next race or to nip down to Ladbrokes the next day like us men. No, they will basically forget about it until they are invited to Ascot or wherever the following year.

There's a part of everyone's brain that is susceptible to addiction. This part is more active in some than others. People with an addiction in one area are more likely to be addicted in another. Addiction is the evil twin of the human desire to stick at something, the persistence and hunger not to give up, to stay strong and push on through whatever problem you face. The mountaineer, the workaholic research scientist, the parent all have that determination to achieve something come what may. Being an addict is no different although addicts also have a blinkered view and carry on regardless. The wise and ruthless exploit this human frailty; the bookies, the drug dealers, the lap-dancing clubs, the drinks industry...

iii. They know you better than you know yourself

The porn sites make most of their money from monthly subscriptions from men with credit cards and money to burn – and often wives to hide it from. So too with gambling. Just with gambling you end up setting everything you own alight even from the very beginning. It's only a matter of how soon you notice your assets are burning and then how keen you are to put the damn fire out. If you are in the DFC you think it ok to let them smoulder and you ignore the fact that this is still burning through what you own. Not to mention the fact that the heat inside is building up and one day it will engulf the lot. By the time I put out the fire, there wasn't too much left.

'HOW NOT TO BE A FOOTBALL MILLIONAIRE.' I always thought Keith Gillespie looked a little skinny, a little gaunt, a little worried looking. Now I know why. He may have been lighting down the right wing but it seems he was almost as quick getting down to Ladbrokes after training too. He really was! The fact he lost millions is almost a side issue, a headline-grabber. It doesn't really matter what the figure is for the individual. Whether you are on £10k a week or £100 a week, if you lose it all then you arrive at the same figure. The fact that you lose *everything* is the point. Even if you don't end up in the bankruptcy court as did Keith – one of the Class of '92 at Manchester United – you might well put yourself into serious difficulty. It's only when the celebrity ends up here do you take notice. People somehow think these excesses are the downside of celebrity – regular people don't do this sort of thing. I did.

WHAT ARMADA? According to a BBC documentary on YouTube, there are more than one million alcoholics in the UK. Alcohol is mainstream, as is gambling; both are encouraged by government, both attract people across the whole spectrum of addiction from slight to overwhelming. The one million figure can equally be applied to gambling. Many of us need an extreme experience. You can go base-jumping or just ride your bike down the hill at the edge of being out of control. Got massively pissed on a New Year's Eve night out when I was 16, and woke up in a pool of vomit. Although 'Never again!' passes from a million people's lips, by the following Friday night they are doing it all over again. I actually learnt from it and never again went on any sort of bender. Shame I never learnt from my gambling benders. These actually got progressively worse until I was almost OD in the gutter. We see in our bank statement what we *want* to see: working capital outlays, costs of beginners' mistakes, pure bad luck – we can spin whatever bullshit we like to convince ourselves of, usually to *easily* convince ourselves. When the gambler starts cashing in investments (but it's only stake money, right?), lying to his wife and maxing out credit cards, does he still delude himself that things are ok?

COST-BENEFIT ANALYSIS. Do not try to rationalise your gambling. You set the wrong parameters; your own terms and conditions make no sense. Gambling will not relieve any underlying problem that you have whether personal, professional or emotional. It will heighten any pre-existing condition that you have, such as depression or anger issues. It will also bring on psychological problems in others.

HOPE. As something in your life gets worse, such as your job or relationship, you find hope in gambling. Religion also feeds off this emotion. When life isn't working out quite how you'd like, when things are not going your way, you find hope and comfort in both religion and gambling. As your job or whatever gets you down even more, your stakes go up even more, possibly in direct proportion. You cannot gamble yourself out of the gambling loss you have built up. You cannot gamble yourself out of any personal mess you have built up. You cannot stop as gambling gives you hope; hope of wealth or success or identity. If you stop then you are without hope and will have nothing. If you continue then you will just be, rather perversely, that 'hopeless' gambler. You will not be on your way to becoming Phil Ivey; your identity will be that of a naïve loser who has wasted time they could have invested in making something of themselves.

There are a fair few others who are doing very well but want to do even better and take up gambling as something exciting, something where they can hustle to become richer and more successful. Unfortunately, the reverse will happen and your life could end up spiralling downwards. I could have gone around the world instead of round the fucking bend. I have not become some playboy, some Mile-High Club member, a millionaire trader. The only club I have joined is the Dumb Fuck Club.

Then there is gamblers' hope; the gambling companies love that you rely on it all too often when your perceived skills desert you; hope for that next card, the market to rise, the number you need to complete your bingo winning line. But there is also that *true* hope that is actually on *our* side. This is the hope that we wake up one day to our madness and actually stop.

PRIDE COMES BEFORE, during and after a fall. Did I fall so hard for gambling because of a need to prove to any potential conquest what an alpha male I was, how I can use my intelligence to beat the system? This reason goes out the window as I was still doing exactly the same thing *after* I had got the girl. In fact, my gambling side got massively bigger. Seems that I was just trying to prove how much of a man I was to *myself*. There was a financial element and I also needed to prove that I couldn't be beaten – I would come from behind and beat those bastards. That's what drives us men and that's what ends up destroying us. We are not so good at cutting our losses and running. A damaged sense of pride is worse than a damaged bank balance. We just don't want to lose. You need real maturity and strength to quit when you have put so much time and energy and money into a venture that you feel you can't just pull out of. Just as with hope, the gambling industry feeds off your emotions, even the positive ones like determination.

If you knew you were in the ring with Mike Tyson then you would lie down on the canvas as soon as he took one step towards you. But with online gambling even though you keep getting pounded, you still keep getting back up. You are alone in there. Your gambling is a secret so there is no one who will throw in the towel. The regulator, that bloke in the bow-tie in there watching on, isn't going to help you. He's a snooker referee anyway – he's only interested in sorting out issues in another arena (this is how I felt towards the FSA). If you've just entered that ring then grab hold of the ropes and *catapult* yourself out. If you've taken a few beatings then hit the floor and crawl out under the ropes and never come back.

ANTE POST. Where does my desire to gamble come from? I don't come from a privileged background, so to some extent it was a desire to make money. There were few luxuries in my house and we were careful with money although we were far from poor; I felt lucky if I got a dollop of Beejam's raspberry ripple with any actual raspberry streak in it! It is unconnected to peer pressure either. For most gamblers, it is less about the money. Just look at Keith Gillespie. He was a millionaire, so why did he do it? For me, I think it was largely the desire to become really successful at something. For Keith, he actually was world class at something yet he still wanted more. Maybe football was almost too easy for him so he needed to get a buzz from something else. A millionaire footballer like Keith proves that we gamble out of an emotional need rather than a financial one. I could never be the pro golfer I wanted to be, so I really needed to get a kick out of an alternative to normal life. We live in an 'on demand' society be it TV, sex, drugs; almost anything can be acquired through an internet search; although the 'anything' is often just a sticking plaster for a much bigger issue. Many, if not most, have some sort of humdrum job and often not that interesting a personal life either, whatever they dress it up as on Facebook. So we try to escape by drinking or taking drugs or gambling. You will not find a new life surrounded by beautiful women through gambling. The only chance you will get of snorting coke off of the belly of some foxy nymphet is if you do a line off a porn mag – or book an escort. Women are not going to flock to you because of your new-found wealth and success, as that ain't going to happen. You will not need to think of which baseball cap and sunglasses you should buy for your appearance on late-night poker TV. Being a poker star? Yes, it happens to a few – but chances are, not you. Being struck by lightning will also happen to someone. Do you wander around thinking that one day you will be struck by lightning? No, you don't so why do you contemplate other equally unlikely events happening to you?

MONEY, MONEY, MONEY. Yes, there was definitely a financial drive behind my gambling. As I was determined to win tens of thousands and quit my job, money moved to the forefront of reasons to gamble. But this motivation for many is less so than people think. Those in the working-class bookie, inhabited by those who get bullied at work, who have menial tasks, who have no sense of power or achievement or success or a simply unemployed flock to these places where they will experience, for the briefest of moments those little victories as their horse comes in first; they achieve a minor albeit fleeting moment of glory, something they cannot experience in any other aspect of their life. This momentary thrill give you that buzz and like anything pleasurable you want to feel it again. Sportsmen have this urge, so too businessmen and so does the man in the bookie. Unfortunately for the latter, pleasure is addictive and in the wrong environment it can become destructive. The FOBT and the B3 feed off this. Horseracing has the disadvantage in some senses for the bookie, that it throws up an infrequent winner for the punter and also that infrequent near-winner too. That horse you backed was never going to win which you knew a long way before the winning post was in sight. So you suffer as a punter from many a disappointing race. But play roulette on the FOBT. Here you get very frequent winners and near-winners too; you are always in with a shout until that little ball finally settles. Far easier to become addicted to this. Even though the machine states that it is not pre-programmed but is random and pays out 97%, these machines make more than half of the high-street bookies profits. Those frequent winners and near-winners somehow disguise the overall loss. Their users are being conned without them seeming to realise just how.

YOU CAN DO IT! Most golfers can hit the ball 400 yards and get it into that little four-and-a-quarter inch hole in four shots. But most of the time they won't. They are more likely to get a five. But you can easily visualise doing it every time, even getting a three. But you are more likely to get a six or a seven than a three. But the times you get a three keep you going. Just like the times you have a big SB win or a poker win or a bingo win or old skool, come out of the bookies with a wad of cash after your horse comes in first for once or your football coupon works out. After 18 holes the course will have beaten you. You will be over par, most golfers between 10–20 over par. There will be some ugly scores on some holes. This is true of the majority of golfers. Your playing partners encourage you, the pro supports and guides you (and takes your money for lessons). The SB company does the same. So does the poker site. Doesn't really matter with golf; might lose a few balls. Spread-betting? With all that bullshit encouragement and support they give you, they will cut your balls *off*!

'BOILER ROOMS'. Boiler rooms operate in much the same way as the spread-betting companies and the gambling industry. They go about it in a similar way with similar results. The BR cold-call people or email them, telling them how they should buy this and that share. They are exactly like the SB execs in the respect that they sell you something that is essentially worthless; the SB firms sell you a product just like the BR ask for your money; you have to fund your SB account – you fund it just like you would a BR. Chances are the BR won't actually buy any shares at all but will present to you in a year or so just how much they have increased in value – by cherry-picking those shares in retrospect that *did* make a good return. You see this and fund and buy some more! Only when you come to cash them in does the BR phoneline go dead. The SB companies also give you the impression that you can make money – and you carry on believing them even after you have lost – and fund your account again and again and again. They 'trade' in shares in exactly the same way as the BR – they buy and sell nothing at all. You look at the graphs and see where you *could* have made money – just like those BR graphs of share price rises. The SB companies' marketing has sold you the bullshit SB dream – and you fell for it, just like those BR scams. They both use high pressure techniques when you are on the phone with them (hence the term 'boiler room'). The SB companies don't have to contact *you* though; no, you do the job for them by contacting *them*!

For the BR scammed, those people who ignored their advice the first time will be phoned back in a week or so when the share price has risen and will be told how they missed out and if they only had listened to him blah, blah, blah. But hey, he's got another tip for you. The SB bookies will also show just how easily you could have made a wheelbarrow full. The spread-better funds his account as does the BR client. Of course, the BR are not registered with the UK regulator (they say they are or pretend to be from a reputable company who are), you send them your hard-earned cash, you may well receive back a (worthless) share certificate that he ran off his computer… you may even invest more if your 'investment' does well. He never invested a penny – not for you anyway. He 'invested' it in his Porsche and a hooker – maybe at the same time. The guy who kept phoning you to increase your investment is uncontactable. His business address is fictitious. You will never see your money again. Madoff did much the same thing, just on an industrial scale. The SB bookies encourage you to invest bigger amounts but they do this very subtly, almost subliminally – murmuring 'just the minimum then', thus embarrassing you or at the very least pointing out how low the bet is, so that you bet more – which you will. But there are differences: they are regulated, they might well be listed on the stock exchange (under 'financial services' to enrich that illusion – and themselves), they are a legal business, they advertise and sponsor. But does it make any difference to the client whether they lose their money in a legal or an illegal way? Not sure which is worse! I feel like I have *legally* been scammed. Either way, someone else will be enjoying the fruits of your hard work, your day job, your inheritance. Think how hard you worked to make that £10k and you will never bet again. Chase it and then you will soon be thinking how hard you worked to make that £20k…

Stake money. You believe you will get this back, especially when spread-betting when it's only the equity requirement to support your bet. But any stake money you allocate to gambling will soon disappear. You will impale yourself on your own stake money sooner or later.

THE TROUBLE WITH GAMBLING IS THE WINNING. Winning leads to big, big losses. If you only ever lost you would give up very quickly. But sometimes you win and sometimes you win big. The gambler has a fond memory of their big wins, usually from a young age; in my case that wide-eyed 11-year-old feeding tarnished silver five peseta pieces into that most basic of gambling machines. I am sure that Spanish hotel bar has upgraded to an all-singing, all-dancing computerised system for extracting cash-rich tourists of their Euros but these machines are still popular in amusement arcades – and still played by kids. And when a nice little pile topples into the win tray below, dad will smile and laugh and congratulate. 'Well done son,' sends out the wrong message; you cannot get money for nothing, there was no skill involved. Well done is even less applicable to his dumb-ass dad. I went from five peseta bets to £5000 bets. It's an easy journey to make.

SO CLOSE! But it is not only the wins that keep you going. Those near-wins give you a buzz too, remember. And those wins you also believe will turn into really big wins, maybe even massive – with a little more skill, knowledge and experience those wins will occur more often and will be bigger. To borrow from spread-betting, let's call it 'Gamblers' Slippage'; that winning cash you imagine is already in your hands has somehow disappeared. You persevere even though you are soon in the red. No matter, this is just some transition stage, you believe. I remember thinking as a 17-year-old how my Yankees would pay me hundreds next time, and not just £80. With SB, I often won a few grand but I believed I would soon be winning money into the tens of thousands. I still believed this when I was tens of thousands down! When I finally quit I was six figures down. All this from that original £2 bet!

You will have many 'if only...' and 'thank God...' moments when you are spread-betting. Those perceived 'missed opportunities' and near misses will keep you gambling. Same as those 'near-wins' on the fruitie, losing by a short-head on the horses or that final card. These scenarios are all *losing* scenarios. They trick you into believing that you were close. If you shoot a basketball and you hit the rim, you were close. If you spin four melons and that final one is only one click away, you were not close – that machine has given you a losing spin, exactly the same as if you got a mixed fruit salad across those reels. Our brains and our DNA have been conned.

Every gambler has their own 'gambler's CV' with dates of big wins and losses all over the place. The gambler quickly develops the idea that if you won big in the past why can't you win big again? So you stick with it and over time, you lose. And win. But you lose more, much more than you win even if you were up big at one point. I was up £18k–20k early on. But I ended £130k down. Makes no difference whether it's a two-pence coin pusher or online gambling. The pattern of wins and losses are more or less the same: it's only the scale of the overall loss that changes. Mind you, I wish I had been addicted to two-pence coin pushers!

SUCKER LITERATURE. There are many books on the shelves of WHSmith about how to win online, and the guy who lost it all sports betting then made it all back and more. No book here about the thousands of guys who lost it all and *didn't* make it all back or those who lose thousands year in, year out. (There is now!) Seems that people only read about what they *want* to become as a gambler rather than about what they *will* become. Would you buy a book about off-piste skiing, having never even skied before, then book a solo heli-skiing trip and slide off down that corniche over bounders and vertical drops? But you are happy to do the financial equivalent. You might not think so but you are. Yes, you might even start on spread-betting's or poker's nursery slopes but before long you will find yourself trying to dodge trees.

The Naked Trader became a big seller. The front cover draws you in when it should really frighten you away: a bloke who trades from his bed 'naked' in between eating toast (actually on the front cover too!) and gets that girl with the cleavage. The author has expanded his portfolio so now you can purchase *The Naked Trader's Guide to Spread-betting*. This is obviously the natural progression. There's that cleavage again and that naked guy. Might even be his actual wife – then you believe that you get the girl for life by following his advice. Those who lost money in the financial crisis amongst others thought they'd buy the former book to try to recoup their losses. Others just wanted some investment advice. Do you really need guidance on how to invest money in a rampant bull market!? He launched the book at just the right time and now has his followers. There will be those who think they have outperformed the market by following some investment book or another but this is more than likely down to the laws of probability, as there will also be those who underperformed. I would suggest that on average, followers of some book exactly perform the market. If you have invested in a basket of shares and held on then you are a winner, regardless of any system you may or may not have followed. The great investor in property or shares can make money in a downturn. Let's see how your favoured book holds up then, shall we? Now 'The Naked Trader' has that following, he is leading them into the world of spread-betting. You think you made money from him before, he sold a lot of books so he must be some great oracle then. Unfortunately, even though I am putting out a warning, there will be those in whom I have sparked a curiosity! His tag-line about making money in up and down markets reads to the spread-better as making money whatever you do, whether you are long *or* short. It reads like you no longer have to wait for your actual shares to rise in value; now you have the opportunity to double your money. You do not realise that this doesn't apply if you are facing in the wrong direction.

For the writing of the book, he was a guest at a couple of spread-betting bookies. He brings in business for them. He's impartial, is he? He also sells us his and his affiliates' seminars and offers within – so when you lose money after he suggests you can win, you pay even more to find out just how that happened! Psychological entrapment – this 'lose money, re-educate then lose even more' pattern is common for the spread-better and also for the gambler. Don't forget, IG's turnover last year was almost half-a-billion pounds! The financial press gives him great reviews: this is the same financial press who take advertising from share dealing companies and the spread-bet industry who naturally appreciate anyone who drums up more business for them. My book will undoubtedly receive terrible reviews or just be ignored and I personally will be ridiculed and vilified. I am prepared for this.

Instruction books are there to encourage and motivate and increase your confidence. If it is something that you might be able to handle then that's ok. But just as you wouldn't subscribe to *Freeclimbing Monthly* magazine, do not sign up to *Financial Armageddon Daily* either. No, stick to something where encouragement and support has a positive outcome for you. Buy a Jamie Oliver book instead.

'Free' money. Signed up with about ten different SB websites in the end, receiving at least £1k in 'free' money. Casinos and poker sites and bingo sites will all give you 'free' money – after you fund your account. It doesn't really cost them anything, as you can't just refund these 'credits' back to your account. What do a few free spins on a roulette wheel actually cost them? They might even fix it so you win at first – not difficult to do when the whole IT system is set up by them. When you see how easy it was to win you go ahead and fund your account with real money. True, you could then refund your winning balance as you have used the credit they allowed you – but you don't. You think you are on to a good thing. Once you sign up and get this 'free money' then you are doomed. You know full well what they are trying to do when you accept those online free credits and you think you will just take advantage of their generosity. The fact is, they will take advantage of *you*.

*

Gambling is heavily marketed as a normal hobby and we fall for it because we *want* to – it legitimises our vice. But no one admits to just how much they lose. We gamblers seem happy to carry on with the same behaviour, gamble increasing amounts and expect eventually to come out on top. Isn't this the definition of madness? We all repeat the same mistakes over and over again; we all think the outcome will be different even though whatever has preceded it is pretty much the same. Just think of your job, your career, the type of partner you fail to chat up, the type of partner who is attracted to you, the lifestyle you have...

You believe what you what to believe. I assumed that if I made £18k before it was only a matter of time before I made this and more again. In the end I was just funding the beast which in the end bit my fucking hand off and half my arm! Looks easy to feed, as in *The Life of Pi*, but as the goat finds out, it will take everything if it can.

iv. Getting their message out

People are so easily herded like sheep towards products or places that are really no good for them; the marketers know this, even some of the customers know this but try to ignore it; many others actually believe it. People believe gambling can actually make them money and that they might even be able to give up their day job. Why do people herd themselves to the same old bars every Friday and Saturday night, waiting in the cold to pay their £7 to be allowed in to drink coloured drinks and be surrounded by so many idiots wearing clothing with massive lettering? Does the F1 driver look at his shiny watch whilst driving, wondering if he'll get home in time for *EastEnders*? They always wear a chunky Swiss watch during the post-race press conference. Remember watching Carlos Montoya win the Monaco grand prix (I remember this as I actually had a winning bet on. Nice £50 win which I thought was a lot at the time. Little did I realise...), reach into his team's arms across the metal fencing for hugs and congratulations, only to emerge with a lovely shiny watch someone had discreetly slipped onto his wrist? A sort of reverse mugging. No, we are the ones being mugged. To most it would appear he'd been wearing it all the time as he sped around the streets of Monaco.

I used to work in marketing, so I should have been more aware. No, I *was* aware. I just thought I was *better* somehow. Used to design adverts telling how our new socks wick away moisture or how durable and grippy the new sole of the boot is. Stick a few coloured tabs on them, give them technical names and people love it! I never had the audacity to actually label our socks left and right as they do with 'technical' socks now though! Just like the spread-better with his box of 'trader tools', the golfer with that new drivers and shiny putter; these never lose their appeal, in spite of the evidence when they play 18 holes with them again and again. The golfer will persist in investing in new 'better' equipment; the 'trader' will try different tools and strategies. This is no better than Wile E. Coyote with his latest delivery from ACME. You find it comical how he falls for these gadgets and then you fall for the exact same thing in some aspect of your life with that tech illusion. You need to restore your pride and you tell yourself that things which are difficult to achieve take effort, and you will prove to yourself that you can do it then to others too. The newer equipment won't do a lot for you, though. Just like taking all that 'investment' advice or reading all those 'improve your poker' articles and books. Although you think it will help, you think surely it must. There are always successful 'traders' in the ads, after all. You must be doing something wrong, you think. The spread-better, the poker player, the golfer will all keep on putting in more and more money. Once you get to a certain point you have to keep on feeding it. You have invested too much already; if you pull out now you will be left with nothing; you still need to believe even though all the evidence is against you so you continue to throw good money after bad. You would also have to think of an alternative use of your time which subconsciously you find frightening. The skilled poker player knows when to cut his losses. The skilful business investor will pull the plug on investments they can see are going nowhere. Gamblers don't. I used to use a TaylorMade R7 driver. Now there is an R9 driver. If they marketed one with a specially weighted sole, people would buy it even if they called it the RSole.

The marketers know their psychology. You are not immune. If you think you are, then just look at the clothes you are wearing, the things around you, the laptop/iSomething you are staring at. There's the rebranding of economy to ecology. Where once I washed my clothes on the economy setting, I now wash them on ecology. Appeals to the issues of the day. We often think people must be nuts if they fall for this or that targeted product but we only think this way because that product is clearly not aimed at us. The obvious example are products aimed at women if we are looking at it as a man, and visa-versa. Jimmy Choo shoes? Women go nuts for them. Any man would think it is crazy to spend £500 on a pair of shoes. Then us men walk into a Porsche showroom and splash out £100k on some car only really suited for a racetrack. Gambling? We men are the hunters, so it is appealing to us. Women, quite rightly, think it is a dumb-ass idea that makes no sense in any way. Men and women do not think and act in random ways. Yeah, women may be from Venus and men from Mars – but only because there's a branch of Ladbrokes there. We are targeted and sometimes conned by those who understand us. You need to be on your guard. The clever and cunning shouldn't exploit people's flaws and vulnerabilities, but they always have and they always will. You need to put up as many barriers as you can to protect yourself. A gambler believes in what they want to believe in – although you don't even realise you think this way. It is easier and more convenient for you to think and act this way – at least in the short term. A few years or ten down the line then it finally dawns on you that you have been living in a dream rather than living the dream.

SPREAD-BETTING AND POKER. James Nesbitt is happy to take the SB bookie's money to star in their advert and plug their free training programme. He looks like a bloke in his 30s, maybe 40s – the target male. He is successful – but not through spread-betting. Celebrities often endorse products that they never use, remember. Why would any SB company train *you* in how to get money out of *them*? Be like the store detective training people in how to become an effective shoplifter. The emphasis is, once again, on how you can be a successful trader. The more accurate term, 'gambler' has been banished from any of their marketing. They tell you what to want to hear. And you believe it. James is just like us – or what we'd like to be – and he's happy with spread-betting so it seems. No, he is an actor getting paid. You will become a gambler, not a trader and you will be paying someone else.

The poker sites often have a girl with a big smile and bigger tits to entice you in. The SB sites have the successful, male businessman type somewhere on their site and in their marketing – the poker sites too are also coming round to this approach. Convince the target that they will become this guy rather than the old-skool tits and arse method. Better still, make them feel that they *are* that guy already. But the real successful businessman will be the one who works for the SB bookie or poker site and the big-titted model will be *his* girlfriend, not yours. You think you are the clever one, the one in control, the one making the decisions. But they control you and direct you and the decisions you make are more theirs than yours. You may be the one entering your decisions on your lovely, shiny, so-easy-to-use smartphone but they know what you're going to do before you do it. Try to think of it as your so-easy-to-*lose* smartphone otherwise they will long continue to tap your savings as you tap their little icon on your phone. You use the same technique as those playing slots – you tap a few buttons, make a few adjustments then never see your money again. Control and involvement are also illusions. Those 'nudge' buttons are the same for the spread-better as for the fruitie player – they have no real effect other than that 'control belief' you hold. If you think you have the control then you think you determine the direction and the outcome. But you are not driving a car – you are no better than a passenger. People are often scared of flying as they have no control – it is all down to the pilot. They feel the opposite about driving, even though statistically air travel is safer. So give the gambler as much bullshit control as possible and they will stick with it. You think it's a game of skill but it makes little difference what you do. Doesn't make any difference what game you play, from spread-bet to bingo. The only choice you make is whether it is death by electrocution or death by drowning. Not much of a choice.

Gambling sites use all the established tricks that casinos have been using for years plus a few more. All those bright lights and attractive women enticing you in with possibility, no the *probability*, of winning. You will win at this game then have sex with the girl advertising it. If you think the second part sounds nuts, it's about the same likelihood as the first. You might not actually think that you will have sex with her – just someone very much like her; this will be possible after your online successes. These are the feelings that these adverts stir inside you and your trousers and these are the things which will never happen. Never. You may think you are wiser than that but I'm sorry to say that you will find it hard to suppress what millennia have evolved you to be. Blame Darwin if you like. Shooting the messenger won't help you. You must find a strategy to help yourself. Just step back and look at what you are doing rationally. Talk it over with friends of both sexes. If you've got more of a solitary disposition, then hopefully after reading the chronicles of my fuck-up, you'll get the picture. Think of this book as a proxy friend; it's more of a friend than any real voice you'll hear when you call customer services. Or when they phone you, demanding payment. Won't happen to you? Never even crossed *my* mind until it happened and I was asked for more than thirteen grand. The only previous time they had ever phoned was to open my account. No calls of concern about my problem gambling. That's because it was hardly a problem to them! Thirteen grand is a lot of money. Fortunately, I had it. Many don't.

You will not have a party on partypoker.com or get much joy out of jackpotjoy.com. Those behind 888.com do not trust to luck; they know they will make millions. You belong to the DFC, the only honest club out there that you are a part of – you just didn't know you had joined until too late. There are Websites and there are Web*shites*. Seems that many people spend too long on the *right* ones let alone fuckwits like me who spent almost their entire time on the wrong ones.

SPORTS SPONSORSHIP. Bookies sponsoring sport achieve three desired effects although the audience only really notices one. When Betway sponsor snooker's UK championship, they obviously get their name out there and in the minds of the predominantly male viewership (I could choose almost any ranking event as they are almost all bookie sponsored, from now-household names like BetFred who sponsor the world championship to F66.com whom I had never heard of, who sponsor the 2017 German Masters; they are big in Asia. It is a similar picture with PDC darts). But there are two other reasons: it puts the gambling industry as a whole out there and most importantly, it normalises gambling as an activity. You play snooker and darts, you go to the football – associate having a bet with regular pastimes and you turn gambling into an everyday, socially acceptable experience. Now you do the shopping and pop into the bookies as if they are one and the same. The betting slip has now found a home for itself next to the Sainsbury's receipt in your wallet.

'The game finishes 2-1 to Man United. 8-1,' announces today's celebrity voice-over for tonight's bookies-sponsored televised match, offering you a 'great deal' during the half-time break. You just can't escape advertising for the twenty-first century's new western addiction, now the twentieth century's addiction sponsors have been banned or banished to the developing world where unsurprisingly they are doing very well. The gambling industry fills the hole in sports sponsorship left by the forced exit of the cigarette and alcohol sectors. Football clubs have bookies adverts running around their touchline advertising hoardings, it's on team strips, on their website – every club has a bookies of choice. There is now every angle of bookie sponsors emblazoned across players' shirts – online casinos, financial spread-betting companies, bingo, poker sites, everything.

How many years before this too is banned or restricted? Many decades away and by that time the damage will be done. Sports sponsorship has long been favoured by companies whose products are no good for us. Splashing your company's name across a shirt worn my sportsmen and women at the peak of health and fitness makes your product appear to be another winner. But an online casino and a player kicking a ball about are completely unrelated in every sense. Do not believe you will somehow become anything like the latter by consuming the former. That's how you absorb the message at a subconscious level. If you get taken in by it all then you will be staring nervously at those market numbers every morning whilst the footballers are slipping on their bullshit branded kit ready for training.

I watched Man United lose on TV after having a karate-kicking midfielder sent off a few years back. First goal scorer was a second-half substitute (Modric). The bookies loved that! They offered you great odds-on first-goal scorer before the game – they flag these up and get thousands of takers. And your player *nearly* scored, didn't he? You were that *near-win*ner (yes, you were, in fact, a loser). Many players will nearly score, remember. Everyone's favourite 'geezer', amongst others, Ray Winstone, giving you those odds again at half-time. Doesn't matter if you think the bet is good or not, it gets you thinking and then betting. Take what they offer or try something else, maybe with someone else. They can afford to sponsor ITV's coverage of the Champions League. They will do very well out of the night. *All* bookies will benefit from another bookies' sponsorship or adverts. The idea of having a bet is established, the target male shops around and places a bet. And as he's there, he skips through a few other sports and ends up sticking a tenner on The Open golf too. Yes, this cunning punter will end up like the rest of us. DFC member for all his cunning. No, as cunning as a fox who didn't see that Range Rover until a split second before it splattered him all over the road. Some will end up clicking on poker, casino, slots or scratch cards whilst here too; the high-street bookie now offers you a broad choice online for you to lose your money. Did you predict the score or were you a goal out? If only... next time... I was so close, I *nearly* won. Nearly winning is losing. That near-win means you will bet again. It suckers you back. The fact that you nearly won more than compensates in your mind for that fact that you have lost – because you will win next time – and the time after that, win bigger. When you actually win, that brings you back too. As the 'geezer' would say about you trying to make some easy wheeler dealer money out of gambling: 'You muppet!' I would call you a DF as you are, like so many, in the DFC.

Embassy used to sponsor the world championships in darts and snooker. The advantage with both sports for the sponsor, up until they tried to clean up their images, the participants in each sport also partook in consuming the sponsor's product whilst actually competing! So did many down the pub or club who then think of themselves as Alex Higgins or Eric Bristow. The sport and the product merge and become one and the same. Embassy loved Eric Bristow, who never even referred to it as the darts world championship but simply as 'The Embassy'! This caught on amongst others. They were still sending him free cigarettes long after he won his last Embassy. But unhealthy product manufacturers don't restrict themselves to sponsoring essentially pub sports. There was also Benson & Hedges cricket, Marlboro Formula 1 teams amongst others, whilst the whisky industry sponsored football teams. Now the snooker stars are only allowed bottles of Highland Spring or something similar. Bradley

Wiggins had 'IG' emblazoned across his arse when he was winning the Tour de France. Even Nutella sponsored the Italian football team. They have nice images of nuts on the product and advertising but I don't see too much reference to the 56% sugar it contains, and yet they still managed to advertise themselves on British TV as a nutritious breakfast! At least the ASA upheld complaints but the damage was already done, so what do Ferraro care. Those who complain or just those who know their claims are bullshit are not the target audience for their sugar-saturated 'nutritious' product anyway. Then there is McDonald's, which sponsors all manner of sports from the Olympics to kids' football in the UK. Throughout my youth the wholesome Milk Cup was played along-side the FA cup. It has since been rebranded as the Coca-Cola cup and the Carling Cup. Carling also sponsored the Premiership and even brought out a draught beer called 'Premier' so that football and drinking became one and the same too. Red Bull perform a similar trick. You believe subconsciously that you are a 'risk taker' when you consume the product and that it will somehow make you like some BMX bandit who hurtles off boulders. Gambling companies sponsor many other football leagues, and many premier league and championship clubs and have a presence with most, if not all, 92 clubs. Won't be too long before a bookies sponsors the premiership. It's the next logical step. And we think we are clever enough not to be influenced by advertising. We are not or else why is it there? This growth in bookie sponsorship shows both how it works on its target audience and the massive growth in the industry itself. It's a virtuous circle – but only for the industry. So now parents buy their kids football shirts with a bookies emblazoned across the front. This doesn't bode well for the next generation, who are being worked on at yet another level.

I sometimes watch PDC World Championship darts over Christmas. Now it seems, if you don't fancy running the London marathon but still feel the urge to dress up as a penguin or a centurion for a few hours then this the event for you. William Hill did not put up £1,650,000 in prize money for the 2017 World Championship for nothing. Sky Sports are not going to miss out and sell their subscribers the complete package; now we get Sky Bet too. William Hill will more than make their money back on increased betting on the event itself and the follow-through on everything else you can bet on – which is just about anything. Bookies draw the line at predicting celebrity death dates but that's about all. In this day and age every bookie needs to keep their name in the forefront of everyone's minds. Back in the day, pre-internet, you basically had the choice of Ladbrokes, Coral and William Hill. There were other players but these three dominated. Not anymore. I can now think of at least 20 household names in internet gambling, not to mention the SB, poker, bingo and casino sites. They are household names where there is a gambler in the household. There often is.

Ladbrokes see an increase on betting on the darts even though a rival sponsors the event. We are constantly reminded of the odds on every aspect. Take it or shop around before the nicely proportioned models lead on the badly proportioned players. This is made easier by websites that compare the odds from the different bookies. The easier it is to bet, the likelier you will bet.

AND THE WINNER IS... not you. It is an award *for them*, not for you. The magazines who give out awards for spread-betting or the best poker site are the same ones who take the advertising revenue from them. The award itself has been invented out of thin air as a marketing trick. Men like to think they are informed, they like to have a dangerous, exciting hobby so they will buy this sort of magazine and buy the 'spin' within. Go for that 'award-winning' company or choose another – your dumb-ass hobby is now justified. Awards are basically adverts – from spread-betting to the Oscars. An award for 'Innovation' means that they have devised another ingenious way in which to con money out of you although like everything else, it will be marketed as offering you something wonderful, that final piece of the jigsaw that will solve all your problems. They've got an award for it, they say, so they must be good. I can't say that investment magazines are complete bullshit, but just remember why they were published in the first place; to advise people on proper investments, which shares to buy when you are not just trading the 'difference', the best mortgage to go for etc. They have now picked up on spread-betting as the public are now interested due in no small part to the massive variety of marketing strategies they hit you with. They create these awards to please the SB industry as they supply a lot of advertising revenue. These magazines now perpetuate the vicious spiral of increasing the coverage and driving even more public demand for the product. Whatever award they receive will only mean that they are better than before at squeezing more money out of their unsuspecting client targets. They are getting better and better at inventing new gadgets and gizmos on their trading platforms, they say, to help make you a better trader. No, to help make you *think* you are a better trader so you trade bigger and more often. And make them more money. They know their market. They know their psychology. And they know men will fall for gadgets and gizmos just like any woman knows a man will fall for a nice slender set of legs.

Whatever game you want, they will brand themselves as being in the business 25 years or be the market leader or be award-winning or industry-leading or be a 'trusted provider' or whatever other bullshit they decide to hit you with. All the bullshit will be generally true and you will be reassured by this. But all it means is that they are getting bigger and better at taking your money. It does not mean they have been giving value to customers and delivering something good. They are not Colman's mustard or Raleigh bikes. The gambling companies try to put themselves at the heart of the community, funding local initiatives. But they are not the local church or village school. Are they in fact, the lowest common denominator? Unfortunately, they have now become as much a part of the British landscape as the oak tree. Or Dutch Elm Disease.

THE BBC

I saw a woman from Ladbrokes on the BBC, talking about the betting on the new pope and how it was the biggest religious betting market in history, back in 2013. It's passable to report this as a news story but using a representative from Ladbrokes is not exactly sticking to the BBC non-commercial guidelines. Gets us thinking about gambling. We might well log on then. That's why she came on. Would a BBC reporter have said that if you think that one of the candidates was going to become pope then why not have a bet? If you bet £1 at 50-1 then you make £50 or £2 then you make £100, says the girl from the bookies. What bullshit. Gave Ladbrokes free advertising. And this is the BBC, no less. The fact that the bookies open a book on just about anything is a news story but it shouldn't be presented this way. In the papers this would have to be called an 'advertising feature'. The BBC should not allow any bookie on in whatever guise.

David Buik always seems to pop up on the BBC. There he is again, BBC Breakfast TV in January, 2017, standing next to someone representing his former employer of City Index. They know they need these 'partners' to come on; it's cheaper for the BBC to have on these so-called experts than have on their own experts. Having an 'expert' on anything give news stories credibility – even when the experts are not even credible! And the BBC, despite having their 'sticky-backed plastic' policy, still invite on 'guests' who are appearing in panto or recording artists with a new album out so why not have on the gambling companies? But unlike the panto stars, these SB companies are presenting themselves as economic commentators as if they are representing a bank or the OECD. The BBC give them free publicity. Why don't they get someone on from Ladbrokes to comment about the latest premiership management appointment? The BBC don't do this because they would be inundated with complaints. They allowed on that pope pundit though. These spread-betting companies masquerade as something wholesome, a valued organisation that cares. Just remember their core business. Whatever they have been invited on to talk about, do not let them sucker you into the believing that they come on because they really give a shit.

And as for David Buik, who spent most of his career getting rich working in spread-betting, was awarded an MBE in the 2016 New Year's Honours List (for 'services to the financial services'!) whilst George 'Johnny' Johnson, the last Dambuster still gets nothing!

Lee Dixon and 'Wrighty' (both ex-Arsenal) can advertise for a high-street bookies with their ex-professional colleagues, encouraging us to a put a 'cheeky punt' on football at Ladbrokes whilst appearing on the BBC's flagship football programme, 'Match of the Day' around the same time. The rules were relaxed in 2007 to allow bookies TV ads. I would imagine that both the commercial TV industry and the gambling industry lobbied for this. It benefits no one else. The BBC do not allow their newsreaders to make adverts. This should be extended to all presenters. If you are a BBC presenter you are well respected and people will value what you say, even if it is an advert. Then there's Gary Lineker with his crisps!

Even those who are not even working for an ad agency employed by a gambling business become their messengers by proxy. With most sporting occasions on TV, one of the commentators will announce what odds you would you get on such-and-such. Often when watching snooker I hear a commentator mentioning what odds would you have got on so-and-so coming back from 4-0 down to win 5-4 etc. or something. Gets people thinking. The BBC especially should be more responsible and put out a policy to their sports, and even political, commentators. I would imagine that commercial TV do exactly the opposite. The BBC seem to be unknowingly influenced.

I love the BBC but they need to watch themselves as much as we watch them. Another example: Evan Davis on BBC *World News*. Programme about the gambling industry. Now I like Evan Davis and his boyish enthusiasm but he admits he is not a gambler so doesn't exactly ask searching questions; it was like some sycophantic government interview from the 1950s where the deferential interviewer basically allows them to tell us what wonderful things they are doing. Everyone on the show, all big players in their gambling businesses, seemed to view their industry as something wholesome. They seemed to be excited about it as though they were revolutionising health care, bringing hope to the sick. They harped on about the new technology in their businesses and how wonderful this is. No, it's not. It's just a faster and more convenient way for the punter to lose money. I got involved with spread-betting with a mobile back in 2008 and it didn't help me. I thought it did, having constant access to market prices and even graphing tools, but it just ensured I lost more and quicker. The industry is pushing mobile betting big time. Just look at sports sponsorships from bookies with 'mobile' in their brand. Most will download that convenient little icon so that with one little touch from their middle finger they are in. Should turn that finger around and show that to the little bastard app! Then delete it and keep it deleted. For most, they will only lose less than £100 a month, maybe just a tenner. But who would effectively set up a standing order to send to someone they don't know to live the life that they themselves want? And then for some this £100 a month will grow massively. The SB bookies will also do their best to speed things along a bit too with a variety of tricks (see Chapter 2). The bingo and casino sites are 'synthetically' constructed to make you lose. 'Knowledge is power' – but without intelligence it's dangerous. If you really had the intelligence to pick apart the 'knowledge' they were presenting in that SB seminar then you would know what they were up to. I thought I knew their game but they still suckered me in from a different angle. Whatever 'intelligence' I thought I had they skilfully bypassed. The con artist or salesmen often talks fast and will overwhelm you with information so you end up doing what they suggest. You don't realise this until too late. Even when you know this fact, the best of us can still be victims.

Now rebranded as 'gaming' not gambling, they are attempting to whitewash their business: It's a game, a pastime like any other, one you can win at. Reminds me of euphemisms used by the military. 'Collateral damage' has now rightly received so much bad press that this has now evolved into the snappier, 'CIVCAS' for civilian casualties. The pseudo-Latin term is far easier for someone in fatigues to utilise and to avoid the actual true description of any unfortunate bloodbath. One of Evan's guest's compared gambling spend to the cost of going to the cinema; this idea of gambling as entertainment is a common theme put out by the industry. Told us what the average spend is; using their definition. Here's mine: You might easily open 20–30 accounts across the spectrum of providers. Just use a dozen bingo sites and a dozen high-street bookie sites and there you have it. All gamblers use multiple sites. So their 'average spend' number is not per user – it is per account. This is a whole different number. Let's say I used 10 SB providers and lost £130,000. Using their criteria, the average spend for the user is £13,000. No, this is what one gambler lost on one site. This is not the average spend of each gambler. I wish I had only lost £13,000! How about average gambling spend per household – easy to conjure up a low figure. Just include those households that only bet once a year on the Grand National or once a week on the Lotto. Or why not just include those households where nobody bets at all. This will reduce that figure! Use this to show how little people spend on it. You employ a completely different trick when you float on the stock exchange. Then you get a completely different idea and a truer indicator as to how much the nation spends. Any 'average' figure hides some monstrosities. If you averaged out the spend on my street, I might only have lost a thousand!

COMMERCIAL TV

TV adverts for gambling remind me of the TV ads for cigarettes from 50s America claiming '8 out of 10 doctors recommend Camel cigarettes', or 'The cigarette that is kind to your throat'. They even marketed one brand for smokers with breathing difficulties! Don't believe me? Look on YouTube. We laugh (or shiver) at them now but people believed them back then just like people believe in gambling now. Will people view these bookies and SB adverts in the same way that we view the cigarette adverts of the 50s? Will it take another 50 years? Difficult to get the genie back into the bottle then. And it's a fucking evil genie who only grants himself three wishes.

The media are happy to take the bookies' millions and not just the print press, who are desperate for any source of income. TV too is fighting the internet so they are as happy as the sports promoters for them. Jeremy Kyle, whose appeal is generally female and working class, regards himself as a reformed gambler, has his programme sponsored by bingo companies yet has on guests with gambling problems.

SPAM!

A Cypriot-based SB advert keeps popping up in my inbox. I allow it through as a reminder to myself what a gullible idiot I have been. They ask three multi-choice questions: 1) Do you have experience SB? 2) How much time do you have to SB – 1 hour, 2 hours or 5 hours? 3) How much do you want to make a month – £100-500, £500-1000, £1000-5000? Even if you laugh at how the question is phrased you still believe that you really can make option 3 a reality. These may be dumb-ass question but they get you thinking, they get you believing. That's why they ask them. How much time do you have? This question indicates that you can make money at your convenience. No experience. It's so easy to make money, it doesn't matter. That third question – or really fantasy suggestion – again: how much money do you want to earn? Numbers range from those who believe a small amount may well be possible to those whom are greedy or desperate.

Any SB bookie already knows the answers to the above – whatever you tick. This time, let's see it from their point of view. Q1: Yes or no – this makes no real difference. If you are new to trading then we will take just a little as you begin your apprenticeship to idiocy. You don't walk into Coral and place £50 straight off for your first ever bet. I started at £2 a point. If you are experienced or have just been lucky, then we will take a whole lot more money off of you more frequently; just means that we are not the first to take money off of you. If we are lucky, we will be the last as we will fleece you. Q2: You will think about it for an hour or two a week but before too long you will think about it every waking hour. Q3: You are naturally greedy so in the end you will want to win as much as possible and one day even give up your job. The question is really the mirror image of how you read it: how much can *you* give *us* per week. You will find it hard to admit your mistakes and you want to prove you are right so you chase your losses.

They do not operate out of some internet café or backstreet set-up. Some of them are quite large: 'ITRADER' sponsor Manchester City (as do the mainstream bookies, 'Betsafe'; now there's a name! Like the National Lottery they come up with the unimaginative tagline; 'In it to win it'. For you, remember it's, 'In it to bin it').

THROUGH THE LETTERBOX

Used to get a regular stock bulletin from TD Waterhouse too, recommending whether to buy, sell or hold. This does much the same as those SB seminars or newspaper articles. It reminds people, encourages people to buy and sell whatever stock, regardless of what they are suggesting; their ideas are to some extent irrelevant. The buy/sell/hold recommendations get you thinking then get you trading. It is a marketing trick to drum up business. You might also get a leaflet that slips out of your newspaper. That's what did it for me!

v. The Ace of Spades

I have already referred to the following strategy throughout this book. It's like some evil creature that they set loose on you. Let's call it: **'The Cerberus Strategy'**:

OVERWHELM: they overwhelm us with data (the information illusion) and with gadgets (the tech illusion). Don't forget the education illusion. All those graphs look so crisp and clear on our lovely, shiny iPad. Anything presented this professionally must be useful, right? They overwhelm our senses, our urges, whether that be in front of the fruitie or the smartphone. They give us so many options, so many graphs or flashing lights. Information, the platform itself, the website – they use it to confuse and disorientate although they sell it to you as the opposite. They overwhelm us with images of successful men that we want to be and beautiful women that we want to be with.

DISTRACT: we are hurried along by customer services or market movements or 'urgent' funding requirements or simply those flashing lights on the fruitie so that we do not think clearly about what we should be doing. This results in us losing more and faster. It also confuses us, mesmerises us, disorientates us so that we cannot see what we are doing and what gambling actually is. We cannot concentrate when gambling; they will throw something at us unexpectedly.

The spread-better is constantly distracted by new data, new developments. Log on to BetVictor or any other and you are overwhelmed with betting categories and options within; you place a bet then are 'distracted' by another possibility. From that tiny device in your hand to the grand scale of a kitsch Vegas monument, you will be overwhelmed and distracted, which work hand in hand.

MISLEAD: Fundamentally, we are led to believe that we will make money when the probability of this long term is mathematically zero (except for the pro poker player and sports better; those who really do make a living from it, that is). We believe the marketing that says we will be that success. We believe in the information illusion and the education they supply. We believe that those trading tools are there to help us. We believe that Las Vegas is 'Fabulous' and is a city of glitz and glamour – it might well be but not for us. We unknowingly take an oath of allegiance to our vice.

They advertise using winners and not the losers that virtually everyone will become. No other product could be advertised that delivers something so unlike what it claims. The ASA, trading standards, the regulator and government all accept this. And so do we.

SIMPLY THE BEST. Some people think they are too clever and can beat the system, whatever that system is. That's what I used to think... Just because you've got an education, doesn't mean you can do what you like and it will work out. Middle-class arrogance. The SB industry has tapped into a liquid gold fountain. They exploit both the middle-class's ability to pay and the arrogance to play. The middle-class do not view themselves as the blue-collar guy in Ladbrokes. They... no, WE regard ourselves as far more sophisticated, far more educated and intelligent and as we are far richer we will end up losing far more money too. We are *exactly* like that guy in Ladbrokes. If you think it crazy for someone to go down to the bookies and put a fiver on some horse after they've stared at the betting shop pin-board for ten minutes and you are wiser, much wiser after you've stared at websites for hours before placing your £5 per point on some index or another, then think again as that horse runs past that oversized horseshoe and the punter rips up his photocopied slip and then gets on with his life while you have palpitations as you are now £2000 down and don't know what to do when your wife comes in from work.

Only birds and aeroplanes have wings. I was the perfect target for the SB marketing team. Single, male, no girlfriend, wanted to be a success at something with barrow-loads of cash. And disenchanted, disempowered so consequently disengaged with up my job. I was just waiting to be devoured by the SBs. Their marketing team and the product itself can appeal to someone who only ticks one or two of the above boxes. They will hit you where it hurts emotionally then hit you where it hurts financially and you will feel you have been hit where it hurts physically – in your nuts (although you might get a stronger feeling in your stomach). You will see those good-looking, toned guys in the adverts successfully playing the markets whilst their good-looking, toned girlfriend looks on and you think, 'That could be me.' No, you actually *believe* it *will* be you. For those slightly more cynical they will produce more or less the same advert but instead of the George Clooney/Brad Pitt lookalike they will substitute in the average/slob guy that more men can actually relate to and think, 'He's just like me yet *he* has a gorgeous girl in his bed.' Yes, this guy successfully plays the markets, like you may or may not yet have done but unlike you he has an attractive girlfriend even though he's nothing special – like you. Yes, let's become like him then and get a woman into bed through money and success. If you are already a 'trader', you try harder. No, you will soon discover that he is completely unlike you ; you will not be a net winner with spread-betting nor meet girls who are on the homepage of foreign dating sites but do not actually belong to one – much like the customer service girls on any website who don't actually work there. Apart from the fact that this average guy is a low-budget actor booked for the day, as is his model girlfriend. We fall for these marketing tricks for two reasons: 1) the marketing men know what they're doing. They know how to get under your skin and pick at your desire for something new and exciting, something far better than you have or can even expect to get, your hope for the girlfriend you've always wanted, the success you've always craved, the respect you've always longed for, the easy money where you no longer have to sit in traffic twice a day with everyone else in the rat race. 2) You are all too willing to believe in it because you *want* and *need* to believe in it.

Marketing is everything these days although I guess it's always been like this. Coca-Cola knew how to get their product seen and sold almost everywhere more than a hundred years ago and even marketed it as a health drink and had it sold in chemists! Now their marketing budget has crossed over the billion dollar mark. Hard to believe that as a percentage of revenue, nowadays no one can spend as much as Red Bull. And to compete with Coke I guess they have to. Vodka-Red Bull seems the drink of choice for the young, whereas Bono maintains that it's JD and Coke. But the twenty-somethings drink more than the forty-somethings; they are more susceptible to watching Red Bull-branded off-piste skiers hurtling down rock-faces or someone jumping out of a space craft with a parachute or strapping rockets to their arms… the list of adrenaline sports they sponsor is almost endless. Now if I drink Red Bull will that make me able to jump 50 feet over rock to land on a nice bit of powdery snow and ski away like James Bond? No, I know it won't. But it somehow gets into your subconscious. Red Bull marketing clearly doesn't work on me as I have never bought a can. It does not give you wings. But SB marketing clearly worked. Coca-Cola had people believing long ago it was a health drink. SB firms still have people believe that they are selling an investment product! I saw myself as being a winner. Yes, I knew that the vast majority lose but if you were smart, did your research then you would win. Easy. Easy for *them*!

Advertising could be subliminal, could be appealing to the aspiration side of you, the greed side of you, the hope and fear within you. They will appeal to both the gullible and the sceptical – they'll both give it a go. They know which models to use, which actors to use, which celebrities to use. You can fill your smartphone display with any number of graphs and charts that the SB company will happily supply you with. You now feel like that trader sitting in front of those eight full-size screens as you ponder your next move. That's what they want you to think. Walk into any high-street bookies and you are also confronted with a bank of screens; that 'Cerburus Strategy'. You are a hard-working guy, you are rational, you are a great father to your child and partner to your wife – but you are a delusional gambler. If you carried over this way of thinking to other areas of your life, others at best would come to question you – or just regard you as fucking nuts.

The Grifter. The 'confidence trickster' swindles you into believing what they tell you, therefore winning your confidence. Put simply, the con artist. Gambling works in a similar way: they advertise, they draw you in, you get a small pay-out then they take large chunks of your money as you become almost a bystander, at the end still dumfounded as to how they managed to achieve this. If you understand the psychology of the con then you will understand gambling in all its forms, 419s, boiler rooms, often internet dating and maybe even your job. You are offered something great, often something you may have been trying to achieve for years but without success. A wonderful partner, a new source of income? There are those big winners that they feed to the media; the guy whose eight-horse accumulator actually worked and he's now got a few hundred thousand, the online poker millionaire at 25 years old. These are rarer than an attractive female punter in a bookies, remember. These winners actually make the gambling companies money; they are the perfect marketing tool. Are the online bookies so different from the guy on the street corner with his three cups and ball that you would never get involved with? You might even get the promise of something great in the future at work if only you work harder or stay with the company; then a few years down the line when nothing has happened, it's too late to leave as you have a mortgage to pay and the wife and kids to feed. Those Russian girls tell you all you want to hear as you email them time and time again. That gorgeous 25-year-old sitting in her Moscow flat really wants to meet you; so says the 45- year-old divorced mother of four as she chain-smokes her way through a hundred paid-for emails from ten lonely guys. The DFC may be the UK's fastest growing club. Cost you more than your RSPB membership and you don't even get a car sticker – not that you'd want one anyway.

*

I knew as a child the expression, 'An apple a day keeps the doctor away' and always felt there was some truth in that. I also knew at an early age what was clearly bullshit; eating a sugar-packed 'snack' does not help you 'work, rest and play' and did Coca-Cola really want 'to teach the world to sing'. (the 'B' side to this record was called, 'I believed it all'!) Yet I believed the SB bookies were keen on giving me *their* money!

There are things we can achieve with encouragement, help and support but winning at gambling is not one of them. But 'I'm Still Alive' (Pearl Jam). I didn't fuck up overtaking on some B-road, full of confidence in my driving skills and my 2.8 litre engine. My confidence didn't kill me. I haven't fucked up anyone else's lives. My egotism, my self-indulgence, my selfishness has affected me alone. For many it sucks in the family, friends and colleagues. It kills me inside when I see those SB and bookies ads on TV. I sit there with my partner and I can say nothing as she knows nothing. I tense up when I hear this bullshit as I know every advert will bring in new customers. It feels like I am experiencing a little of the pain that they are about to self-inflict. I don't want my revelations to affect my relationship with my wife, my friends and my colleagues whom all know nothing about my secret life but I have a compulsion (there's a surprise!) to get the message out. I know I will always be a gambler so of course I'm going to roll the dice and see what happens.

I was suckered into the gambling delusion. I had the money and the confidence. I have a degree in economics so I even have a certificate proving just how good I am. I should bin it and just frame my DFC certificate. I do not have that naivety of youth, the overconfidence, the dumb-ass risk-taking attitude of a 20-year-old. No, I have the balls when I need to and will quit when the cards are against me, don't I? They will get you at any age because you perceive yourself as better than the rest. Youth gives you the confidence you need, right? Age makes you a wise old salt, right? You're educated, you look sharp in your suit, you act sharp in your job… Just forget all of this. All completely irrelevant. Lemmy knows. He wrote a song about it.

7

HOW WE GAMBLE

This is not the section that gives you hints and tips and tells you the common beginner mistakes to avoid so you can win at gambling. There are many books out their which offer their suggestions. They might even have great testimonials too – the law of averages dictates that you get it correct sometimes and one of your clients will vouch for your system. Or it's just completely fabricated. You might become skilled at losing money more slowly – this just prolongs the pain and extends the losses. Brimming with the confidence bestowed on you by that book you ordered through Amazon, you will certainly lose more. Gambling is where the unknowing masochist meets the unstoppable sadist.

Gambling has gone mainstream and is now technology dependent – like most gamblers, whether through the smartphone or at the FOBT. Spread-betting couldn't really exist without it and poker is now largely online; those Texas hold 'em nights at the pub help to feed the nation's interest in playing online and the online sites also get a fair few into the pubs and clubs too. It's a mutually beneficial relationship. The high-street bookie is now also a big presence online. For the gambling providers, all forms of gambling are growth industries. The only problem the bookie has is not so much to get people to bet but to get people to bet on *their* site. Don't know which area of internet gambling has the fastest growth and the biggest profits and it would take a fair bit of digging to find out as it's not just the poker sites that play their cards close to their chest. But to the gambler, it doesn't matter in the slightest which site is making the most profit; it's the site you are losing on that is the only thing that matters to you.

BET BIGGER! Whatever you say about only making small bets, in the end we all make bigger and bigger bets. They sucker you in by emphasising just how small your stake can be. You can often even play for free. This applies from poker through to casino games. But however controlled you think you are, you WILL place bets with real money and then make bigger bets. And some wild bets too. And when you're behind you WILL try some risky plays. You start small then bet big and lose big. Won't do that again, you think. But you do! Start small but all too soon it's the same or even bigger. At the end my bets were so large they dwarfed what I thought was massive only a year before. And these were also massive as compared to a few years before that too! In 2007, a £10 bet was BIG, then by the first time I got out (October 2008) it was up to £22 a point on the Dow. Then I took a break and started small (£1 a point on Dow) but it went up way beyond the £22 within a year or so, to finish in late 2012 where I was betting £250 a point on the Dow and even £500 a point on the FTSE. I did some pretty wild things, but going £500 a point must surely have been the wildest; like downing a bottle of Jack Daniel's. What happens if it suddenly plunges? That was potentially the worst and most desperate thing I did but I got away with it; so I repeated this trick several times! Could have easily lost me £50k! If your thing is poker, then you will do the same thing too. If you've been putting 10p coins into fruities, you will soon find yourself feeding in £1 coins. Those machines in the bookies can cost you £100 a spin if you want and not just the £2 you started with. There are many who can lose a grand or two on these in the space of a couple of hours. Same story at the bingo club. Start with coins then before you know it you'll be letting that machine suck in your £10 notes before moving onto your bank card. This is just like in sport. When you are down you start taking big risks. In football in the last few minutes even the goalkeeper comes forward for the corner kick. In snooker you go for the really difficult pots. In golf you try to hit it as sweet as possible to get the ball over that water hazard 260 yards away and onto the green for an eagle putt. But how often does this work? Even if it works, this eagle will not compensate for those sixes and sevens you got on some previous holes.

The bets will get bigger and bigger until they are MASSIVE! I was £30k+ up at one point on one 'bet'; a 'Legion' bet made up of many ('demons', I would soon discover. N.B. a biblical reference – one of several – but I am not religious). Then within 24 hours I was £10k down. Yes, I should have taken the £30k+. But I could have said this when I was £10k or £20k up. When is enough, enough? I didn't know the £30k would be the height of my profits. Could have made £30k, £60k more in my mind. To grow that pot to £30k I was betting massive stakes. When you are down you bet massively to win it all back as quickly as possible. You then get into the habit of betting BIG straight off. I doubled my losses from £65k to £130k with this strategy!

THE BLOW-OUT. Binge drinking? Easy to spot on a Friday night. Binge gambling? – this is only evident in the privacy of your online bank statements. We all binge gamble sooner or later. A few quid here and there ends up one day with that bender. I had a lot of these. You feel guilty and dumb and that 'never again!' hangover feeling. But you can't stop yourself. You had a Plan A and then a Plan B. You gradually work your way through the whole alphabet. A few years down the line you do not even realise that you have had so many plans you are now working your way through the Greek alphabet! Some plans you repeat time and time again. That original Plan A might have been followed ten times, a hundred times. You might even 'tweak' it in your own mind. You will probably then try many different plans then go back to one you tried months before which didn't really work then either – but it worked once or twice and you *almost* won big... no, you are tricking yourself just like the machine tricks the slot-jockey. The only plans you need to follow are contained within the pages of this book: the plans and suggestions about how to give up, how to control your urge and how to get yourself back on track.

We all seem to want to make easy money. There's even a SB bookie out there called 'EZTrader'! They are one of Tottenham Hotspur's sponsors, along with William Hill. The bigger clubs nowadays tend to have one mainstream and one spread-bet sponsor. Trying to make easy money is akin to trying to make money the lazy way and who can do that in real life. They con you into believing that this is possible. It ain't. Trying to make easy money will generally lead to losing money and usually more than you think. Sometimes much, much more.

'IT'S JUST A FLESH WOUND': You see your losses as part of the learning curve rather than actual losses, which is exactly what they are. You invent your own reality. We all distance ourselves further from reality the more we separate ourselves from our money. We fantasise more about buying that Porsche when we are DOWN! Like Monty Python's Black Knight, you carry on regardless, seeing what you want to see. You elbow aside your morals, justifying yourself in the belief that gambling in work time is only a temporary measure. As soon as you are back on top, you'll stick to gambling outside of office hours. You reason that gambling at work is not your long-term strategy even though you've now been doing exactly this for longer than you care to remember. Gambling will not be a short cut to what you've always craved: success, wealth, self-esteem, respect, sexual prowess but just a short-circuit. We will just end up destroying whatever good reputation we have from the boardroom to the bedroom. Hard-work, perseverance and education get people to where they want to be. They are not the easy options but they are the right options.

GIMME, GIMME, GIMME! Louis: 'Do we just keep playing until we lose?' Tim: 'Hell no! You play 'til you win!' Louis: 'We *were* winning!' Louis was right. You play until you lose! Why? Because you can never win ENOUGH so you keep on playing then you lose more and more until all your winnings are gone then you lose your stake money, then you find money somewhere else and gamble and lose that. Even if you lose, like I did, then win big (I was £18k up) you will never stop – which means you will end up losing again. If you have won £100k, what's stopping you taking it to £200k? You've won BIG, so easy to win BIG again, right? I just about managed to pull up short of the precipice. Many return as soon as their salary or inheritance comes through. But if you can quit with cash still in the bank, then you are a winner! Then it was YOUR decision to stop and not the fact that you are broke and have been forced to stop. If you can stop before you lose everything then you deserve some respect. You have beaten the bastard.

The professional poker player will eat away little by little at their opponents' stacks. The SB companies do much the same. There will be times when they take a big pot off of you. You win some, you lose some: but the latter will occur more often and with bigger numbers. You can split gambling three ways if you like: the wins, the nearly wins and the losses. That means you lose two thirds of the time.

'TAKE THE MONEY AND RUN': We know this advice. It means nothing to a gambler. How could it? You wouldn't have those winnings if you're hadn't been gambling in the first place. There is a paradox here that is lost on the non-gambler who reminds you of this cliché. I lost £6k then was almost £20k up! Did I stop and take the money? 'You don't give up when you're winning, man! What's wrong with you?' Tim announces to Louis when he suggests they just stop now they are ahead. A winning gambler cannot do this, he believes he'd be *insane* to do this; no, he is onto a good thing and he is going to continue bringing home the cash. Anyone who advises him to stop must be nuts! A losing gambler cannot stop either; just needs that little something, that bit of luck, his 'near-wins' to become wins then he'll be back in the black. So neither can stop. The winning gambler will sooner or later join the second category and both will descend deeper and deeper into the world of losses until they hit the third category. The third category gambler is the one who runs out of money.

This takes different forms. All my savings had gone, my income had gone, my car had gone – then I started on the house equity. Some go further than this and lose every last penny and usually have unpayable credit card bills too.

There is also the fourth category where a minority end up; they have an altogether different take on the expression, 'take the money and run'. These are the ones who steal to cover their losses and to continue gambling. Could be stealing small amounts to keep on going to the bookies to put on £10. It could be the teenager who steals from his parents in order to return to those fruities. It could be stealing thousands from an employer or through some other fraud. Most of them intend to 'borrow' the money, to use as stake money. But as they have used their own money as collateral time and time again, they shouldn't be too surprised that the 'temporary undisclosed loan' suddenly becomes a pure and simple theft. How do many try to escape from this self-inflicted mess they have tricked themselves into? 'Borrow' more of course. It is not long before their unauthorised withdrawal becomes a gaping hole in company accounts. Now they are in the shit. There will be an internal cover-up and the culprit will be fired or moved. If they are fired the company and employee may agree on some bullshit reason acceptable to both if the fraudster has some standing in the company – or he knows things that he might well divulge if he doesn't leave on favourable terms. He might even get a nice pay-off. If he has no cards to play, has no bargaining position and if it doesn't put the company in a bad light then the employee will find himself in court and either end up selling second-hand clothes in the British Heart Foundation or be sent down for a few months. Seems these cases are popping up more frequently now as people bet extraordinary amounts online in all forms; poker and bingo seem to rear their ugly heads all too often. But the middle-class who like spread-betting for all its bullshit information illusion and perceived skill of the 'trader' often have large savings that they can draw upon. They do not need to resort to crime; there are exceptions of course and these are more likely to be the ones we never hear about, because these are the company cover-ups. Would reflect badly on the company. No one wants its customers, employees, competitors amongst others to find out just how slack it had been with internal auditing and supervision for all those years. You might think twice about working in an organisation like that or having any dealings with it. No, safer to hush it all up. The high-stakes spread-betting is more likely to be older and higher up in the company than the younger poker or female bingo player. We don't hear about these frauds.

For the middle-class once cash-rich gambler, they kick themselves and hopefully stop gambling like me, before they lose everything. If you can stop gambling whatever class you think you are, before you are forced to then you have your own special category of gambler; the gambler in remission, in recovery. No one will find out about your losses, you hope; it will be your skeleton in the closet that you will hear jangling as it chuckles at your misfortunate once in a while.

RETURN TO SENDER. Several times I took my balance to zero so that it was harder for me to place a bet, but I ended up funding the account time after time. Lose £5k then return the remaining pitiful amount, like £123.34 to my bank account as some trick to call it a day. Whatever game you are playing, you will do this sooner or later. But after a day you will just type in your three-digit security code again – maybe even before that £123.34 has even shown up on your bank statement. Then one day, a long, long way into the future you will do this one final time. Take it from me, do it now and call it your final time.

MINIMISE IT! Unfortunately, this does not refer to your losses. I always seemed to have the SB website permanently on my computer; conveniently minimised so I could instantly flick onto it at will but sufficiently hidden so whatever adult wanders in, can't see it. Sure, I am doing what millions of others do at work, although that hardly justifies it. Any employer or line manager need do is have a look occasionally at what their employees have minimised to find out what they are really working on in company time. Most people will not close down a website entirely even when their boss wanders in briefly as they'll have to go through the palaver of logging in again; this takes far too long. No, just minimise it and wait for them to leave. And if whoever comes in sits at the other side of the desk, then you are free to max that website you shouldn't be looking at, even when they are trying to discuss something of importance with you; it may well be important to you too but not as important as what's happening on your screen, whether you are watching the Dow or the dealer on your favourite poker website. As a teacher, I've even done this during parents' evening! There are very few companies who monitor what their employees are looking at or ask their Internet Service Provider to do so; this takes time and money and as the bosses may well be doing the same as the minions under them at whatever level, they are not going to want to implement any web snooping. So I did the same; I gambled when I should have been doing something else. I lost way more money than I earned from the day job. No sane person would moonlight to *lose* money. What did that make me then?

'PRACTICE MAKES PERFECT'. Whoever said that was a) either born perfect or as near as, or b) they had a vested interest in convincing others that this is true. Take the pro at your golf club – he sells you lessons and equipment and driving range balls. However much you practise at being a poker player, you ain't going to become what you want to be unless you are born with 99% of what's required already. Practice makes perfect if you only have to work on that final 1%. 'Practice makes perfect...' with today's addition of, 'with the right equipment'. Witness all those men on a Sunday morning with their hit-straighter-and-longer driver, slice their little white ball into the trees. Kids always want those magic football boots that so-and-so wears for Real Madrid. It's ok for naïve kids to fall for it but surely as adults we are smarter than this? The SB sites use their 'technological illusion' just like the golf club manufacturers. With the SB bookie amongst others, however much you 'practice' it is basically *impossible* to be that long-term winner.

DAISY, DAISY, give me your answer, do. Sometimes you win and sometimes you win big. This drives you on – together with those near-wins (which, remember, are actually losses) and those big wins that you believe next time will be even bigger. Nearly achieving something in life outside of gambling gets us excited and planning how to achieve our goal. We gamblers believe gambling to be the same – our own human nature betrays us or is simply conned by our excitement over the near-win. We then naturally invent strategies for success – we don't realise it is unachievable. The gambler's DNA can't compute this. We drive ourselves half-crazy over this – we end up as the HAL 9000 gambler.

SELF-IMPOSED STOP-LOSS. I once read an article where one SB client stated how she would allocate £2k to it. If she lost this amount, then she would stop. This is the level-headed, wise decision of the pre-gambler for whatever game floats your boat. Just that it is clearly bollocks to think this way. If you give yourself a set amount for gambling then sooner or later you will reach your loss target. You never intended it to be an actual target number to lose but that is what it is from the very beginning. The other loss number, which the bookies seem keen to encourage and has now become a cliché, is that you should only bet what you can afford to lose. This is just as much bollocks as the former concept. Yes, you have some initial figure in your head when you start out but this is soon revised up and revised up time after time. I too had some idea that if I lost £2k, I would quit. In the end I lost between £130–140,000. The concept of how much you can afford to lose has several major flaws. The first flaw is that the number that pops into your head is likely to be fairly random, fairly arbitrary. This means that when you reach it, going beyond it seems no big deal. Anyway, you go beyond this figure as you expect your next bet to pay off so that part of your £2k loss is returned to you. Any extra money you allocate beyond this £2k is only the stake money, after all. The trouble with this is that, for any gambler, there is no way you can stop after a win so that even if you recoup your losses completely, you'll only jump back in again. Then sooner or later you'll end up back in the red again. You might well regard your initial losses as something all gamblers need to accept as the mistakes made and lessons learned will stand you in good stead for the future. I know this from experience. I pushed on through my £2k loss limit and was £6k down. I remember how angry I was at myself for the mistakes I had made and the loss I had incurred. I had worked hard to build my savings yet had frittered £6k away within a few months. Little did I realise at the time how easy it would become to lose much, much more. That £6k would be almost an insignificant amount. I would soon be able to lose that in a day. No, I even lost this within a few minutes! Actually, sometimes instantly. But back in those early days I was £6k down and pissed off but a month later I was £18k up! I was now beginning to think that I could give up my day job! I never realised my membership of the Dumb Fuck Club had already begun.

REDEFINE, REALLOCATE. The major problem with the sage advice of only losing what you can afford to lose is that you redefine what you can afford. Why not just use up all your savings? You don't exactly think this way but you turn to them time after time after time until they have all gone. Well, they were not doing much for you anyway. You convince yourself that it won't affect your quality of life. This is what I ended up believing. As I was then leaving the country, I sold the car and house. The problem then became the fact that I now had a massive injection of capital and it could only head in one direction. On the one hand I was happy that I had a new source of finance to back up the equity requirement that the SB companies ask for. It would only be stake money, right? But on the other, I was shit-scared. I feared what was going to happen. The car money disappeared in an afternoon. How much can you afford to lose? What an odd concept to consider anyway! Whatever number you dream up, a month or two down the line, this figure is likely to be doubled. A year or two later, this last figure will have a zero added, maybe even two. I know. That's how it works. For the desperate, the concept of affordability goes out the window and they start on the house equity, maxing out credit cards and even stealing from their employers. I briefly entered this territory but woke up to my own madness soon after I had made a sortie into the land that nobody should enter.

The 'only bet what you can afford to lose,' mantra is willingly propagated by the gambling industry either directly in their own literature or through some third-party that they fund, such as GamCare. The advice is oft repeated to new and old gamblers by the industry as they know it's bollocks and they know they will benefit from their clients' false belief in it.

As we gamble, our funds get gradually depleted. Again, in other areas of our lives, if we can see something isn't working then we will stop. But with gambling we do the opposite. We allocate MORE resources to it. We double our bets. Eventually our bets will dwarf what we originally started out with. The industry always encourages you to bet more. The casino fruit machines and the FOBTs incentivise you to increase your stake. 'Just the minimum then,' says the guy in the SB bookie's 'dealing room'. So, as we lose more, we bet more. This just speeds up the process of losing. And when it's gone we find more money from somewhere else. Do you really need that investment that you have? We are uncomfortable with the word 'addiction' but if we keep repeating the same actions and we can't seem to stop, addicted we might be. You don't have to do it every day to be one. You will follow a pattern. Even if you just bet every Saturday then you have some sort of problem. Even if you *only* bet on a Saturday, you will find yourself sometimes upping your stake, betting in the week and betting on that app. It's a slippery slope. I slid down it for five years – I was going fucking fast when I hit the bottom.

REDISTRIBUTE. I still buy a lot of my clothes in the Next sale and buy reduced items in the supermarket as I did when I was gambling. Seems kind of stupid when I had my mobile in one hand, watching the market numbers flashing against me and losing me hundreds, whilst I was deciding if I really wanted to eat the use-by-today yogurt that was 40 pence cheaper in Sainsbury's! But a gambler's mind is not rational. It could almost be described as being a split personality. The way we view money becomes almost bizarre. The gambler will try to spend as little as possible outside of gambling. We reason that we need as large a gambling pot to draw from as we can; money spent on anything else is simply 'dead money' so you spend as little as possible on anything outside of gambling. If we can add that extra £100 or £1000 to our gambling fund, then we can double or triple this number after our successful bet pays off. With SB you believe that £1000 will soon have an additional zero added to the end. No, what will happen is that digit at the front will become a zero instead. You will realise too late that your 'dead money' logic is actually the reverse of what you believe in. Your gambling money is deader than a ZX81. Sometimes though, after a big win or a big loss – it makes little difference really – you might go out on a cash bender. Only when you come out of gambling do you start to properly reassess the value of money but to reconnect with its true value is one of the hardest things for a reformed gambler to get their head round. For me, I have become more generous. I still remember when I lost a grand or so and almost didn't bat an eyelid. So why not just spend whatever amount you feel with friends or family on whatever. These gambling spending sprees are the result of two realisations, possibly only subconsciously: 1) Money has lost its meaning. 2) Spend what you have quickly, as you might have squandered it by next month or next year. It still seems odd though, when I spend £450 on a new laptop (to write this book!) when this was less than the 'buy-in' on many 'Legion' bets and on a few individual ones too. I work hard to make £450. I must try to remember this more than how I spent it in the past, otherwise I can feel blasé about any sum of money. If you've squandered the lot, your attitude to money is decided for you.

OLDER AND WISER? If you are in your 60s and think the spread-betting companies only make their money out of those younger than you who don't have your wisdom, then think again. They actively market to the elderly. Why should you be any better a poker player than the rest at the table? The SB bookies don't discriminate. Whether you are 22 or 72, the SB companies and the rest will take your money. Whether you have a degree or a Ph.D. or nothing at all, it's all the same to them. The only questions they ask you that they really care about concern your financial status: are you a homeowner, do you have savings, annual income… and if they get their way, they'll take it all.

Maybe you lose big when you are in your 20s but decide to try again five or ten years later when you believe you have lost that naivety of youth. The only difference will be that you probably have more money at this point. So that's good; no problem with margin calls or running out of chips or cash to back the horses. Just means you lose more. You feel renewed confidence returning to the table with your lovely new chip-stack. But it didn't come from playing poker but from your day job. Those true professional poker players do not have to resort to savings. Yes, they do use the money earnt from their day job, as winning money off of suckers like you *is* their day job. I had loads of equity at various points. Did it make a difference? Yes, instead of betting £1, I bet £100; per point, that is... And as 'bet' equals 'lose', the experience of having more equity at hand is not a beneficial one. If experience tells you anything, it's that you just can't win. If you really think you are older and wiser and get back in, then you really have learnt nothing. Maybe you just thought you were a bit reckless and now you know better. Was I reckless? Sometimes. But I had a plan and usually stuck to it. Did it help? Answer: I lost £130k.

HOLIDAYS. Gambling in the last few days of my holiday in Cuba means I am in and out from the pool, up and down from the beach to go and look at that CNN rectangle. But the relaxation of a holiday is destroyed if all you do is watch those market numbers and worry, or sit by the pool without access to market numbers and worry. I told myself not to do it, I warned myself not to go through this self-imposed stress, I insisted to myself that I go to the beach and relax, I fought against this constant desire to watch the markets and place a trade. And what do I go and do? Let's not be too hard on myself – most of the holiday was bet free. Might only be because the flight over cost me £10k in losses, though, as well as the £10k I was up less than 24 hours before. How did that happen? Held a large sell position, then the president of the European Central Bank, Mario Draghi, gave his 'Whatever it takes' speech about supporting the market, and I got wiped out when I was at 40,000 feet. I needed a holiday to get over that! I was doing well before I boarded our long-haul flight when I secretly checked my account in the departure lounge in the few minutes my partner went off to get some coffee. This was risky but as there was no connection in the tomb-like airport toilets I had no choice! I even funded my account and logged into my bank account from Cuba! The first day I just checked my then closed position. A week later I reinstated it. God knows who was reading everything that went into the hotel computer! A year before, I had been on a cheap holiday to Turkey and as there was free wireless everywhere, I bet everywhere; hotel room, corridor, whilst eating, by the pool. There is no escape for the gambler! Then when I was back in England I visited the public library several times to use the internet to check the IBEX on the BBC website. Damn waste of time, having to return to the library every 30 minutes or so. And I didn't exactly saunter there either, which turns a pleasurable, leisurely wander around the shops into more of a trolley dash. So there you are; a gambler's holiday will always be a busman's holiday. If you are down you want to win it back as soon as possible. Why wait until you are back from your hols when you can do it during your hols?

TIME ALONE. What do you do when you are away on business and find yourself alone in your hotel or your partner is out? Spread-bet? Poker? Phone for an escort? Too many people get drawn into gambling online when they have a quiet night in then before long they *only* want to have a quiet night in so that they can gamble. Could be spread-betting, which at least stops at nine o'clock on a Friday night. There is no respite for the poker player. There is always a game available. I am sure they even do well over Christmas when people want to take a break from their families and spend time with what they now love the most.

A NEW BREED OF GAMBLER: It's the internet that's the killer nowadays. Online gambling is hidden and growing and pervasive. The middle class are adept at stuffing skeletons in closets, so unless something dramatic happens it will remain so. Those who would never have entered a bookies or a bingo hall or a casino or been to a poker evening now do so online. Financial spread-betting has now tapped a new and lucrative market. People are too embarrassed to admit to it. They still think they are alone in their nightmare. But what do people search for when they are losing or before they even start gambling? They search YouTube for those video seminars with those who will coach them on how to make money. People are more interested in these than hearing the tales from losers. What relevance is this to them? They will become winners. They just need some guidance about how to make money. That's what people want to believe and is what they actually still believe even when they start to lose and keep on losing.

WIN, LOSE OR DRAW. Takes a rare gambler to actually stop when he's back to break-even again. Takes a rare gambler to stop when down too – or up! The fortunate gamblers who get back to break-even will continue gambling and inevitably lose. Every silver lining has a very big black cloud: they will just prolong the day they finally give up and will have bigger losses than if they had lost and given up the first time they were in the red. The gambler who wins it all back again is more likely to bet bigger in the future – like myself or Nick Leeson, for instance. If you have lost before then make it all back, when you once more go negative, it doesn't overly concern you as you've been there before and emerged as a winner. You might even be confident enough to bet bigger to get yourself out. But one day you will just sink further down into that hole. I was down then back up then I went so far down I barely knew it was possible. Happens to us all if we continue to pursue the impossible.

FOLLOW THE EXPERTS. Those racing tipsters in the national newspapers, if you look at their profit/loss over the season you will see that they almost all make a loss. The *Racing Post* even publish the form guide to the tipsters. The newspapers' tipsters are very happy to let you know when they get it right, especially those 8-1 or so winners. The stock market tipsters do much the same thing and operate in much the same way and will throw in a graph or two to help prove their point; a few candlesticks and it all becomes very sophisticated. But it's just very sophisticated bullshit. You can always find a graph and a trade you made based on it that made you money. Let's just forget the times it went tits up. I can prove to you why that horse won at 8-1 after it's gone past the winning post if you like – just forget the times that I lost. When there are thousands of experts out there, it is not too difficult for the business channels to find someone who predicted such-and-such that actually happened. There are a fair few who don't take much convincing. The presenter at the SB trading seminar started by telling us something that seemed important then was asked a question which was SB related about how to read markets and he suddenly went off on a different tack, giving us valuable insight and tips and trader secrets. It was like some sort of 'Uncle Albert' market trader plant, although I doubt if it was. He tells us how there is nothing in it for him when he directs us to his website. His trader blog is subscription free. He doesn't tell us that he runs adverts on there from third parties who pay him a fee for each new sign-up! There were even people taking notes at that seminar – I have seen this in another arena: church. They will either write down notes or get their highlighter out and block out sections in their Bible. Both congregations are looking for an answer. But they are essentially, if not entirely, recording *someone else's* ideas. He needs to give those with little imagination something to work with or else they might not bet at all. Do not be fooled by *The Hangover* or *Rain Man*. You are not going to card count and win back your losses. You are not going to gamble your way out of your gambling losses and debts.

OVERWHELMED, OVERLOADED AND OVERDRAWN. However you gamble, you are not in control. The gambling companies insist that they inform you, they educate you, they allow you time to practise. What they really do is overwhelm you, distract you and encourage you to play. When you play, you lose. Go to Sylvester Stallone's Hard Rock casino in Las Vegas. They employ showgirls as croupiers. This is more of a distraction than those flashing lights on the pub fruitie or the breaking news that pops up on your trading platform. Yes, she is interested in the contents of your trousers – as that's where your wallet is.

STRINGING YOU ALONG BEFORE THEY STRING YOU UP. They pride themselves on customer service. It's in their own interest to try and appear to be as helpful as possible. They need the gambler to stay with them for as long as possible in order to lose as much as possible. They do all they can to keep you with them and to stop you switching to a different provider – which you will eventually do – where you will receive the identical treatment and get that déjà vu experience both from what *they* say and what *you* do. You will switch after you have lost a considerable amount and believe the next online firm will be better for you – this is where you will make your fortune. Little do you realise that you will lose double here what you lost in the first. You are like the blackjack player at the casino who changes tables. You might even give that original site another go.

ROOM 101: Motivate, encourage, support are the goals of customer services and the ultimate Holy Grail is to get the target to attend a seminar. Any gambling firm knows that the more a client gambles, the more they will lose. It's a simple formula. The seminar allows them to make more money off existing clients as well as tapping some new ones. After you have quit gambling you will feel like you voluntarily and unknowingly attended something akin to an Orwellian re-education session at the Ministry of Truth; you come away thinking differently, thinking 'clearly' – and thinking how they want you to think. Most clients will have already lost money by the time they attend these seminars to find out where they went wrong. Then they go away conjuring up some new strategy in their head now they have been given some more knowledge, that extra bit of information and insight that will make all the difference, right? Almost all clients who attend these seminars are chomping at the bit to start 'making money' because they are now educated and have the edge, right! They go to find out where they went wrong. Should never have started spread-betting, that's where it went wrong!! The poker sites also offer you education. They explain the rules and give you tactics. There are 101 attributes you will need to win at poker. Unless you have at least 100 of them then you will lose. As soon as you log on to any gambling website then your fate is sealed. The bookies give you all the form guides you need for almost everything online, not just the horses. Or you can just read the form guide from the *Racing Post* pinned around the bookies' walls or read a shop copy for form on other sports. Or go online and you'll have heaps of information. Yes, heaps of ultimately useless information. If I read everything there is online about swimming and trained my body professionally, I still would have no chance against Michael Phelps, even if he swam in his pyjamas. But you are not swimming in an 'Olympic-sized swimming pool' at Maplin's or elsewhere anyway. You are swimming in a murky lake, filled with all sorts of creatures and old rusty shopping trolleys hidden beneath the surface. They are just handing you the key to the gateway of illusion; or more exactly, the gateway of self-delusion. I remember remarking to the girl at the desk in Ladbrokes when I placed a bet (when I was 17) that I should take their recommendation from their 'Bet of the day' board. 'What does it say?' she asked. 'Nothing!' I replied chuckling, as the board was blank that day. She laughed – as she took my money! Yeah, I really should have followed this advice.

MARTINI BIANCO. We all end up Martini gamblers sooner or later; the internet has allowed us to gamble anytime, anyplace, anywhere. That smartphone you bought to help control your life, it now controls *yours*. I used to check my SB positions throughout the day when possible – the gambler always makes it possible. I wonder how many people watch the market numbers change like I did, whilst operating machinery, high up on a crane, driving a car, lifeguarding a beach… I would imagine one day someone will be in court accused of this, just like people text messaging then being involved in car accidents are now. It didn't matter too much when I never even owned a smartphone. I would just take my Sony notebook with me and find a café or shopping centre and connect up to the Wi-Fi. I remember sitting in the shopping centre all afternoon once. I only went there to buy a drill. My partner never queried why it had taken me so long. I sat there outside the underwear shop for the simple fact that that was where the comfy bench was, watching the girls go by. I sat there for hours and hours just like I used to stand in the betting shop when I was 17 for hours and hours. At least there were attractive women around – never the case in a bookies. And no one reported me for hanging around outside a ladies' underwear shop all day with a webcam inadvertently pointing that way either.

Even when you leave your smartphone at home you will still manage to take the Martini Bianco approach. I have on several occasions popped into the Apple shop and spread-bet from the shop's MacBooks themselves! Maybe you use the free internet in the hotel lobby. Done that too from various countries. You might just even resort to phoning them up, old skool. Done that too. Again, from various countries! But sitting on the toilet, stuck in traffic, squeezed into a standing room only train or bus is not quite as romantic or sophisticated as those 70s adverts.

I have placed bets before and after work and, as we all do eventually, during work too. Worktime and free time then becomes a blur as any conceivable time just becomes gambling time. You will gamble whilst eating, you will even gamble whilst having a shower. Yes, this sounds difficult but I managed it and so will you; I would put the laptop on the toilet seat facing me so that I could keep an eye on the market numbers. I have even stepped out mid-shower, made a trade (bet!) then got back in again. You could do this playing poker too, no problem. I became like the alcoholic who has that bottle of gin in the office desk drawer who takes regular swigs when no one is paying too much attention. In fact, it was often easier to gamble when I was working as I always had a computer at my disposal. There must be millions upon millions who check their email, Facebook, even bid on eBay whilst at work. I have seen people do it, if not on the computer then on their phones. I am ashamed to admit that I have placed bets whilst teaching. Set the kids some task, they return to their desks and you return to yours – with that computer on it. Even if you can resist the temptation to actually bet, your mind is still on it. And as a teacher with that massive smart-board fixed onto the wall, connected to your computer, you need to be extra vigilant. I have walked into someone's classroom before and even though she performed the minimising trick as I approached it was too late as her dating site had been projected for all to see. Fortunately, the children in her class were too young to notice.

You will bet all day sometimes. I could miss breakfast and never get out of the shirt and boxers that I had worn to bed. I may barely eat all day. These days remind me of the story of a frustrated wife whose husband plays computer games all day. Sends him to Brazil for two weeks to see the rainforest. So what does he do? Never leaves the terminal but finds somewhere where he can play computer games all day for a fortnight. Is this true? Not sure, but there are people out there who actually piss in a bottle rather than have to get up and leave their computer. At least I never got to that stage. But I never had to. I could take the laptop to the toilet with me.

THE PROFESSIONAL GAMBLER. Some people think they can make a living out of gambling or use it to supplement their income. I have believed this at various stages of my life. By the time I reached my mid-30s, I reasoned that the only place where you can win is the stock market. After all, this is what the world economy is based on, not horse racing. There are professional golfers knocking a ball about making a great living too. Does that mean I can turn up with my clubs and tee off next to Sir Nick Faldo and join the party? So why did I think I could trade against the traders? But I'm not even trading against traders; I am trading (betting!) against a professional gambling company who lead you to believe that their website is somehow identical to real traders' screens in investment banks. But it is an artificial device similar to a fruit machine with all those flashing lights and buttons you can click and nudge to get a lovely pay-out. If porn is your thing, do you really believe you are having sex with the girls you are watching? You can *imagine* having sex with them but you know at that moment you are not and never will be. So why believe you are an *actual* trader? You may be sitting at the poker table and trying to hang with those few who actually know what they are doing but you are as much a professional or winning poker star as the naked guy who sprints onto the football pitch and manages to kick the ball about a bit is a professional footballer. You will have a not too dissimilar experience to the streaker; you will feel great for a short time as you join in before you are brought smack back down to earth. You will one day realise that the only outcome for what you did gambling was to get your arse kicked just like the guy displaying his wedding tackle is tackled to the ground. That Android device is what you have become too for those gambling sites. They know how you behave as if they have programmed you themselves; you are their Android, their robot device for making them money. The only difference between the online betting companies and online porn girls is that it's only the former who will eventually fuck you one day.

SWITCHING. Gamblers transfer from one website to another in the belief they will do better elsewhere or at least the deal they get will be fairer. Why would walking out of Ladbrokes and across the road to Paddy Power or going online make any difference? You might get that 'free' £50 'golden hello'. Yes, you have that shiny shilling in your hand and you haven't even realised you've been hit over the head by that sign-up girl in the customer services chat box.

It's not that you just chose the wrong sort of gambling for you. Do not think you should try poker after failing at roulette. For you, they are both a game of chance and you will do equally badly in both. If you lose betting on the horses would you really believe betting on the greyhounds would be any different? Or in my case, the stock market? True, there are professional poker players – and they will fleece you. Play with your friends. If you think you are good then try tournaments, face to face. Do NOT start online. NEVER play online unless you are that one who wins every face-to-face tournament he enters. Forget casinos too! Just do the maths. The zero (or double zero) is there for a reason on a roulette wheel. It is IMPOSSIBLE to win at blackjack over time. Slot machines are programmed to take 90–97% of your money over a given cycle (So if you start with £100 you will soon be down to £90 then £81 – at 10% – and so on). They even play internally when no one is playing them, so don't think you can beat them by waiting around for others to lose their money before you nip in. Or those Monday morning gamblers who convince themselves that the machines make so much money at the weekend that they pay out far more easily after the weekenders have left. SB gambling or bingo or whatever you want in many ways is just like that slot machine; it gives out and it takes in but the money you have to gamble will reduce and reduce until there is nothing. The machines cannot lose. There is NO winning system. There are NO professional slot machine players, only consistent LOSERS!

TEA OR COFFEE? The only relevance to which betting form you choose online is which one loses you the money the quickest, which one will lose you the most and which one you get stuck in the longest. To me spread-betting seems the worst but that's just my personal taste. Can easily lose a fucking fortune on poker sites, casino sites, bingo sites, in the bookies, FOBTs, any of them. Gamblers always up their stakes and play longer than they intend. You can easily start off playing simple one-card bingo but end up playing multiple cards for big stakes. You can easily start just playing poker for an hour then start skipping meals and then start going to bed at 1 a.m. then 2 then 3… you will lose money and time and so much more. You will always end up chasing your losses. Gambling is gambling. If you spread-bet and think bingo is just nuts, then think again. Whatever form you prefer, it will become your worst fucking nightmare.

WIN IT ALL BACK! Fighting spirit, eh? But it is not like a rematch in golf or chess or something. There will be no different outcome. Your DNA and evolution is being conned again here. ""I'll get it back…I know it sounds sick and demented. I will get it back," says John on *Gambling in Las Vegas* (BBC, Louis Theroux). Even the gambler recognises his behaviour as 'sick and demented' but he's powerless to stop himself doing it. As my losses grew month on month, year on year, I was beginning to realise I was no different from John: "I just need one good streak and I can get it done." I needed the market to fall faster than an Austrian skydiver. A winning streak is purely and simply a lucky streak, no more. It has to be lucky, as the odds are stacked against you which means you cannot be a long-term winner. The fact that both expressions exist should really set alarm bells ringing – just that for the gambler, the idea that they might get a winning streak excites them! It is not like Ronnie O'Sullivan's winning streak; this really is down to skill and control. A gambler's winning streak, other than in poker, isn't anything of the sort. That first 'night of the long dives' back in 2008 destroyed me as I was facing the wrong way as the market went in the same direction as my bank balance – my lucky streak had ended. You are walking through a minefield. Just how lucky can you be? There are undoubtedly many shorts who thought all their dreams had come true with Brexit or Trump only to be replaced by that sinking feeling as the markets failed to sink. You might switch your gambling around in some way. Switch tables playing poker. Switch casino game. Switch from high street to online. In the end, I switched from stock market indices to Gold to Brent Crude. What do I know about gold other than it's some cheesy/classic (take your pick!) Spandau Ballet song? I would then worry about how much I've lost that day or week, where I went wrong, what I should have done, then come up with some bullshit plan to get it back. Once the baby was on its way, I became desperate to win back my losses and tried 'harder'; eventually, after doubling my loss with this approach I woke up to my madness and took the remaining money and ran! This I really would need for my new-born; the loss I just have to accept and move on. It wasn't an easy thing to do.

You can win at heads or tails. Maybe five times in a row. But can you do this 92 times in a row? No. Unless your name is Rosencrantz (or Guildenstern?) and they are dead! You will get that end game feeling at some point – it is likely to be later rather than sooner as you will keep allocating new funds to chase your losses. Once my baby was on the way, I actually tried 'harder' to win back my losses as I would need this lost money in the future. I was backed into a corner which I needed to escape from. With this renewed fighting spirit I was set up to lose in a way that I hadn't imagined possible before. You are playing against a player with all their pieces. You have a king and a pawn. And you're playing the Grim Reaper for your life back again like that knight on the beach. 'Winning back your losses' is as much of a pride thing as a financial thing. You just hate the fact that someone out there has got the better of you. But chase your losses and they'll get the better of you again. And you try to win it all back in big chunks; this mean your bets get bigger, massive even (see 'Bet bigger'). They don't even think of you. It's just how they make their money. But for you it even starts to get personal. No, you have lost, lick your wounds and move on.

RISK AND REWARD. It is human nature to take a risk to get a reward so we view the artificial construct of gambling to be no different from anything else in the millennia of human existence. Do not confuse the concept of 'life is a gamble' with the adulterated version presented to you through gambling. They are unconnected.

Returning to gambling time and time again when we have never succeeded in the past? To continue filling out that football coupon, to return not only to the same amusement arcade or casino but to the same slot machine within it. Yes, our minds have been tricked into believing what you are told in childhood, "If at first you don't succeed, try, try again." Doesn't apply to gambling although we try, try again 10,000 times. In other areas of our lives we easily stop when something clearly doesn't work. If you discover that you have a peanut allergy then you don't give it another go; no, you will be sick or maybe die. A young rabbit who tries to eat a stinging nettle gets a nasty surprise so sticks with lettuce leaves. It has learned its lesson, can recognise a stinging nettle and won't do it again. Do we just hate being taken for a ride? Do we believe that we will get the better of that dammed machine or that bookies, the 'I'll show you!' mentality. Our positive human characteristics of determination, perseverance, and endurance have been used against us. We have been skilfully manipulated. A beekeeper uses smoke to send his bees away from the hive. They have been conned into thinking that the forest, their natural home, is on fire, so fly away to protect themselves. They have a better excuse for their repeated actions than we do. Then there's that little lemming, of course. No one really knows why they seemingly commit suicide by falling off cliffs to their deaths. We commit financial suicide, a few actually suicide. That lemming must surely see that others have not survived the fall before they too plunge to their death. Is the gambler any different? He even knows that with gambling you can't win. But then there are a few who do win. Does the lemming think that he will be the one whom walks away? Some naturalists say that lemmings are just following some migratory route that they have followed for millennia but unfortunately for them, the geography has changed but they carry on regardless. We have taken risks for millennia but now the geography has changed and we carry on regardless. The gambler is the human lemming.

THE GAMBLER'S TRIPLE WHAMMY. Once you have invested a lot of time and money into something it is difficult not to stop feeding whatever it is with both of these. That is because you have invested three things: time, money and *belief*. You cannot give up on something that you believe in. The result of abandonment would be worse than not believing in anything in the first place. This belief also gives you hope; hope for something better. Give it up and all hope is gone. That's how I felt when I finally gave up. You have this massive void in your life. You are standing on one side and can't even see the other side. You don't really know where to go or what to do. But the bridge of gambling that spanned the void before was some rickety old wooden structure. It was never going to last. Just be thankful that you weren't actually standing on it when it finally gave way and you fell into that chasm. No, you need an Isambard Kingdom Brunel construction to join up the old part of your life with the new one without gambling. Get something solid in your life, find something sustainable. 'All things are possible if one believes,' Mark 9:23. Not with gambling.

THE INFORMATION ILLUSION! One of the positive effects of the internet for the bookies is regarded perversely as a positive thing for the individual. The information illusion is just that. Yes, let's use the internet to research how the Dow will perform over the next few months or the price of oil or sugar or gold. You'll end up convincing yourself of just about anything then betting based on your convictions and your research. This is the main reason why the bookies pin the *Racing Post* around the walls of their shops. It is to give the illusion that you will actually be informed about the 7.15 at Newcastle. You need something to base your convictions on or you are much, much less likely to bet. The more information they can supply, the surer you become over some selection or another, the more you will then stake. So the high-street bookie even goes to the lengths of providing you with their own in-house TV.

The internet has ratcheted up this level of illusion of control. If you are a stock market bull or a bear then you will find a website that will further convince you that you are right. You can research individual companies, next year's Derby, the future price of copper, the winner of the PDC Darts World Championship... Do all the research you like, it's just an illusion ('Imagination'. From the 80s, if you've forgotten. Sing it over in your head whenever you need reminding that what you are doing or thinking about doing is just that). The business channels also add to this information illusion. Yes, tune in for the cheap thrill you get from seeing a pearly white smile and a tantalising bit of cleavage but don't fall for the idea that you are gaining any useful information and getting ahead of the game. It's not the history channel but it comes a close second. They are never going to brand themselves the 'recent history channel' but don't forget, that's what they are.

IT BLINDED YOU TO ANY REALITY. Sometimes the information illusion was replaced by information overload; you were overwhelmed by data, 'trading tools' and charts and information. You used to think you were in control. Somewhere during the extremely frustrated stage, as the losses grew, came that information overload. Give the punter too much for them to take in. Con artists also do this. A good old-fashioned overload of the senses: 'shock and awe'. You were overwhelmed just like the slot-jockey with all those flashing lights and nudge buttons and options, the poker player with all those strategies swirling round in his head. Or the guy with his *Racing Post* trying to cross-reference races. The high-street bookies started all this with their very twentieth-century paper information illusion. It's just the law of averages that you win sometimes – it's not your skill at selection. You might as well just choose the name of a horse you like the sound of as anything else. You switch from one direction to another with this overload. You read poker websites, you buy the books, you study economic theory... but you will never find the answer because the answer is not out there. You are asking the wrong question. It is not, 'How do I win at poker or spread-betting?' and for the really delusional, 'How do I win in the casinos?' No, the question should really be, 'Can I actually win at all?'

PRIVATE AND CONFIDENTIAL. A little bit of privacy. Betting is a secretive activity. If you gamble in secret, if you do *anything* in secret, you know it can't be a wholesome activity but you still con yourself into thinking that it's not a problem, even when you do it time and time again. Take it from me, you have a problem. You might have realised this yourself by now but carry on regardless. You can sneak into the betting shop and no one from the outside can see you in there, hidden behind its floor-to-ceiling shop window display boards. For the home gambler, where do you go? The toilet was my favourite – the toilet is *every* gambler's, drug addict's, drinker's favourite. My trick for staying up a little longer than my partner, was to say that I was waiting for the dishwasher to finish its cycle so I could open it before I came to bed. This was my Sunday night routine. And Sunday night, I wanted to see how the premarket opened. No, the more accurate way to put is to say that I was usually *desperate* and often shit-scared of this opening number. You can also hang about in your car a bit longer; pull up in a lay-by maybe before you get home. The gambler will always find a way to place a bet. I have placed bets between aisles in Sainsbury's on a mobile. I am not sure which is worse: being in front of the laptop or being away from market numbers but then worrying about it nevertheless. I even thought about having a smartphone on the handlebars of my bike so I could view the numbers when I went for a long ride one day. This could have ended up with me being in the canal if a dog or child ran out in front of me!

Gambling can be such a solitary, secretive activity. Remember seeing a TV advert for a SB company: sexy girlfriend in bed asking "Where are you?" to her average-guy partner i.e. you. Partner replies that he is in Tokyo, in New York etc. i.e. he is betting on the markets there. Makes it sound cosmopolitan and sexy, like you are a sharp stock trader with your finger on the pulse. No, you are no better than the unwashed man in the high-street bookies with his old carrier bags and mangy dog, putting a few quid on the 4.15 from Wolverhampton. Now, if the guy had shouted up the stairs that he was in Wolverhampton or in Carlisle then that might not sound so sophisticated. Truth is though, most clients (i.e. gamblers) would not shout out that they were in Tokyo or in New York but more likely shout out, "I'm on the toilet" as they secretly watch the market numbers spin for them and generally against them on their smartphone or iPad. Do you really feel like you are having a party playing bingo by yourself (or with your online bingo friends)? Are you feeling like that suited-and-booted poker hustler? Are you shaken not stirred playing baccarat or roulette? No, you are sweaty with old coffee mugs and cigarette butts scattered around you. You will not be turning up at poker tournaments to stroke your coloured chips and your coloured hair. There will never be that pinhole camera revealing what cards you have. Your kids and wife are asleep and you are secretly tapping into your savings. Feeling sharp or feeling shit?

Gambling's secret nature will eat away at you; you have no one to share the joy of your wins with and no one to share your frustration when you lose – although for the latter you probably wouldn't want to. You can't reveal it to anyone, not least your partner. You have to button it and bottle it when you something goes against you. This kills you – the deceit kills you, not being able to share it kills you. But you remain on your own. The exception to this is the occasional casual, largely unintentional boast from a work colleague or friend about how they won this or that. But you don't hear about their losses. People keep quiet about these. Yes, they went to York races last year and came back with £500. But they don't tell you about the other 20 occasions when they lost a couple of hundred each time.

KEEP TRACK OF IT. You can even make yourself a spreadsheet. With spread-betting, by them daily closing and reopening your positions, you can no longer see if overall your position is running at a profit or loss. You might well have lost many thousands on it over the last week yet for that position it could easily show a positive number. Confuse and disorient, remember.

So you try to be professional about it – just like you are that professional trader or professional poker player. I could be a professional golfer. I would never win anything but I could do it as a job. I could pay all those entrance fees time and time again and never see any winners' cheques. But recording your gambling wins and losses won't help too much. As your losses mount up, the figure you record will be just the target number to win back. But as you bet more frequently, you will lose track of just how much you are losing. You will choose to spend more time gambling than to 'waste' your time actually recording what you are doing. In the end, whatever your dedication to accountancy is, won't count for anything. Your bank balance is reduced and whether you know the exact number or not, it doesn't make a lot of difference.

MARITAL STATUS. Yes, it could end in divorce or separation in the end. Whether you are married or single, you'll bet what you can with whatever form of gambling you choose. I had no one looking over my shoulder seeing what I was doing. So I managed to lose £60k. Then I got into a serious relationship, she moved in and I had to curtail my gambling. We would need the money. That would follow, right? Over the next few years I managed to lose more than double what I had done when I was single. Now I was £130k down! So it never seemed to matter what my relationship status was after all.

If you are single, then you can use up all your savings. So long as all you do is lose this, then you can hide your losses, at least in the short term. I also cancelled my health insurance and my monthly donation to Amnesty. But what the hell, it's only temporary. When I'm back in the black big time I'll treble what I used to give. And you actually believe this bullshit! You might fuck up and even have to sell your car and then your house, though. Then you have some explaining to do. I *did* sell my house and car but I was going to do this anyway as I was leaving the country so the link to my gambling was hidden. Whatever you do, just don't try to win it back. If you are in a relationship then it is to harder to cover your losses, but the gambler always finds a way. But if you try to win it back, you will make your job harder. There are a few tricks the married gambler will use: he has a credit card or two, has a separate account, doesn't tell his wife about any bonus he receives, tells his wife it's been a bad month at work, sells any investment or shares he owns...the list goes on. Easier to hide than being a drug addict or alcoholic and easier to function as a person too. Can still work although a gambler's mind is always distracted; no adverse health effects apart from the stress. The gambler can still end up re-mortgaging the house, stealing and finally committing suicide. This has all happened too often in the past. It will happen again. I would never let it go so far. So said the man five years before he hanged himself. But for me, I know I never would. Too much to live for. I actually sold the house and gambled away part of the capital though. Stupid. How the hell did that happen? These things do happen, though. You might sleepwalk into your problems. Time to wake up!

YES, YOU ARE RIGHT! You will find a website that convinces you that what you already believe in really is correct. For me, it was that the stock market will fall – the second time, that is. We all missed the first. ZeroHedge.com gives valid reasons but is preaching to the converted. I am sure I can equally find the opposite website but you will stick with the one you believe in and only make a cursory visit to opposing sites. You will also devise poker strategies that some website will agree will make you win. Or what to base your horseracing selection on. The *Racing Post* gives you all sorts of info. You might convince yourself that how far the horse travelled to get to the racecourse is key. Or any number of things. You have become information delusional.

TAKE IT TO THE MAX! At several times, I also contemplated using the maximum I could on my credit card; £6k. But it wouldn't matter as it would only be my stake money, right? I wouldn't lose it. Back in 2008, I tried to double my overdraft to £16k to keep my positions running. A wise woman at First Direct questioned all my recent payments to SB firms which I declared to her as 'investments' – yes, I knew they weren't but couldn't come up with anything else; she must have been inwardly laughing her fucking head off in the call centre somewhere in Scotland just before she refused my dumb-ass request. I was actually partially thankful at the time she had as I could feel I was losing control; little did I realise what was to come. I still can't believe I actually behaved the way I did. A gambler always thinks that they will just 'borrow' the money whether it's from an account, your house equity or stolen from someone else. Most draw the line at criminality – but not all, that's for sure. They are not the same type of person as a crackhead who will burgle and pick-pocket. But the middle-class fraudster must be reminded in their arrogance, that they are no better than the shoplifter, the ATM bank card duplicator, the counterfeit clothing peddler. You only gamble what you can afford to lose, they say (bullshit). But it's just the equity (the stake money); you're not going to lose it. You just need it to get back in the game. Then you lose it. You are now in shit. And you cover and keep hiding your losses from your wife. But unless you win it back, then one day she will find out how much you have lost and how you have deceived her; how much she loves you and how easy it is for her to leave you are now *her* thoughts. *Your* thoughts are still about how unlucky you were, if only this or that trade (bet!) had worked, if only the market had risen or fallen, if only this or that card had come up… This is all bullshit and is the fucked-up mind of a gambler… If only that goal-line clearance hadn't happened and the team you backed had won 1–0, if only '45' had popped up and completed your line in bingo, the queen had been turned over on the 'flop'; you were so close, a near-winner, just unlucky. The only thing you should say is, if only you had never started gambling and were so stupid to believe that you could actually make money.

Just remember that whatever game you are playing, it is set up to make you a 'near-winner' (i.e. a loser) to keep you going. And losing more. To make you believe that you were just 'unlucky' and that next time it will be your turn. The gambling world is full of 'if-only' men (and a few women too). Tell it to your wife, if you dare. But you're a dumb-ass if you do. Tell it to the barman if you need to tell someone. He's heard similar tales before and will feign sympathy as he pours you another drink. You are now a badge-wearing member of the Dumb Fuck Club, just like me. Accept it and move on. If you one day think you can win it back again, then dust off your DFC badge. Take a long, hard look at it. No one wants to be a gold member of the DFC!

HOPE. Hope is usually a good thing – not if you're a gambler, it ain't. The professional poker player knows the percentages, they really know how to play, they do not rely on hope and luck. They are the opposite to you whatever you may believe.

CHIP STACK. Another perceived problem for the gambler is the idea that if only they had enough financial clout, then they would succeed. Lose all your money playing poker then save for another six months and return to the table older and wiser. You have a nice stack of chips and can win back what you lost the first time. But nothing has changed. The people who win at poker are the ones who return to the table with a stack of chips funded by the money *they have won playing poker*. This is not what you are doing. Believing I could win back my money spread-betting now that I had a £100,000+ kitty was a crazy notion. But it did scare me somewhat. I wasn't exactly unaware of what had happened to my savings. Seems no different to giving any other sort of junkie a windfall; they will be straight round to their dealer as quickly as I logged onto my dealer. I also got a windfall from my dad. He once gave me £10k for no apparent reason other than he was getting old and didn't want it. I lost it within a few days. Then Christmas time I get the question, 'How did you invest that money? Did you get some more premium bonds?' Unlike the SB bookies my dad understands the word 'invest'. Of course, I lied. And I never told him that my £20k of premium bonds had also long since disappeared. You should never give or loan a gambler any money – unfortunately, most of the time, like my dad, you have no idea that's exactly what you are doing. Fortunately, my sanity chip kicked in before I squandered everything I had. For many others, the true point at which the gambler calls it a day is that final hand of cards or market numbers going against you when your funds are emptied entirely. You are broke – and sometimes in debt.

CUT TO SHREDS. Gambling is not a double-edged sword – some bets you win, some you lose. No, it is just a sword. You sit on your sofa with your smartphone in hand as the wife has gone out. You are in that gambler's bubble, just like the woman sitting in front of that B3 for five hours. You are alone, isolated. You concentrate on that poker hand, on those market numbers. Nothing else matters. You eat something from the fridge that doesn't require heating up and get back to the Dow or that deck of cards. You did this the night before too. And on the way to work this morning. And you think it's a hobby? Just a bit of a bad habit sometimes. No, secretly picking your nose is a bad habit. Secret gambling is a problem. Recognise it as such. If you don't it will get worse.

I GIVE UP! The trouble is, we give up only to give it one last go – several times. Your staying away may last a few hours, a few days or even a few months. You just want to win it all back again. You just can't resist the urge. You end up returning to the ring – but you are a featherweight up against a heavyweight. And you don't know how to box. The longer you stay in the ring, the more you will get hit – you are not suddenly going to discover ring craft. Do not think that it's just 'rope-a-dope' then you will come out fighting and win. I gave up for a few hours and days or even months but I always got back in. I usually got back in slowly and performed the same merry dance repeatedly. It was only after my bets got massive and my loss doubled from around £65k to £130k in about six months that I really did finally call it a day. Maybe it was the future birth of my boy that finally did it. I'd like to think that it was just some blinding light (non-religious) that hit me one day from somewhere that snapped me out of my madness. I hope this book will do the same thing for you.

Giving up sounds like you are not trying hard enough, even a bit lazy – but it is the harder option. Carrying on is lazy. Don't see the market numbers or that 8-1 winner you fancied before and think, 'I stayed away because of that Chris Stringman book!' and next time place that bet or else one year you will curse, 'I was going to stay out because of that Chris Stringman book. I wish I had!'

8

EXIT STRATEGIES

i. How to spot a gambler

Whatever form of gambling you go for, it is likely to be a secretive activity. After a while, it becomes so secretive you even start lying to yourself about it. You try to ignore just how much you lose and how much of your time in takes up. It is often easy to spot a drug-taker or drinker; those subtle giveaways of being wasted or pissed! With a gambler, there might be no obvious physical signs – unless you know how to spot them:

MOOD. The winning gambler will be overly and overtly happy for no apparent reason as far as you can tell, and when he's losing, he'll be the reverse: tetchy, rude and extremely pissed-off. They might claim it to have been a good or bad day at work. When this behaviour repeats, you might start suspecting something else. Women might start to think that they are dissatisfied with them and have sought the attention of another woman. But it is likely to be something much simpler.

FINANCES. Middle-class gamblers often have money to burn – or so they think. They might still have their own bank account with statements that only they can read. They might claim that they received only a small bonus that year whereas they have really siphoned it off into their gambling habit – she'll never find out. Maybe he has cashed in their savings – but I'll win it back, he thinks, and replace the money before she notices. Should be fairly easy to check the family's finances if you are that concerned. Your husband's attitude to money may change. Yes, he might always have been tight but not in all areas, although you might feel he is even tighter now. Maybe he used to change his car every few years but now, even though he shows the same interest as before, he decides to stick with the old one. He makes up some excuse but he doesn't sound convincing. He has spent the money on something or someone else. Again, the wife will probably think it's the latter as cheating on your wife is well known whereas cheating on your finances isn't. Yet, when you combine this with another suspicious activity, it can add up.

TIME. Late home from work? That's because he's been parked up in his car, playing a few hands of poker to win back what he lost in the morning, watching the Dow move this way and that; waiting for the Fed's interest rate decision so he can react to this undisturbed; always getting up first so he can secretly check how his positions have done overnight; checking his smartphone a bit too often; staying within the privacy of the bathroom far too long as he plays online poker, spread-bets, backs the horses – yes, the toilet becomes the best room in the house. But if this is you, you are no better than the alky who secretes a bottle of vodka in the cistern. How did I think up all these scenarios? I just *remembered* all these scenarios as they relate to spread-betting. Sometimes the deceit of oneself and one's partner is worse than the actual financial loss. You have jumped onto the back of a crocodile with your gambling. Yeah, you think you are Tarzan and it does excite you for a short time. But you are not Tarzan. He never existed anyway. If I was a gambling man (!), my money would be on the croc.

INTERNET/TV USAGE. He spends longer and longer online. He will come up with some excuse. He might be watching a film online – he never did this before or rarely. Yes, he might be doing this but he's flicking between this and his poker site or trading platform. You can also get both partially on the screen at the same time. I used to do this. Watch YouTube, watch the market numbers simultaneously. He'll delete his search history and recently viewed website history too. We will always cover our tracks! But this is a giveaway in itself. Been online and no history! What's he been up to? You will find him staring at his phone late on a Sunday night when the premarket opens – if something major has happened over the weekend then he will be looking tense and any distraction will annoy him. He might flick on a business channel in the morning or sneak it on during the ad break in the evening to check that little rectangle in the bottom right-hand corner which displays market numbers – although he'll come up with some bogus excuse for doing this.

Whether you are an alcoholic addicted to red wine or cider or special brew or vodka, it doesn't make a lot of difference; the result will be much the same sooner or later – it's just the severity and speed that varies. So now I have done the equivalent to 'breaking the magician's code' for the gambler – throughout the book, in fact. Sorry about that!

ii. How to stop a gambler

The outgoing commander of NATO forces in Afghanistan, John Allen, once said the military was on the verge of success and on 'the road to winning'. This is how I felt during various stages, even when I was massively down. You can perceive things however you want to perceive them. Oceania's perpetual war with whomever it was – Winston Smith hears some news bulletin about some 'decisive victory' – sounds remarkably similar. The coalition had no exit strategy when they began the campaign. Neither does the gambler when they start out. Why would they?

SUPPORT STRATEGIES. A gambler unable to bet will pretty much get the shakes like a withdrawing alcoholic. If you are a wife, just support your husband and try to divert his attention. No, it ain't easy but do whatever you can. Go on holiday to somewhere you've never been before. Gamblers like the rush that it gives them so try something new, try to overwhelm his senses to replace the buzz of the bet. Then there's sex, of course. The gambler should avoid medicating their way out of it. And watch that you don't slip into another addition – the classic move for addicts. An addict in recovery is often an addict in discovery – of something else destructive.

I don't need some quasi-religious 12-step programme of The Priory or Alcoholics Anonymous (or more pertinently Gamblers Anonymous) to sort myself out. Why do the most recognised help organisations just follow the same one-size-fits-all strategy, not a lot different than just going to church. This is distinctly off-putting to many. GA users are generally older, have long-standing gambling issues, may be addicted to something else and are generally working class. Now we have a middle-class spread-betting gambling epidemic and there is no organisation that they have an inclination to attend. Plus there's the younger generation playing poker online and all those bingo women. AA was set up when church attendance was the norm. Society has changed. Help organisations must adapt.

Luckily, in my case, I can sort *myself* out. Whilst writing this book I think I have discovered my new addiction. Writing this book! But it's better to replace a destructive addiction with something so positive it can help others. Competitive sports mostly go out the window when you get into your thirties as you just can't compete at the level you want to. That's where gambling enters as a pseudo-sport. You have the cash and you think you have the wisdom. Soon you will realise that you don't have the latter and no longer have the former either any more. Gambling gives you some sort of buzz similar to that which you used to feel playing sport. When you are young, you believe you can do anything. Whatever you want to do is possible. Once you hit 30 you realise your sporting dreams and your career dreams are no longer possible. When you get to 40 you realise that they never *were* possible. You never stood out as a sportsman and you never really improved. Class sportsmen are already competing in their teens at a level you could never ever hope to achieve. Jimmy White and Ronnie O'Sullivan were knocking in 100 breaks when their cue was taller than they were. Sergio Garcia was already playing on the European tour before he had left school. Ryan Giggs played for Manchester United when he was 17.

I did give GA a go a few times but as is my wont, only online. Chatted to fellow strugglers like me but 'Keith' bet on the horses and 'Dave' on the dogs. This is far removed from my style of gambling. Asked Dave, whom I assumed was betting on greyhounds rather than pit-bulls tearing each other to shreds in some illegal set-up somewhere, what can be worse than the £60,000 I have lost gambling? His reply: £61,000.

The greyhound punter made me laugh but I'm not sure GA online really works for me. Expensive joke though. Maybe if I had persisted I might not have more than doubled this figure. If I'd tried it again a few years later, I'd have to have asked what's worse than losing £130,000. Not sure how much comedy value I'd get out of the reply this time. Not sure how much I got out of it the first time either.

Thousands go to the cinema and watch bullshit films like *The Hangover* then go back a year later to watch *The Hangover 2* – and then *The Hangover 3*. We now believe as a society that we can do in our 30s and 40s what we used to fantasise over in our teens. We now believe anything goes. Yes, you might get away with it. But just like anyone who enjoys doing something, you'll want to do it again and again. We all have an AWOL time in our lives when we go a bit nuts; might last a few hours or a few years. You need luck on your side and a greater degree of self-control to survive today's temptations. You might get away with sleeping with girls-who-advertise for years and years you think, but there will be a consequence, even though you choose to ignore it. You might only go out once on a one-night bender but then fall into the river on the way home and be recovered by police divers from the sluice gate a few days later. Actions have consequences and they are almost always not unexpected. Now I am sounding like some temperance society against all things 'wicked'. No, life is a balancing act; without these things that could kill us, life doesn't seem worth living.

If you go nuts, then having someone around you who can save you from your excesses would be the easiest answer. But who is going to admit to sleeping with pay-as-you-go girls, drinking a bottle of Benylin every day, watching porn, voyeurism, gambling or binge eating? If you haven't got the willpower to stop it yourself then you need a plan B. Anonymous phone helplines don't do it for me; I can just easily ignore them and they ain't gonna come around. Might work for you. Would be good to tell a trustworthy work colleague or friend or uncle or someone who can really help and give you the support and check up on you. Maybe if I had talked through my gambling problem with someone I knew well from the golf club it would have helped. I suppose you could find Jesus. Works for some, I guess. Not for me though. My wife now drags me along to church with her regularly. I must be the only atheist in the congregation. At my most religious moments, I could concede that some sort of God-character could exist. I'll call myself a 50/50ist if anyone there asks. But one of the main tenets of the church is that you should get yourself into small groups as some sort of support network. Works for many who attend AA or GA, so I am in no way going to dismiss them. So in 2017, I attended. GA is for those who have given up for a day or a decade or just want to give up. For all my reservations, I found it wonderfully cathartic, only notionally religious, even entertaining and the most valuable environment for 'therapy' as they call it, is in the company of other gamblers. I implore even the most atheist to give it a go.

We all need someone to talk to, where you can meet real people in similar situations, although you need to meet someone you actually like, who is similar to you, who would be your natural friend in different circumstances, for it to work well. Many are put off by the 12-step programme with God at its core and the fact that there are too many Keiths and Daves and no one whose addiction is online and certainly no one with a spread-bet addiction. Dave had never heard of it. I felt a little uneasy having to explain it to him just in case he decided to give it a go. I could have done with a support group where we discussed and even joked about our problems; a DFC, in fact! I should have given GA a go before; a gambler is a gambler after all. Doesn't matter if you get pissed every day on Pimm's or pints, you're still an alcoholic. Actually felt that the greyhound punter was somehow inferior and an idiot for betting on dogs racing around a track. I was better than him. Now I know this is complete bullshit; we are exactly the same. 'Where are you darling?' 'I'm in Romford.'

We feel sorry for those afflicted with alcohol problems and then we go out and drink the very stuff that killed them. Too many people suffer but it's only when the famous die that we pay much attention: George Best, Alex Higgins, Jocky Wilson, Pat Eddery. Paul Gascoigne is now looking fragile. These were all once greats in their sports. Gambling doesn't kill you in itself but it can lead to other things, such as suicide. But just like alcohol it is sold as something cool, something fun – much like cigarettes were marketed too. When you're still on the 'inside' you go along with this, you even believe it.

Even if you have the help of others, you still have to walk down that bookie-littered high-street, you still will have to use that work computer, you still would like a smartphone, you still need to look online at home for car insurance. You can phone GamCare from time to time. Even though they are funded by the industry, there are some good people there. They do their best, they provide some care. But it really will come down to you alone when you're alone.

Most gamblers never admit to their partner or family that they are a gambler with a problem, due to the financial loss and the deceit. Many don't think that they have a problem – they just need to turn that corner, a bit more experience, then they will win and so on. We all know that term 'denial' – it's just that we believe it applies to someone else. Gamblers fear that if they told their wife she would go nuts: because of the financial loss and the deceit! There is a good chance she would. So he says nothing. At some point the gambler believes his deceit will be only temporary, it will 'pay off' and that he can be open about it once those regular winnings start hitting his bank account. That's what I believed. The usual way for the wife to find out is for him to be discovered. Then what to do? Like many addictions, the gambler has to *want* to quit. All the partner can do, rather than to rant and rave, is to try to bring that date forward as much as they can.

My best advice is to give him a copy of this book. When he understands more about the industry, it will kill him to remain part of it knowing that others are taking easy advantage of him. He must understand that it is as much down to the fact that he was born male as anything and only partly down to his own personality and urges, albeit still a large part. His wife cannot compare herself to him; it is just not a level playing field and unfair to do this. He needs to realise himself that he is in the DFC rather than the wife constantly reminding him. We men are too stubborn, too proud for that. Men are supposed to be the stronger sex, so it is difficult to acknowledge that our great plans were wrong from the inception; we find it hard to admit that we need help and to accept it, especially when another man has gotten the better of us, when someone else has conned us. The partner needs to try to understand the mind of a gambler, however hard that is as you regard it as just nuts (you are right!). He is likely to be stuck in the belief that he will win it all back, that he's in control. It hurts our egos to admit defeat. Try not to whinge at him – we gamblers do not appreciate such unspecific and unhelpful complaints. Encourage him to follow the suggestions in this book. When he understands more about himself and the industry that preys upon him, that mocks him, that scams him then even though he will always be a gambler he might never gamble again.

CARELESS MEMORIES: There are some good organisations out there who do what they can. GordonMoody.org.uk offer a residential programme for those with severe problems. Again, they are funded by the very industry that they are trying to rescue sufferers from but you can't hold that against them. If Marks & Spencer or someone came forward to stump up the cash, then I am sure they would only be too willing to accept an alternative form of funding. But this never happens. Big business prefers to build temples to themselves, such as art gallery wings or football stadia, or fund something the public view favourably. There's also Gam-anon, for those affected by others gambling (gamanon.co.uk) and cnwl.nhs.uk/cnwl-national-problem-gambling-clinic/about-us/, as the name suggests.

REDUCTION STRATEGIES. Do I still hanker after a bet? I need to gamble a little, like a recovering junkie needs methadone – but the urge is waning. Now into my fifth year, it's almost gone. Trouble with class 'A' replacement on-prescription medication is that it becomes a legal and prescribed addition to what you are already taking illegally, even if you reduce. Best thing is self-control and, better still, abstinence and to stick to the plan – not easy for many but it's what GA recommend for a reason. I now only indulge in methadone gambling on the rarest of occasions and am abstinent online – a few quid on a horse when I am back in England only; like the ex-heroin addict having the occasional cigarette. A few £1 coins on a race is a world away from my previous pattern of entering three security digits to release a four-figure number to the SB bookie. I only place small bets in high-street bookies now. It's the safer way (to lose). Of course, I miss the rush of high-stakes gambling but I don't miss the desperation, the guilt, the remorse and the rest of it that results from the inevitable loss. I used to get up in the morning and think of it, just like any addict but after about six months this desire was sufficiently weak. I try to fill my life with other things, preferably something difficult or risky, that's what makes my life worth living. Now, after four years, I am almost completely off and don't 'need' to visit the bookie; once a year almost for its novelty value coupled with a bit of nostalgia, but mostly it gives me a deep satisfaction that when I walk out I know I won't be back for another year. I have no real interest. In fact, I find the whole idea of gambling ridiculous and laugh inwardly at myself and others as we stand there. Mine is a niche approach and can never work for the truly addicted but it's only honest to tell you what I do. This transformation can only be down to me writing this book and exploring everything there is to know about gambling. I hope it has the same effect on the reader.

From five peseta pieces to bank card transfers of £10k. It's an all-too-easy a journey to travel. Wherever you are on this trip, please get off. The internet did for me. I was happy enough betting tiny amounts on Saturday football in my local bookies. I also signed up to a dozen bookies, they sent me a 'membership' package and card and I phoned in my bets, taking advantage of the 'free' bet – actually a matched bet – that they all offered before moving onto the next one. Managed to break even this way but once the list of bookies was exhausted I knew any continuation would put me in the red, so I basically stopped. Strange that this obvious fact didn't dawn on me until five years down the line with spread-betting. This telephone service is not that efficient for the bookies. They need to employ customer service people at the other end who often have to deal with naturally dissatisfied and sometimes abusive customers. The customer has to enquire about odds on this and that and may well ring around half a dozen. This takes time, delays the bet and leads to fewer bets being made via the internet. Also, you actually have to say aloud the amount that you want to stake. Five pounds is easy to say. Five hundred pounds isn't. Then the internet came along. Or more precisely, high-speed internet came along to replace dial-up and I had 24/7 instant internet access for a flat monthly fee, so I no longer had to worry about how long I stayed online for. Now the customer can clearly see the odds across different bookies and can easily place the bet that took them ages before, so they'll now place far more bets – then bet on other events that catch their eye on the website. And typing in £5 then adding a zero or two becomes oh so easy. You can stay online all day if you want – which I did. I even left it on at night so I could quickly check it then too. Then to make it even more convenient for me to give away my money, wireless was invented so I could now bet whilst sitting on the toilet. Technology has revolutionised gambling. Since about 2006–07 the size of the industry and the revenues and profits have rocketed due to high-speed and Wi-Fi and smartphones. A gambler can't do anything online without flicking onto their favourite poker site or SB site. Trouble is, they will stay longer on it than on the website they had all those good intentions about looking at. Whatever else you should be doing is easily postponed with just a few clicks. It's just too tempting. Especially at work where what you should be doing could well be very boring. Giving a gambler internet access and not expecting them to log on to a gambling site is like giving an alcoholic a tenner and sending them to Tesco's for a pint of milk, and not expecting them to get a few super-strength cans for the walk back. It's difficult for the best of us to use any computer without flicking onto our email or Facebook or whatever. Cancel your internet subscription (this is unrealistic), go work in a café or a park where there is no internet or just be stronger willed to fight the temptation. When it comes down to it, we must all go for option 3 in the end, as internet access is not hard to find when we want it. I took an extreme measure of moving abroad but the internet was still available, of course, so it made no difference. I even contemplated moving to somewhere like Saudi Arabia where many websites are blocked – but a proxy server would circumvent it. But I had no interest in working there anyway. But living abroad does give me a challenge so it does help; it takes my mind away from gambling. The high-street bookies here obviously have none of the familiarity, nostalgia and comfort of those back home and look rather too grimy for my liking so bookie betting is clearly off the agenda. To really avoid the internet, you'd have to get a job on a North Sea fishing trawler as Apple haven't invented the 'Sat iPhone' yet -and when they do they can market it to the maritime industry as the iiPhone!

If you are trying to give up gambling and take all the precautions I suggest, yet you have to work where you must use an internet connected computer, then you have temptation staring you in the face every day. This is difficult. As gambling is embarrassing, then turn that computer screen around for all to see – this way you are less likely to log on. Never sit near one during your lunch break. Turn it off completely when you can so you are not tempted to just 'check' something! Leave the office at lunchtime and leave your smartphone somewhere else too. If you are really strong, confide in someone who can monitor you. If they ever catch you then you owe them a tenner! If you incentivise them they will check up on you a lot – as you know this then you are even less likely to bet. If it's possible technically, get betting sites blocked – for you and all employees. This way you'll be helping others too. If you feel like clicking on the wrong site then just get up, leave the office, go and talk to someone about anything else then come back later. This might distract you enough. Get enthused with your work so that the hours go faster – if not then change jobs. Company bosses would be wise to put something in place to stop their employees spending too long on the internet or some (many?) will take the piss. I should have just stuck to gambling using a half-size pen although that's hardly a heathy option. Abstinence is really the only way to go whatever your addiction. Just don't have that first bet – this opens the floodgates. But if you give up narcotics, it's no good saying you are clean when you have just switched to alcohol. Swapping NA meetings for AA meetings is not really progress. I will remain off-line. Base-jumpers never retire. Neither do many gamblers. They carry on regardless until they have smashed themselves to bits. One or two take an overdose, others just destroy their finances and their marriages. Many just stop their own career in its tracks. I was never going to throw myself into Avon Gorge and I never had any marriage or career to ruin. Just my bank balance. I can hobble away and rebuild. But I need to get my kicks elsewhere. Base-jumping? I'm afraid of heights. Alcohol or drugs? Abusing my body, even though it might well feel great at the beginning, is just not my thing. I see the stupidity in it just like millions see the stupidity in gambling – even many gamblers.

No one really knows the true level of gambling addiction in this country. There are figures out there but I don't even think they are worth quoting. Online has taken off in the last decade and research hasn't even really seriously attempted to compute its effect on the nation. You can only really guess at the size of the problem from the other end: the size of the industry, the number of providers and their revenues and profits. Ask people how much and how often they gamble and you will get a distorted picture. Another statistic is the suicide rate. This would have to be investigated as it could be for a whole host of reasons. But gambling has always been one of them and it seems likely to be more so in the future.

My father used to smoke then just gave up overnight. For some, it's easier to stop than for others. I think I will be one of the fortunate ones. I can suppress it – I just get on with something else. This must be partly down to my genes. Alcoholism seems to be inherited to some degree. Most things are. You are like your parents in so many ways, even though you prefer to think otherwise. Gambling wasn't really around when my father was in his 20s. Nowadays, men in their 20s with money to burn, do exactly that. They might as well light their cig with a £20 note as type in some dumb-ass bet on their phone as they sit on their sofa, scratching their ass with their other hand. Understand yourself and try to understand how others will try to manipulate you just like an abusive partner controls the other.

If anyone learns from my story I would even feel that I have had some wonderful careers by proxy; I will become that doctor or architect or research scientist. How? Because I have helped to give their lives back to them. I'd be happy to give people's lives back whatever they do. If Einstein had been around today, maybe with his mathematical genius he would have spent much of his time playing online poker rather than on quantum physics.

I needed 'gambling' every day from the second I woke up. Even got up in the night on far too many occasions for a quick fix. I even set my alarm once for the middle of the night so I could monitor my rolled-over positions when chairman of the Federal Reserve, Ben Bernanke, was giving a speech. I had to check my positions almost the second I woke up in the morning. When I was single, I would sleep with the mobile or laptop next to the bed, just like the alky has his can of special brew to hand so his mouth can open a few seconds after his eyes. If you are still tempted to use your app or keep reinstalling it after it's deleted, then leave your smartphone at home. But people need to call me, you say. Buy a flip phone with no internet access. And whatever you do, do not enter the phone number for customer services on it.

Regulation? Self-regulation? The former should be tighter by the government but as this isn't really going to happen then self-regulation by *your*self. No, not self-regulation by the industry – this already happens to some extent and what a surprise, the results ain't great. Like letting Dracula regulate the National Blood Transfusion Service. Government should be there to protect us from our own stupidity. Hats off to the FCA in 2016 though (see 'Regulation')! We have freedom to choose but many choose destructive lifestyles, some without even knowing it.

The voices encouraging us to choose this lifestyle drown out those advising us not to.

Having no internet access may be the only way of stopping some people gambling, although it would be difficult to police it. You can ask bookies to bar you – a self-exclusion form; works like a self-imposed ASBO but only for each individual shop where you fill out the form. But *you* must ask *them*! They're not going to offer it to you. This is an inefficient method. The bookies like it this way! Very easy to circumvent. They're not likely to have a wall of mugshots of those self-barred customers behind the counter so you could easily return to one where you filled out that form but you don't recognise the cashier and they won't recognise you. Or you just go to the next town. Or online. You can self-exclude here too but as there are almost unlimited number of providers, you will always find somewhere. In my opinion, bookies are paying lip-service to any sort of system that encourages responsible gambling. Let's face it, they benefit from irresponsible gambling. All gambling is irresponsible if you look at it rationally.

Can I ever stop being a gambler? Short answer is no. I will always be a recovering gambler just like an alcoholic will always look down the drinks aisle in Sainsbury's longingly. If you really want to enter the bookies, if you really *need* to then here are some survival tips:

1) Do not study form in the newspaper or online in the morning. This will usually mean that you go to the bookies earlier and spend longer there. You will bet on races that you never even looked at before that morning in your paper. And don't read form when at work. If you are bored at work

find something else to read. Only read form whilst in the bookies, as this will take up your time and you will place fewer bets. Reading forms does not help in any way in selecting the winner, even though you are convinced otherwise and everyone and every bookie will confirm this bullshit belief.

2) Visit the bookies as late in the day as possible, so there are only a few races left. If you delay your visits until later and later then one day, with a bit of luck, you will find that you don't end up going at all, then you start to get into a routine of not going and find something more interesting to do instead. Nowadays though, bookies open until 10 p.m. so this is much harder to do but try to avoid the 'meat' of the day.

3) Give yourself a set amount to bet with. The only way you will stick to this is to leave your wallet at home. Do not go there with your cashpoint card. Walk to the bookies with a tenner, split it between a few races then go home.

4) Never bet on any machine. If you are fascinated by the 'crack cocaine' machine, then feel free to surreptitiously watch others play and lose on them. And don't bother with CGI horse-racing. If I bet, then I place a few pounds on one or two horses then leave. This is the true methadone approach, rather than continuing with the 'H' and using the methadone to make up the difference. Don't reduce your online gambling then just increase it in the high-street to compensate or vice-versa.

5) Phone up those online sites you are using and self-exclude – it can help, at least as these were your preferred providers, where you felt 'comfortable'. Cancel all your credit cards too.

6) If you are confident to tell the wife then get your wages paid into her account. After she has calmed down she will be more helpful that you think – after all, she married you and promised 'in sickness and in health', and you are afflicted with some sort of psychological condition if you're at this point. Best not bring up the 'for richer, for poorer' too soon as she'll blame you!

7) Agree with the bank *not* to give you an overdraft facility.

8) Do not sign up for new online accounts: those incentives that the bookies give you are not free amounts of cash. They are the hook to draw you in. They offer you them as they work. In total, I took more than a £1000 in free credit. I lost £130,000. Hardly free money then. Only for them.

Fear of failure stops you from trying. But if you don't make any attempt then you have definitely failed. You could try some of these reduction strategies but there are major drawbacks: cutting down means that you may be doing this for a lifetime! To avoid blow-outs and increasing the frequency of betting requires more discipline that stopping entirely. So just make the decision to escape from the self-delusional financial and emotional pain that you suffer week-in week-out. Commit to quitting. Apart from heroin withdrawal, giving up any addiction is not as hard as you think. You only believe it is from a lifetime of being fed misinformation, often by those with vested interests. After you have read my book (read it *all*!) and understand how you have been brainwashed by the media, popular culture, marketing and advertising – and by yourself ever since childhood – how could you ever gamble again? After being conned, would you knowingly and willingly let yourself become a victim once more? Why bother with this half-way house of reduction? Just quit entirely.

But gambling is now in the past. Now I go away to a hotel, get up for breakfast and have no interest in checking the markets. If I pop up to the room during the day, I do not flick on CNBC or the laptop to check the markets like I used to. Now I sit and write whilst glancing up at the sea; I feel like Agatha Christie although the only mystery in my writing is why I believed gambling was the answer. Take some quiet time somewhere to reflect, don't dwell on negative emotions but just laugh at your own naivety and get on with your new life.

If you have a desire to get online at any conceivable time, then you have a problem, that's for sure. We tend to avoid the word 'addict' because of its drug and alcohol connotations and 'problem gambler' sounds more acceptable these days and better than compulsive gambler too. Who wants to tell someone else they've got an addiction? Although most don't admit they have a problem either! 'Compulsive' gambler makes it sound like they have something continuous, like Tourette's; it's usually not that every waking hour thing like this – although it can be. I finally managed to stop due to a combination of impending fatherhood, simply being busy and coming to my senses regarding spread-betting and realising it was not trading at all. I had really believed the 'spin'; their deception had suckered me in. There are many tens of thousands out there who are not really even gamblers – but they spread-bet thinking it's something else. It is pure and simple gambling. And it really is simple even though they sell it as sophisticated; you are betting higher/lower in the same way as I did in that amusement arcade when I was 14. If you are spread-betting, then realise that it can lose you money like you'd never believe possible. Take my suggestions on how to quit gambling but quit spread-betting straightaway! Do not try to win back your losses. These will grow exponentially. Bets will grow in size and so will the losses, like bacteria.

I still have my relationship and money left and no debt or criminal record. I guess I'm one of the lucky ones. The luckiest are those who never start down this road. I only told her recently, years after I gave up. I didn't have the strength to tell my partner before but conversely had the mental strength to quit by myself. This is a risky strategy but it works for some. I can't keep a secret from everyone else now that it's available in paperback! But owning up to your past – or your present – will be a release, whatever the short-term consequences.

I know I am an addict to some extent. I know this because I realise that the best thing about being an addict is the addiction; of course, I want to repeat something over and over again, I want something to dominate and take over my life because I enjoy it. It gives me an almost sexual rush. No addict really wants to stop. Why would you want to give up taking ecstasy at weekends? The 'E' poppers can always cling to the belief that if you survive your first tab then there will be no long-term effects; they can ignore the fact that they are the guinea pigs to their chosen chemical compound. I more or less ignored my dwindling bank account balance. A gambling junkie sees what they want to see and just carries on regardless. Even the lows give you an intensity. And the highs are just great! But one day for most junkies like me, there comes a day of reckoning. For H junkies that could be prison – although it is often only the cessation of being that means the cessation of addiction. For the gambler, running out of money is the most obvious, but some don't let this stand in their way; they always have stealing to fall back on or maxing out credits cards (and combining the two). The wife finding out is another. But even if she does, it might well not stop you. You need to *want* to stop. At some point in your life, you will hopefully reach that point. Took me many years though and several almost apocalyptic days. I guess I just felt any more losses and my child's future would be in jeopardy. Stop now and you might be able to absorb your losses. Any more and you'll have lot of explaining to do.

If you've already gone beyond this point, then you must tell someone. You cannot stop yourself. There is NEVER a point of no return. Don't struggle on regardless. The true gambling junkie will beg, borrow and steal ad infinitum – this is the warning for you if you haven't reached this final stage. If you have then seek help; visit the GP. Thankfully, my brain chemistry isn't this way. I have stopped and I will stay stopped. The wise junkie will know they can't carry on with what they are doing even though they'd love to. They just have to control themselves. Drug junkies need to change their environment and their circle of friends. As gambling is usually a lone occupation and is now often done online alone, it will take a different approach. You should delete all those gambling site apps for a start but you can't just stop using the internet or your smartphone. Keeping yourself busy helps. Occupy your mind with other things.

"I'm not a quitter, I'm not a quitter," as John says on

Louis Theroux's *Gambling in Las Vegas* before he goes on to lose even more. Fight or flight? The law of survival. Don't believe you have failed when you give up because you never could have won; stopping and staying stopped is a victory in itself. Giving up has negative connotations and human nature means that we want to persevere. But this is not universally applicable. Your DNA tricks you into sticking at things which you really shouldn't bother with. You should know when to quit with many things: gambling, relationships, jobs. If you can't fight something and have no chance of winning, then run a fucking mile! John misses the point. It takes a strong man, not a weak one, to give up. Sometimes being a quitter is the best thing in the world. It can save your life, save you a lot of pain and save you a lot of time and money. Do not chase unobtainable dreams. Do not throw good money after bad. You will find it refreshing when you quit and find something more meaningful in your life. Yes, it might leave a hole and you feel that all hope is gone. Just readjust and refocus. You will never, ever be that millionaire gambler.

We all like a challenge. Gambling presents itself as a challenge but it is not. It is a death wish for your bank account. Try thinking of something else to do in life that you might actually achieve some success in. Gambling is for those with no imagination, no stamina, no guts, no sense of adventure. Gamblers believe it is exactly for these factors that they become involved.

Never realised there were so many episodes of *Magnum*. The quality of the show goes rapidly downhill once the opening sequence has finished, just like with *Miami Vice*. It's a meaningless activity watching *Magnum*, but so is online gambling. But apart from the nostalgia you get, it also has some distinct advantages over gambling: I can admit to watching it more easily than admit to watching market numbers whilst my bank balance moves the wrong way. If I have to watch all 162 episodes, then that's what I'll do.

No one will help you when you are engaged in the act of gambling. You stay in your gambler's cocoon; you are not even forced to leave it when you need the toilet when you gamble wirelessly. If I stayed online all day spread-betting, there would be no pop-up reminding me how long I had been gambling and how much I was losing. But I always thought I was trading, not gambling. I was doing exactly what those City boys do. Even though I could easily log on at 6 a.m. and log off at midnight when I went to bed, no one questioned this, no system flagged this. I will say it again to all those delusional 'traders': you are GAMBLING. You are sitting in front of the laptop in exactly the same way as those women sit in front of the B3 in the foyer of the bingo hall. If you have accidentally deluded yourself that you are not really a gambler, you don't really have the urge to go to the bookies, then wake up to the fact that this is exactly what you are. Quit now whilst you are... well, behind (or well behind).

Actually had a relaxing week or so after going through gamblers' cold turkey (when you become a vegetarian do you experience cold turkey?). My body actually felt looser (rather than loser). The real cold turkey actually kicks in a few weeks later. But for this briefest of honeymoon periods you think you are fine. Have lost a small fortune but after six months I was strangely relaxed about it; for the first time in years I actually didn't want to spread-bet. When you quit, especially with spread-betting, you believe that you have missed some golden opportunities to make easy money. But the biggest problem is now that void in your life; what do you do now to fill that time? This freed-up time should be a good thing but in those early days, it isn't. That's because you long to fill it with the old you. You have also given up what you believed was the last chance you had for change, for a new life; all hope is now gone, replaced by emptiness or even despair. Gambling gave us hope. That's why it is so hard to stop. Who wants to give up hope? We know this, perhaps only subconsciously, so we stick with gambling; it's the security we need. We must think and try a bit harder to put our energy and hope into something meaningful and attainable if we want to achieve, to be satisfied with our lives, to be at peace with ourselves.

Close all those accounts to put some distance between you and your chasers. Assign those marketing emails to spam. Change your email address if you can. You need to avoid any temptation. If you get through a week or a month without gambling, then buy yourself or your family something with your 'winnings'. Try to laugh at your own idiocy rather than feel guilt, remorse, embarrassment or shame; might take a while but you'll get there. And if you are confident enough then try to dissuade others from joining you in the membership of the DFC.

Maybe you play poker just to beat your fellow man face-to-face across the table. This is acceptable with friends for low stakes (the true addict should NEVER even do this!). But online? It will likely get out of control. There will be professionals taking easy pickings. If you want to pit your wits against another man – because you are a man and as such that's what you need to do to satisfy your manliness within – then think about taking up something else. If you can't hack physical sports anymore then take up darts or snooker – gambling is not the experience you are looking for to replace competitive sport and that feeling you used to get when you won at something, when you beat another man. The gambling industry know your desires, they know you are a *man* – but don't try to compete against them. It is just not a fair contest. You may think you are strong, quick-witted, intelligent, resourceful. These characteristics help you in life. But here they give you a false sense of invincibility. They prey upon your desires – they know you want to beat them. They know you want to puff your chest out after your successes. They know your male DNA is programmed to compete against other men. But you are not competing man against man. You are subconsciously tricking yourself into believing this. This is not a game of football, a game of squash, a wrestle with some kid at school. You are like a man in a rowing boat up against an aircraft carrier. Why not try something non-competitive but still a challenge, like scuba diving. If sports are not your thing, then do something for charity. Get involved in local politics – there's always a good fight to be had there. Think about what you enjoyed all those years ago. Art, photography? Remember, gambling is the lazy person's pastime, the pastime of the unimaginative. Is this really you?

How do I now get my kicks? '*Get your kicks on Route 66*'. Wonder what that involved? If you sang about a modern-day Route 66 it would have to have small-time brothels just off the main highway as it would pubs offering poker nights and the occasional lap-dancing bar. You'd also be able to pull in pretty much wherever you wanted to meet the local drug dealer. But I need something else. Bizarrely, I get a little buzz from bidding on eBay, even when it's only for £10. That 'You won!' message from eBay gets you excited; a great little marketing trick and one of the reason for their success. It turns us all into winners at some point and for some, this will be the *only* thing in their lives where they win. eBay is only another form of shopping and there are a fair few desperate shopaholics out there. Can't see me becoming one. It hardly replaces the buzz you get from sport or gambling. But it's competitive shopping so I'll take what I can get.

I didn't have to make a New Year's resolution; I gave up in November – 10:50 a.m., 29th November, 2012 for the record). I never had to go into rehab; DIY rehab worked for me. For some, going to somewhere like The Priory gives them that little extra they need to get on the road to recovery. Others end up as serial rehabbers. Sad to say but some don't survive. Most can't afford it anyway. Most muddle through life, ignoring the real fact that they have a gambling problem. They've seen the ads, their mates do it, it's legal so there's nothing wrong with it at all then. Much like alcohol, in fact. Rehab is mostly concerned with substance abuse of some kind. These are more life-threatening than gambling, on the face of it. But you don't have to attend Alcoholics Anonymous groups to have a problem with alcohol. People who drink regularly, who binge drink do not call themselves alcoholics. They do not need a tinny when they wake up and can do without alcohol for days even. Most are not alcoholics; they just drink an unhealthy amount. People gamble unhealthy amounts too.

What do you call compulsive gamblers when they stop gambling? Usually the word would be 'skint', but what if they choose to stop? Always been, 'In the hole,' so maybe I'm now, 'Out of the hole'? Or just, 'Back in pocket'? Yes, you are 'in recovery' and 'born again' without having to be dunked in the lake. You will be bet free. You are now set free.

9

REGULATION

If anyone wants to sell us something we all know there is something in it for them. With gambling, we seem to believe there is something wonderful in it for us – because of our own stupidity and because that's what they tell us! Regulation and law making take a long time. So does educating individuals and the nation. The bookies have almost infinite resources to educate people in the wrong direction, and, many would argue, to slow down regulation through whatever means they can get away with. Any decent regulation might well take the 18 years of my new baby's childhood to get something decent in place. I think this is on the optimistic side. History tell us this. Just look at car seatbelts – something that is patently obvious and necessary and not some dumb-ass lifestyle choice like smoking, drinking or gambling, each of which supports a multibillion pound industry. That took decades to enact. As I said, the genie is already out of the bottle. And this genie is a fucking evil one.

If you legalise an addiction, then the morality issue that stops many is removed and the floodgates are open, as is the case with cigarettes and alcohol and gambling – people think it is just the normal thing to do, like having breakfast or having sex. Now with the internet, porn has become mainstream. Fifty years ago, it was the preserve of sad men in 'flasher macs'. Gambling is not what it once was; the preserve of working-class men filling out little carbon-backed slips of paper with tiny pens in smoke-filled betting shops with windows that essentially let in no light and allow in no prying eyes to the secluded world of the gambler and his circled selections in today's *Daily Mirror*. Not anymore.

Recommendations:

MULTIPLE ACCOUNTS. All gamblers will have multiple accounts. This should be banned; no gambler should have more than one account at any given time in any given sector of gambling AND there should be a cooling off period of one month until an alternative account is opened. This will result in some hanging onto their original account longer than they wish, but if they are somehow dissatisfied with it, they will use it less. Delay and restrict and the gambler may reflect and reject. Gamblers do not realise the futility of 'switching' anyway. They will still be allowed to have accounts in multiple sectors but as us gamblers 'specialise' they are unlikely to move from spread-betting to bingo. The multiple account ban cannot be applied to traditional high-street bookies websites as here the punter likes to shop around for the best odds. An alternative restriction for this sector needs to be applied. Any spread-betting and bingo they offer on these sites must be separated otherwise they will just exploit this loophole.

GAMCARE. GamCare give their stamp of approval to bookies' websites – you can see it at the bottom if you scroll down: 'GamCare Certified'. Like a chartered accountant or a certified healthcare specialist. Makes it sound reassuring, trustworthy, like they've had to undertake rigorous tests. The gambler then subconsciously believes, 'Hey, what I'm doing must be alright then.' It legitimises it and reassures you that what you are doing is acceptable, it's fine. It's certified as safe and healthy then much like the Soil Association give out certification for organic food. GambleAware/GamCare are funded by the gambling industry. How can they be truly independent? The industry paid for that rubber stamp.

The industry always cites GamCare as a positive initiative by them. Like the drug cartel who pay for the building of a new school. GamCare costs the industry a few million each year. Ladbrokes' revenue for 2015 alone was £1,199.5 MILLION! (That's over a billion, in fact!) They employ over 14,000 people. The government are happy to receive corporate and personal income tax revenue and to support an employer of so many. They too would cite GamCare, as would the Gambling Commission, which is there largely to just implement the law and to make sure pub landlords, bookies and the like are aware of it. It presents the industry as being responsible and as far as possible, respectable. They want to present gambling as a normal activity, much like the alcohol industry have successfully achieved. There is an advert for Bacardi where the scantily-clad bar girl stands on the bar counter, spraying the crowd with two bottles of the stuff before the last shot of the product and the line, 'Always drink responsibly'! They are required to say this. Would they prefer if you didn't? The bar girl didn't seem too bothered. Would the gambling companies prefer if you didn't gamble responsibly?

GamCare reform: impose a half of one percent levy on gambling companies' profits then use this to fund decent gambler education that visits schools and universities, for instance. GamCare's primary focus is on the extreme end of problem gambling although it is questionable what they even achieve within this narrow band. GamCare is a smokescreen that allows the bookies to carry on making money out of the 99.99%+ of us whom they ignore as having any problems. The industry fund GamCare. Who sets the agenda? When I was at school, we watched an 'alcohol education' video, funded by the industry. It actually informed us about some of the benefits of alcohol but even as naïve teenagers some of us laughed at this. I would be fearful of an industry-funded gambling education programme for schools from an industry that describes itself as entertainment.

GamCare is far from proactive. The gambler has to essentially find *them* or the more likely scenario that the girlfriends, wives and mothers of gamblers find GamCare first.

Needs a name change, a funding change, and it must broaden its reach and scope. It must be separated from its possibly abusive and controlling parent. Education, prevention and not just the 'care' of the truly addicted.

RESEARCH. If you look closely at the bookies' websites and scroll right down to the bottom you will find the Gambling Commission logo and the equivalent for Gibraltar where many of them are based. You will also find organisations such as GamCare. You will have to look hard as these are all written in grey on a black background underneath the forms of payment accepted which are all written in full colour on a white background! This is Ladbrokes' site but most perform similar tricks. You can also read research carried out by GamCare if you click on their camouflaged logo.

The latest report, January 2017, analyses the effect of the £50 limit, with its 'nudge' policy, for the FOBTs.

This is unrelated to the nudge policy employed by fruit machine players but refers to the fact that users must request at the bookies' counter to be allowed to go above this £50 limit. The 'nudge' here is that gentle 'Are you sure?' reminder. A very 'thorough' report basically says that the £50 approach is ineffective. Point 16 of the summary states that it doesn't reduce harm or make play more responsible. Did we need to wait months to discover this? No, but the industry did...

There have been various research projects on the FOBTs. There could hardly not be! So GamCare consult with some of the major players in the industry (Ladbrokes, Paddy Power etc.) and the machine manufacturers for their October, 2016 report. Their 'Player Awareness System' (PAS; a tech illusion?) is a 'work in progress'! The data itself is collected by the betting shops themselves. The system is overseen by the Responsible Gambling Trust (now operating as GamCare), funded by the industry (as is the rebranded 'BeGambleAware'). Of course, they are not going to attack these machines – no, that's what some of the customers do! So, consult with the industry and the manufacturers! From the report it seems to me the bookies are rather disinterested in cooperating fully. Research needs to be carried out under the auspices of the regulator. When someone with power enters the room, people sit up. Under the RGT/GamCare, the reverse seems to happen. The researchers should take on a more Nuclear Weapons Inspectorate approach and not just repeat in their reports what the industry supply them; this can only be achieved if the whole process and system is fully independent. It isn't.

These research projects are often focussed on problem gambling as I can see, for the following reasons: 1) to prove they are doing something 2) when things go wrong, such as ending up in court for fraud, it is the problem gambler; this puts the industry in a bad light in the eyes of the public, the regulator and the government. If they can quash this problem, then they are free to get on with their business of extracting millions out of the 99.99% of us. 3) It is a delaying tactic. When reports take months, are inconclusive and state that further research needs to be undertaken it begins to take on the appearance of an episode of *Yes, Minister*. How many more are we going to have? The bookies suggest some initiative to show that they are doing something. It proves ineffective. We move on to the next one. No! The regulator should step in and suggest something with teeth! A watchdog should bark AND bite! I have put forward a few suggestions. Here's another. FOBTs should be switched off every morning and all day Sunday. Also applies to those bingo hall B3s. Yes, it may shift the problem to another time of day but it could make a difference.

THE RESEARCH TEAM: Who do you award research contracts to? Researchers who viewed you favourably in the past or those whom didn't?

GAMCARE: they set the researchers the task; this is often focussed on problem gamblers. Compare this to smoking (might even have happened 50 years ago): the tobacco industry focussing all their attention on those whom smoke a 100 a day and underage smokers (surprise, surpise! Gamcare also commissioned a report on underage gambling). With these reports it is always the problem gambler and not the problem product!

What data do the industry release to researchers? I am sure they are none too keen to release the most revealing.

The research is highly technical; like they are 'blinding us with science'. As well as being difficult to read they are also just dull! Is this intentional?

Who actually picks up on any of these reports? The media whom are partially indirectly funded by the gambling industry? I am disappointed that the BBC don't; it is as if the media only report on topics that other media outlets report on. Your local MP, perhaps? Write to yours!

GambleAware does not speak up for the gambler; they are not like a trade union. Research, to some extent, is pointless. But not for them.

We all know GambleAware/GamCare as it's on the bookies websites and in the shops. You have been brainwashed into believing that they are truly on your side. Here are two organisations that you have probably never heard of who are: Gamblingwatchuk.org and fairergambling.org. Organisations like these should be supported by government if they are really interested in protecting us. We may be in for a long wait.

LIMIT SETTING ON LOSSES LINKED TO DECLARED INCOME. How can any responsible gambling site not question where a guy, who only made £16k a year, who was placing massive bets and losing shedloads, was getting the money from? He surely had to declare his income and assets on any application; the gambling sites want to know how they can get their money when you fuck up. I am sure, like with me, no one emailed or phoned him about his massive bets. There is no IT system in place to flag up problem gamblers like this. Why would the bookie do this unless they are compelled to do so? They set up their system to maximise profit. End of story. It is usually working-class losers who make the headlines and make the courts.

This is simply down to their inability to pay. The middle classes hide their losses by actually paying them off so we don't discover the true scale of the problem as it is hidden. Neither the providers nor the losers are likely to own up, are they? But I have. Someone has too! They can stick the GambleAware logo somewhere semi-hidden on their website to satisfy the regulator and give the veneer of being a responsible company. They clearly are not. They are only responsible to their shareholders and employees.

Limit losses to a quarter of declared certifiable income in any given year. This would automatically limit someone's losses, keep people out of jail and keep them in the real world rather than some zombie-like state where they dream of winning back the money they have lost and *more* so that they can *still* buy that BMW. This mindset will result in bigger bets. I remember once looking at a Porsche website and I was *down* at this point! And down a fucking lot! Could have bought a big Porsche with the money I had lost. And one for my partner. I expect this is exactly what some employees at the SB bookies have done with *my* money! So, set a total loss limit linked to income. This will apply to any gambling site, whatever it is and the record of loss will transfer when the gambler 'switches'.

Bet-size limit linked to declared income (linked to the above). I shouldn't have been allowed to hold such big positions with such low relative equity or stated income. £500 a point on the FTSE!

I feel for that teacher over in Tipperary, Ireland who checked his computer, in class, like I used to do, after receiving a warning text message – he discovered that he was liable for a loss of almost £280,000! He only earned €25,000 a year. Having that dazed 'I Wanna Be Your Dog' moment in class ain't good. He was not the only one to sustain massive losses when the Swiss National bank did its thing on the 15th January, 2015. Don't think that 'stop-loss' would have saved you. They are not obliged to trigger it in a rapidly moving market – just read those caveats that *you* signed up to. So manually close it then when you can see it moving? Again, you will be prevented from doing this, as many found out. Those caveats again! IG, amongst others was keen to get back from its clients all that it could! It was probably a good thing that that teacher *didn't* own a house!

ADVERTISING. I would not want my child seeing 'Carling' on a football shirt as used to be the case, nor do I want them seeing 'FxPro' either. The actual warning on these SB ads should be spoken and not hidden in faint onscreen text, or they should use much larger warning notices similar to that on cigarette packets. It should also remain on the TV long enough for you to actually read it. There should be a warning notice on ANY bookies' ad, not just the SB firms. A ban on people appearing in the ads as with cigarettes too.

Lotto and scratch cards. Minimum age raised to 18. It's ridiculous how you can buy these on the way home from taking your GCSEs!

It should not be permissible to market a product as giving you, for instance, a one in four chance of winning if one of these winning categories is in fact, the cost of the ticket! If you 'win' £5 from your £5 Monopoly Millionaire scratch card, many will just buy another one, subconsciously believing it to be free! For this reason, they offer the cost of the same card as a prize for most if not all of their 'games'.

Minimum age is also currently 16 for the football pools but this has a much older client base and is not the instant gratification appeal of Camelot's products but for consistency's sake, this must also fall in line.

AMUSEMENT ARCADES. Many city centre arcades have a 'No under 18s' sticker slapped on their front door. But down at the seaside you can wander in and win a fiver legally when you are 12. Many machines are designed for the primary school child. They can play those coin-pushers and underpowered claw lifters on their own or with an adult; it makes little difference as there is no minimum age requirement. These places are open-fronted; the sound and lights draw in the unsuspecting child and their complicit parent. The parent lifting up their child to put coins in the slot should be aware that even though the neon sign over the shop reads 'Family Entertainment', it isn't. These places should try to think of something that *is* actual family entertainment, then any regulation imposed could be absorbed, whereas it seems likely that any restrictions brought in without any forward thinking on their part would sound the death knell for these places. They need to adapt, as many a British seaside town already looks a pale imitation of what it once was.

ESTABLISH A DEDICATED SPREAD-BETTING REGULATOR: As spread-betting comes under the Financial Services and Markets Act 2000 it is classified as an investment. Bit of a misnomer which they exploit to the fullest. It should really be reclassified so the public can clearly see what it is.

I waited six months for a reply from the Financial Ombudsman Service (FOS) about my concerns over 'slippage' and requotes. They then had no idea about spread-betting: like I was explaining the rules of cricket to someone who had never seen six lengths of wood hammered into the ground before. I can only imagine that they got little or no education in spread-betting or perhaps the guy who was given my case, whom I spoke to, was just off ill on training day. If you want to progress your career, then stick with the mainstream and take those courses and exams in pensions and investments (the FOS work with but are independent of the then FCA). It would be nuts to have Ladbrokes *et al.* regulated by a financial regulator, so why spread-betting? Spread-betting is not an ISA. Having a financial regulator overseeing spread-betting is like British Airways having their planes covered for breakdown by the AA or RAC. The regulator seemed primarily concerned with pensions and misspelling of PPIs. Having your industry regulated by a financial regulator gives spread-betting the appearance to potential customers that it really is an investment. The SB bookies build on this with their tax-free marketing bullshit, the idea that they have a 'portfolio' of 'opportunities' in different sectors and so on. And you can't offset your spread-betting losses against tax, as some desperate losers briefly cling to the belief. To me, the regulator was like a football referee trying to officiate at a rugby match back. SB affects hundreds of thousands directly and millions indirectly (gamblers' families, employers etc.) so they need to establish a dedicated body. All well and good the regulator's employees having this accounting qualification and that qualification, but if you know nothing about spread-betting then you are lost. Takes a gambler to know a bookie.

The FCA was the split into two in 2013: now the Financial Conduct Authority and the Prudential Regulatory Authority. December 6th, 2016 hopefully marks some turning point when the FCA have announced some new regulatory plans including the banning of financial incentives to start spread-betting and new rules on leverage. They have recognised that in some instances it more closely resembles gambling than investing. So you don't have to just take my word for it! Those financial incentives will still hold for the casino and poker sites as the FCA has no jurisdiction here. They also plan to force the SB bookies to declare the historical performance of products they offer and state that most investors lose money (82% wish they weren't referred to as investors though). This news had a devastating effect on IG and CMC's share price. This just goes to show how much the spread-better is currently being exploited with the massive leverage they are allowed. The spread-better believes this helps him, the SB bookies and the stock market know differently. The regulator should have been more proactive and not just stepped in late in the day as the SB companies pushed the limits further and further; took the piss, actually. The increase in leverage should have been restricted right from the start. But still, much credit goes to the FCA team; they didn't mess about with years of industry consultation but lanced the boil straight way. Compare this to FOBT/B3 reform. As for the casino/bingo/bookies industry, any reform seems to be crushed under the weight of deregulation. Someone at the FSA deserves an MBE and not some spread-betting executive.

It seems that even those companies based in Cyprus will be affected by the new rules. FxPro, who are based there, have now shelved their intended IPO. Richard Kilsby, its chairman was a former director of online gambling group 888. Owen O'Donnell was reported to have been joining the board with the flotation; he is on the board of Rank. Yeah, they would have been listed under 'Financial Services'! Again, don't take my word for it that the spread-betting companies more closely resemble a bookies.

So how can the spread-betting companies counter this? Chief-exec of IG, Peter Hetherington, has taken a two pronged approach. Firstly, he is encouraging his clients to appeal to the regulator directly. Rather like asking turkeys to complain that there are too many people turning vegetarian this Christmas, but as spread-betters cannot recognise the blindingly obvious fact that the rule changes will save *them* money and Mr Hetherington is in fact asking for their assistance in allowing him to continue to extract as much money as he can out of them, then many will take up this self-defeating call. The other approach he is taking is to get on a plane to Germany. We can only guess at what he was discussing with the regulator. CMC are considering their options too. I can't see the UK regulator backing down so I imagine that by the end of 2018 they will be fully established in Germany where the rules are much like the preproposal UK rules. As the majority of their clients reside outside the UK then there's little stopping them. In fact, is there any regulation in place to stop UK IG clients registering with the German IG division? Would take further legislation, comparable to what the U.S. put in place to stop its citizens gambling online. European-wide legislation to harmonise rules would be beneficial but now with Brexit the legislators have more pressing things to formulate.

These rule changes could still result in unavoidable negative effects: gamblers will now not be able to place such large, risky bets and lose big amounts quickly which, on the face of it is a good thing – but it may just result in their continual participation as a spread-better for many more years. Secondly, if you now need a much larger capital requirement for a given bet, then those who can find this will and those who can't will try their best. The gambler reasons that it's only stake money, after all. You can't ask the bank manager to loan you £10k for gambling as he'd politely smile and show you the door. No, you *can* do this. Just apply for a credit card or three; there's your stake money – just pay it back within a month after your bet pays off! Gamblers do this across the whole spectrum of gambling arenas. Even if they don't accept credit cards then just switch your own expenditure to your new credit card then fund with your bank card. You think you are being shrewd. You will avoid that big APR. For all the rule changes which will be finalised in 2017, it must come down to the spread-better to wise up.

INCREASE SB EQUITY REQUIREMENT. The SB bookies are always advertising the advantages of leverage, how you don't have to tie up your capital, how you can make far more money this way. But it's there so *they* can make far more money this way! Warren Buffett warns of the dangers of leveraging. Seeing he's consistently in the top five richest people in the world, best listen to him. Remember that a crowbar is a lever; the SB bookies use these crowbars to access your personal vault. Thing is though, the gambler's vault is already slightly ajar. Not exactly difficult for them to open it right up and take everything. And once it's open they don't even have to waste the effort emptying it. The gambler does that for them. The FCA are now planning on tackling this 'leverage Leviathan' and although it won't be completely destroyed it will at least be partially dismembered. They also plan on distinguishing clients as 'experienced' and 'inexperienced'. The amount of leverage will be allocated differently to each group. But be careful; after you make some losses in your first 12 months as 'inexperienced', you will then try to win back your losses with your new level of leverage and lose more.

In the few years I traded, the Dow requirement reduced and reduced so that I only needed to have £60 in equity for each £1 of a trade on the Dow. It started out at £120. These companies should be forced to up this requirement to

£500. They do not leverage products for *your* benefit. They are not there to make *you* money. Let's see what number the FCA impose.

Things that go bump in the night. They know you will be offline overnight. You should not be allowed to go into the red for more than a few hundred pounds especially when they know you are logged out!

Some SB bookies just close your positions slowly until your balance is zero. City Index let me run up a massive debt! Seemed odd to me. I argued my point to them. They asked for the £13k. I stated my case again. They asked for £13k. I agreed to pay them the £13k. Then I did the classic gambler move: I switched SB providers and lost even more. Still didn't get it. Switched again, bet even bigger, chased my losses, thought about what I would do with my eventual winnings (!) and lost big again. Finally, I got the message. Unlike with that horse you backed that trails in last, better late than never.

There will be the odd occasions on a Sunday night when markets could suddenly open hundreds up or down and it is difficult to legislate against this, but if the amount of leverage is controlled sensibly, then it will severely reduce the chances of some heart-stopping loss. Will stop scenarios like that teacher in Tipperary experienced ever happening again although get too cocky and your loss can still be BIG!

BINGO'S B3 REFORM. For the current headline-grabbing problem, as a simple starter, limit the number of these machines, do not site them within 5 metres of one another so customers can't switch between machines so easily and take out the ATMs. The FOBT and the B3 should be disconnected from that PIN terminal on the counter. They should also have a coin slot as some of these machines are notes only!

Losses limited to a maximum of £300 in any 48 hour period across all FOBT and B3 machines nationwide, recordable on their swipe card; this is not a voluntary code of practice set by the industry or just by the players themselves but is U.K. law. This 48 hour rule runs in conjunction with the losses linked to income rule (see FOBT below).

FOBTS. The industry has come up with some code of conduct and the government restrict each bookies to only four machines. That is why you might be able to walk out of one Ladbrokes and straight into another branch at the end of the road and another around the corner, as I can in my home town. And figures reveal that each single machine, on average makes around £700 profit PER WEEK! A figure that is also growing. These machines are massive cash cows. Government should regulate how many bookies operate in a given area, especially in low-income areas. Should Ladbrokes be allowed to operate three within a few hundred metres of each other? These machines sometimes act like the section of chocolate by the till at a supermarket although most of their custom seems to be from frequent players. These machines are limited in taking £100 every 20 seconds. Yes, that's £100 every 20 seconds! You couldn't do that on a regular casino roulette wheel as it takes a long time for that little ball to come to rest. The computerised system has sorted out that problem for the bookies. They just speed it all up! As you can guess, the self-regulated (!) industry is very happy with this massively high number. Newham council in London called for the maximum stake to be reduced from £100 to £2, but it isn't common for councils to take these steps. Just like the betting shop staff are supposed to step in when they can see you betting heavily – and they know you are betting heavily as you keep giving them your bank card and ordering hundreds or thousands of pounds to credit that damned machine – no one contacted me about my massive losses and massive betting and no one in the betting shop is likely to step in either – especially as they might get assaulted.

A gambler should be required to register as a member. They then have to insert their card into the machine to play; then when their losses amount to a given amount linked to income, they are barred not only from the machine that they are playing but from all the 35,000 machines in all the bookies that are linked together. The danger with any barring system is that many gamblers will switch to playing online. There are currently a few buttons that need to be pressed and restriction controls in place but it seems a fairly weak system. I would like to say that the FOBTs' days are numbered but that isn't going to happen. It already reminds me of the king-size Mars bar. There was eventually enough pressure on the company that the king-size Mars bar didn't particularly help anyone 'work, rest or play' so they withdrew it out of responsibility (!) in what campaigners hoped would be a small victory against the sugar industry and the fight against obesity. But Mars had the last laugh. They basically chopped the 84g King-size Mars bar in half, repackaged it as a Mars 'for sharing' and stuck it back on the shelves, undoubtedly to be consumed by the same individuals who consumed the king-size version alone. Now rebranded as the 85g Mars duo.

I would imagine that some warning will pop up every 15 minutes on the FOBT which the gambler can then click to make disappear. Those pop-ups should be far stronger; similar to those harmful messages and images now required on cigarette packaging: 'the long-term FOBT gambler has 100% probability of losing'; 'Stay on here for one hour and the average loss will be £200' (or whatever it is); 'Gambling can lead to suicide'. The maximum bet will reduce but this will probably only mean that the gambler will stay there longer and it won't reduce that much. Even if he is only allowed to gamble for a maximum of 30 minutes in one shop then he will just pop down the road to another – the machines will not be linked. Any new regulation will be hailed as some victory for gambling campaigners but the industry will give them this in order to mask what they are up to elsewhere; it draws attention away from their online operations, their marketing and expansion into other areas. They will still try to grab some of the credit and claim that they are a responsible industry. The FOBT have become the whipping boys for the entire gambling industry although they are hardly innocent. Yes, they deserve a good kicking (some punters have literally done that – then been arrested). Go into a bookies at any time, even ten o'clock Sunday morning and there's a good chance someone is sitting in front of one in a zombie-like trance.

Who drinks 8% cider or lager? This product is the choice of the alcoholic and the drinks industry profit from it. It would be like if Gillette produced cut-throat razors again so as to attract the self-harm market. Enter the FOBT.

The B3 and the FOBT have drawn so much attention as the players also draw so much attention to themselves. These machines are *noticeably* addictive. This focus diverts any scrutiny over the *secretly* addictive games; there are more online addicts than those on these in-house machines. The companies who run the websites know but what data do they offer up to researchers? Whilst the FOBT acts to create the classic 'diversion' the online firms, many of whom are one and the same as the FOBT operators, make hay. Difficult to research but independent research on online gambling has to happen with companies being required by law to supply any data requested.

The FOBT problem was brought to light years ago, but still there is no action other than consultation and ongoing research. The industry will say this is so they can get it right. Others will say it's a delaying tactic.

SWIPE CARDS. The swipe card needs to be brought in for the FOBT and B3, but why not for other forms of gambling? How can any self-exclusion system ever operate properly without this?

The system should be administered by a third party and the bookies are not permitted the data; they'd just use it for marketing and for market research. The system could also be applied online too – if all parties agreed or were forced by government. But this isn't going to happen for about 100 years! But a swipe card for the FOBTs and B3s should be easier to implement.

WARNING SYSTEMS. Intervention procedures are basically non-existent. It relies on a system of self-intervention; you then self-exclude. The industry will have some voluntary code of conduct and best-practice guidelines but their business is about making money first and foremost. If you are sitting online all day gambling, you will never be contacted, there will never be a pop-up warning. The only time anyone is emailed, telephoned or sent letters is for marketing and demanding payment. They will phone you every single day, several times each day, at home and at work when you owe them. At the counter in the bookies the only questions you will get will be, 'Have you got one of our loyalty cards?' and 'Do you want the SP on that?' Those FOBT gamblers will be left alone unless they try to cause physical damage. The woman who is feeding her and her husband's retirement money into the B3 machine will sit there all day in her 'gambler's bubble'. Management have no desire to pop it and give her a reality check. Her husband knows nothing of his wife's excess – yet. He never chose to gamble but now he is like hundreds of thousands of others – he is that unknowing proxy gambler. Management know exactly how much she is spending – they can easily check the computerised machines. She could lose thousands in one sitting. Those girls on reception see her and comment amongst themselves – but not to the gambler herself. These places adopt two strategies when faced with someone who is obviously a problem gambler: a) ignore them or b) take the Vegas approach and offer them a drink! This system of no checks and balances can't be right. An actual warning system needs to be introduced, regulated and run by a third party. There needs to be regular inspections by a regulator. Establishments with multiple machines must intervene daily with customers who spend more than 30 minutes gambling and keep records of these regular customer interventions. For those online, see the next section.

AUTOMATIC FLAGGING SYSTEM AND REFERRAL. When the representatives of the industry are happy with the safeguards in place, then many suspect these safeguards must be pretty shit! Would like to know how the lad (or his employer and all those employees) who managed to lose £1 million of his company's money on an income of less than £20k per annum was safeguarded? No, the *industry* is safeguarded, not its users and its proxy users. One of Evan Davis' guests says how, as everything is recorded and they have the data on their clients, they are in a far better position than the high-street bookies who just accept the bet from the man who walks in off the street. Far better position for what? To help them? The £1 million loser wasn't protected.

From my own personal experience, I know that they couldn't give a fuck. If they were really concerned they might have raised the fact with me that my stated annual income was £20–25k I think, but in one day I could lose £10k or £15k. Did anyone contact me about this? At the end of the year when I had lost £65k did anyone contact me? Did they fuck! 'Dear Mr Stringman, we are concerned that your losses this year have been three times your annual salary...' This letter was never written. I think they should have been obliged to do something along these lines. No, I have included the letter they emailed me in the final section. All they want is that I start gambling again! Yes, they have collected all that data on their customers. And what do they use it for? For more effective marketing and better targeting of new and existing clients. The only emails I have ever received have been margin calls and marketing. I was exactly the sort of client that their system *should* have flagged up as 'of concern'. But their Java programmers are busy setting the system up to maximise their profits and no regulator has ordered them to do this so they are not going to do this of their own volition! I could have been in serious shit holding such massive weekend positions. Could have lost £50k on Sunday night! But the SB bookies know I am a homeowner, so what do they care? They couldn't give a shit if I lose it all or if I am a problem gambler. Why did they never, ever contact me about my massive overnight and weekend positions on an annual income of £20–25k? The only concern any casino, any SB bookie have about keeping their clients happy and not wanting them to blow it all is this: would they want a customer to lose £10k in a month and never return or lose £2–3k a year for 10, 20, 30 years?

A flagging system should be implemented and the customer contacted through an independent and discreet third party. This new body should contact anyone who has bet and lost that quarter of their annual income online or on the FOBT/B3. Ideally, you should also be required to have a swipe card to place any bet. This won't breach any confidentialities as the gambling client can just sign up to this condition at the beginning. The companies love the long, long list of T&Cs that their clients don't read so adding another one should be no problem. Would really be *Elpis – Hope*, that is – that gets placed into this mountain of unread legal documents; the hope that we will stop.

*

I am well-educated and have a respectable job, am in a stable relationship… This all makes no difference. Just like drugs and alcohol it affects every layer of society. Read about a head-teacher in England who was so much into debt from online gambling that he lost everything: his partner and children, his home and then his life. Hanged himself from a tree. I doubt if the company that runs the website mentioned this at its AGM; just how much profit it can generate, how much it can pay in dividends. Shareholders and government seem to ignore the human cost, they don't see the personal stories behind these numbers. If you're a big and growing internet gambling website that employs hundreds or thousands of people, then you are regarded as a success and your board have praise heaped upon them and are feted by governments.

10

IN RECOVERY

The future looks rosy – for the gambling industry, that is. However, the UK spread-bet industry has recently been dealt a severe blow by the FCA so the domestic spread-bet industry has now taken a few steps back. This could mean that the overseas spread-bet industry takes a few steps forward. IG claim that they are the good guys and that the regulators need to sort the overseas SB bookies out – not sure how when they are beyond UK jurisdiction and as we are leaving the EU there's little chance of any pan-European regulation now. The Cypriot-based amongst others, play by different rules and their UK competitors insist that these are more ruthless. They've been pretty damn ruthless themselves over the years whilst the FSA were busy with other concerns. They are just annoyed that someone has muscled-in on their lucrative business and are now stealing an advantage over them. After you've read this book, there should be no chance that you will switch to a foreign-based provider as you want to make bigger bets. When you are tempted, read Chapter 2 again!

I guess it is possible to unsubscribe to these or assign them as spam (a recommended strategy for those who desperately have to fight the temptation) but these gambling companies' marketing emails actually now act as a positive thing. I know they are trying to entice me back in but now they simply demonstrate to me clearly just how bullshit the whole thing is:

Dear Mr Stringman,

As your account manager, I'm here to offer any support you may need with dealing on the financial markets. I'm writing because I'm keen to talk to you about how I can be of help, but the telephone number we have on record for you isn't valid.

I also wanted to ensure you were aware of our insight, news and analysis centre. You can use this unique resource to quickly identify dealing opportunities and plan your strategy with a range of practical tools.

- *Use sophisticated pattern-recognition technology to identify market trends*
- *See whether clients are going long or short on your chosen asset*
- *Stay informed of the most popular markets and positions*
- *View live data, Reuters news, expert analysis, broker ratings and more*

- *Deal instantly from any chart or information page*

You can launch the insight centre by logging into the trading platform and clicking on the Insight button in the top-right of the screen.

Please get in touch if you'd like to discuss dealing on the financial markets, our trading platform, or anything else that may be of help. To make sure you can benefit from the full extent of our services, please do ensure we have your current contact details.

In the meantime, good luck with your future dealing.

Kind regards
Brad
Client Development Team

I am sure 'Brad' (I changed his name to protect the guilty) from IG is really interested in my welfare and my future prosperity. I have a picture of Brad; mid-20s, hard-working, doesn't think at all about the morality of the business he is in but is only interested in his line manager's performance targets he needs to meet to get his bonus, is 'one of the lads', likes 'office fun', thinks little of his clients other than a bit of schadenfreude entering his head occasionally but for the most part only views them as a means to an end, might be someone who couldn't get a job with a proper bank but is doing nicely here thank you, but equally might be someone who regards this as like any career job with the added benefit that it pays well too, regards himself as a banker/trader – a 'master of the universe' rather than a call-centre worker (nothing wrong with working in a call centre unless you are delusional and think you are not a bookie but a banker), either ignores the nature of the industry he is in or just naïvely believes in what suits his own morality or has fallen for the marketing himself like his clients, likes his sport and even bets on them too but doesn't see any irony in this (why would he? He's not a bookie), looks after himself and thinks he is a player with the ladies (he might even be), might be one of those guys who wear a shirt and trousers one size too small to show off his pecs and quads (and loves his 'Under Armour' too), has that cold, business-like quick manner that all these pseudo-traders are told and taught to use to rush their clients into making quick decisions (that overwhelm trick again. Get the client to place some sort of bet. Do not let him ponder or he might think twice about what he's doing)... I could be wrong about all this but if you run a business like this, that's the type of employee you want. They get the job done. They certainly did a job on me.

I could never take this sort of email seriously, even when I was gambling. It all reads as complete bullshit from top to bottom. 'I'm here to offer any support you need'. Yeah, he will help slip my head into the noose. 'You can launch the insight centre...'; A tech illusion combining with the information illusion. 'Launch' suggests speed – and speed is often what you believe you need to succeed. 'Pattern recognition technology'! A gadget that sorts the information for you so you don't have to work it out for yourself which you've struggled with before. You will try this new gadget as you *believe* it will work; when it doesn't you might try it again or use something else they recommend. You get to use a 'unique resource'; this suggests you have something special that others don't have that will give you the edge – like being guillotined. 'Dealing opportunities.' Hmm. Makes the gullible think that there really are opportunities and they really are 'dealing' like a trader so you can 'plan your strategy with a range of practical tools'. No, they are 'dealing' from a pack of cards – and they are dealing you these cards, face up, remember! They have a clearly defined strategy and those practical tools are designed to backfire – not good when it's a nail gun or circular saw. We all know that tools are there to help and make life easier so again, a good choice of words. They have just given you something that they tell you will work, that you believe will work. Even a child knows their plastic saw is only pretend. Like those 'duck and cover' ads in 50s America, telling people to hide under a table if a nuclear bomb is dropped on them. People believed in this strategy. The spread-better believes in theirs. In both cases, whatever you do, the only result is obliteration (the spread better has around an 18% better chance than the A-bombed). This line also gives you the impression that there is a 'strategy' that works if you plan it well enough. There ain't. You subconsciously absorb everything. Convenience gets a mention. Makes it sound that you can just earn money whenever you like, however you like. The text is crafted more carefully than William and Kate's wedding cake.

Look on any of these companies' websites and the story is the same. Here they can back up their bullshit case with lovely colourful graphs and graphics; that information illusion. Other gambling websites attempt the same but they don't have the scope of the SB firms nor the same requirements of their 'information-hungry' clients who wolf it all down like a *speed eater* (no longer some novelty event but now with big prize money on offer; a symptom of today's 'anything goes' society).

And they sure do want my current contact details – so they can bullshit me on the phone too and send me marketing material through the post – no sorry, I mean 'to make sure you benefit from the full extent of our services'. Not to mention, another genuine address for a red-hot client (for them – this is not your winning streak I am describing); another one that they can bundle up and sell to a third party (IG may not do this but others might). They also need to make sure they have my current address to send their letters of demand. I've had them before (from City Index) and follow-up letters from their solicitor. Then the guy from the 'Client Development Team' whom is 'keen to talk to you about how I can be of help' finishes by wishing me good luck with my 'future dealing'; there's that word again. Double-dealing, more like, by the SB industry. Yes, he is in client development. He develops a client base, that's for sure but he doesn't want to develop anyone in the sense of education; maybe education illusion but nothing else. He works in his interest and his company's and not in the client's. The false sentiment, the hidden truth, the deceit... I don't know whether to laugh or cry. Brad has chosen to do this for a living. It's hard to feel sorry for him, but in some ways I do. But I feel far sorrier for the dumb-ass client – like me. And the millions of other members of the DFC. I also used to get marketing material from high-street bookies that I had registered with. But at least with these, you know what they are. They can send you offers but they can't dress it up as anything other than gambling.

I also still receive surveys. Who would actually waste time completing one? By the fact that they send them out on a regular basis, the answer is thousands. You might even subconsciously believe that they really want to 'improve their service to you', which is the reason given for asking for that five or ten minutes of your time, just like those, 'please let us know how we well we responded to your enquiry' and such like that we receive from every business; makes us warm to them. You must believe their stated purpose or why else respond? Ask me about how it fits in with my 'investment strategy'. Would be about as good a strategy as charging on horseback down a valley in the Crimea to test if those shiny sabres were any sort of match for artillery. This question, this psychological trick is employed so as to engender a belief in the client that yes, what you are doing is not gambling but investing. This survey could even not be a survey at all but just be there to inject their choice of words into your head. Would Ladbrokes ask you at the counter how that tenner you are putting on a greyhound running at Crayford fits in with your investment strategy? No, they wouldn't as it would elicit the response, 'Are you taking the piss, mate?' So why do the SB punters fall for it then when there is no difference at all? Must surely be because investments and financial markets, commodities and so on go hand-in-hand in the real world. Almost all spread-betters will actually have some real investments in these. So we cannot distinguish between gambling on them and investing in them. If it's financial markets then it's investing, if it's a horse running around a track, then it's gambling. Sorry, but they are identical – apart from the fact that that horse will lose you far, far less money.

They always tell us how SB is 'tax free'; again, a psychological trick to make us believe it is no different to taking out an ISA. Of course it is tax free! It has to be. As almost everyone loses, if it wasn't then it would also have to be tax deductible. The government would then lose out this way so the SB firms sell you this notion as a benefit whereas it is no better than a marketing gimmick – which you fall for. Again, there are three parties in this equation. Only two of them benefit although it is marketed to the remaining group as exactly that for them. Get a list of other providers they want to know if I am using. They list about 20. Oh yes, there are plenty of SB bookies out there exploiting the DFC; if people are honest with this survey they will tick between half a dozen boxes to almost all of them. The ones they didn't tick, they were not aware of and will utilise in the future.

Spread-betters keep using different providers, hoping (no, expecting!) different (i.e. profitable) results. This is how the spread-bet gambler's mind works. Would make as much difference as losing a tenner in Ladbrokes on the two o'clock at York races then trying your luck in Coral's with the 2.35 at York. You will take many providers whether consecutively or simultaneously, it really doesn't matter, they will all fuck you in the end. You will probably start with the big players; the well-known and well-advertised. You will do this whether you are spread-betting, playing poker or at the online casino or whatever. They have reached their status in the market by being the best at taking their clients' money and have been doing it successfully for many years; please stop and ask yourself why they grow every year and more companies keep on entering the market. You will try different providers, only to discover they all use the market leaders' platforms, but just brand themselves with their own logo. As spread-betting has the illusion of financial investment, and believe me, it *is* an illusion, banks and financial companies are happy to be associated with it – as they do very well out of it. But it is gambling, in my opinion, pure and simple; that is why high-street bookies also run financial spread-betting books. So is 'trading' on whether the price of wheat will rise or the CAC will rise or Apple will fall or oil will plummet or whatever else you decide you are an expert in, any different from investing on the 3.15 at Haydock Park? The second provider will fuck you just like the first. If you continue then the last provider you take will fuck you the hardest and fuck you till it hurts.

They ask me why I have stopped trading. 'The fact that you cannot win' was not listed as one of their suggestions. What would encourage me to trade again? A lobotomy was also not listed. Would I recommend them to a friend on a scale of 0–10? What sort of friend would that be? Only a friend whom I know has tried to sleep with my wife. By filling in the survey, get entered into a free prize draw! To get to the 'free' draw stage has cost me £130k. They will tell you that they want your opinions so as to 'deliver a better service to you'. It is to gain more insight into their customers so as to make more money from them and to attract new customers. The more data they extract from you, the better it is for them. Some of their questions seem straightforward but they might be gleaning information about you as a gambler that you are completely unaware of. You are helping them with their research project about how to suck people in, and hold them there before they get stripped naked. That's what *The Naked Trader* should really be about.

Once told my future wife to be that I had an alcoholic friend who started drinking car windscreen wash as it has much the same effects but is cheaper. She actually started to believe me until I said, 'Doesn't do that anymore. He's clean now'. Is this a bad joke? The worst joke of all is the fact that we live in a society which appears to value the alcohol and gambling industries that make vast profits out of the likes of you and me. Or worse. Gambling might lead to a quick death through suicide or a long, drawn-out one. Alex Higgins' death was as much down to gambling as it was down to his smoking and drinking. He just never bothered looking after himself, including eating. He just wanted to be in the bookies 24/7. Now with online gambling, this is exactly what most of us try to do. Keith Gillespie always seemed to look unnaturally pale, thin and concerned for a professional footballer. Now I know why. I used to wake up and check the markets just as quickly as the alky reaches for that can of Special Brew they strategically place beside their bed the night before. I used to regularly have a quick check of the markets in the middle of the night too just like the alky wakes up and has a quick swig. So easy to do when your iPad or smartphone is lying next to you on the bedside table; might be nearer to you than your wife or girlfriend. Could even place a bet; this is no different to running down to an all-night Ladbrokes at 3 a.m. in your pyjamas. But this is effectively what you do; and if your wife is lying next to you, you do it secretly whilst she is asleep. If you need a little longer or are more cautious, you will get out of bed and bet in the bathroom. Sometimes, you will bet in your pyjamas during daylight hours too as you will never actually get changed out of them. You will watch the markets and place bets all day and barely eat. Your life will be dominated by gambling, you will be a slave to it.

You have effectively cut your life short; all those hours, days, in fact years spent gambling will be completely dead time. The loss of your valuable time is just as bad as the loss of your valuable money. There seems to be several years of my life that are just a blur. I was so focused on it, I didn't really do much else. Even when I tried to get away from it by playing golf on Sunday, I was thinking about how the markets would open in the evening. You will go through gamblers' cold turkey. You will not suffer so much the physical pains of a recovering drug user but you will be constantly twitchy, you will see all those missed opportunities when the market falls 500 points and you believe you could have been on it. Don't go casting your eye over the 3.15 at Ascot then killing yourself that you didn't put that £50 on that horse that did, in fact win at 16-1. You have been there before and yes, you did have some lovely winners; but you had a fair few losers too. Don't believe you have been unlucky with the markets or with the cards. You haven't. That's just how markets or poker or whatever works. The more adverts you see on TV for bookies enticing you back in with promises of riches should make you run a mile, not draw you in. If they can put up a Porsche 911 for you to win, simply by placing a bet, doesn't this rather suggest that they must be raking it in (bwin, 2017)? The more of these adverts there are should tell you that the bookies are doing rather well – off of the likes of you! Metallica might not be singing about the same thing as Lemmy but to a gambler, nothing else matters.

You are not the next bracelet-wearing poker star, you are not a 'master of the universe' trader but someone who spread-bets on the stock market with your underpants around your ankles as you sit on the toilet. You are not that off-piste skier with a mohawk you see on ESPN, do not enter a triathlon to keep up with the boys at work as you used to be fit twenty years ago and definitely do not try it on with that girl at work under the same delusion. Take up a hobby that won't kill you if you want a challenge. Or one that takes all your money either. What thrills us, sometimes kills us. I hope James Kingston stays lucky; he's a free-runner who hangs from 100 foot cranes from one hand or does a back flip atop a stanchion on a suspension bridge. This may seem irresponsible, it may seem like you are just asking for trouble. Extreme free runners know it is inherently dangerous and potentially fatal. Unlike the free-runner, it will actually only be a handful of gamblers who get away with it completely. There will be plenty of stories and warnings in the media when someone falls from a building site crane to their death. Suicide due to gambling issues will struggle to get a mention, and even then it will focus on the problems of that particular individual rather than gambling and the industry itself, as if it was entirely down to that person's shaky psychiatric state. Gambling kills more than free-running ever could. Those who watch the TV report will think that it was entirely that person's fault for letting it overwhelm them. Those gamblers who throw themselves in front of the express train because they can't live with the embarrassment, the shame, the selfishness of their acts, the self-hatred, the remorse, the feeling of stupidity, the financial loss, the belief that they are a burden on their family, the feeling of bereavement that we have lost something within us is something that all us gamblers suffer to a greater or lesser extent. You are a long time dead anyway so I ain't going to extend it. Do not believe the marketing and drive your BMW like you are on a racetrack. The subliminal or otherwise message has got into your psyche and when you crash you are not secured by your four-point harness and neck restraint, cushioned by that tyre wall with firemen standing by. No, you have bounced up the curb, taken out a pedestrian and smacked into a brick wall. Your prized BMW is now the size of a Smart car and the firemen are unaware and are still eating their fish and chips at the station. No, don't fall for the marketing of cars of alcohol or gambling…

If I had wanted a monthly reminder of my spread-bet delusion, I didn't need to subscribe to fuckup.com to send me texts. I saw it every month in my bank statements. I paid a mortgage, investments, petrol and Tesco's and Sainsbury's, paid my golf membership and car insurance, TV/internet/

phone… yes, the normal items. But these were all dwarfed by those massive payments to SB bookies. Those £20s and £40s you've been putting into that machine in Ladbrokes through the convenience of that remote payment system on the counter now appear itemised every month. Just hope the wife doesn't see. She won't; you have your own bank account and do everything online. You've covered yourself there then! Hardly something positive in your life though, is it? These amounts all add up. And chances are they all add up to a fucking lot! Now, delete your app for bullshit.com and give those FOBTs a miss. If I need any more confirmation of my DFC status, I can find it in my inbox once more. I seem to be getting more than my fair share of 'investment opportunities' emailed to me. As I was idiotic enough to believe spread-betting was my route to success and riches, then I am a marked man. But I am not going to invest in 'pink diamonds' or whatever! I imagine some SB firm has sold on mine and thousands of others' email addresses to some intermediary, and the SB companies have no interest or concerns as to what they do with them.

Gambling eventually makes you really sick of it all, even physically sick. I really couldn't make head nor tail of economic data in the end although at one time I used to believe I could. Information illusion and delusional clarity make way for information overload eventually. Even if the media are given 90% or even 99% of the information, it's that missing information that is the real key. We think we have all the information, all the data, all the charts, expert opinion at our fingertips. We make informed decisions on the information we have, just that they're just as likely to be wrong decisions and based on information that is known to everyone. We are also operating outside the system where the real money-men are, where the real traders and sports insiders inhabit. If you would enjoy a hobby that involves sitting on one side of the road and seeing how many pound coins you can flick into the drain on the other side, then gambling is for you. Information will never be open to all, whatever the internet suggests. There will always be more information outside the internet than on it. I was permanently stressed by constant gambling. I used to subject myself to almost unbearable stress around 'data days' and rate days and key company report days, like the football fan watching the penalty shoot-out with their scarf in their mouth or the poker player feeding the pot, inwardly praying that his hand is better than the bloke's opposite. I sometimes risked almost everything – then I'd have a lot of explaining to do to a lot of people. It's not a list of fucked-up emotions that I want to experience: admission, degradation, embarrassment, guilt… but still I carried on! I still have a whole list of negative emotions built up inside me that will be difficult to exorcise: anger, frustration, an intense feeling of being manipulated – 'groomed' would be the modern word for it – used, dented pride, betrayal even… the list is not endless but there are more than one or two more. I am sure you have your own suggestions swilling around in your head like some rancid dregs of cheap wine. But these are easing themselves into the distant background. They will always be there as a reminder, to draw upon if I ever need reminding, if I ever feel tempted again.

The internet is a wonderful thing! Just that you and I abused it! A close friend told me the internet had worked for him and he has found his partner this way. Never worked for me all those years. BUT always be careful of someone who says that he 'got his girlfriend off the internet'. Makes it sound like Autotrader. If he had said he *met* his girlfriend *through* the internet or *on* the internet then I might have taken him more seriously. I knew it wouldn't last. It didn't… Okay so that wasn't the best example I could come up with!

I *did* actually see a picture of a winning gambler leaning against the side of the Porsche he had bought with the fruits of his skill at gambling in one of those I-made-a-fortune-gambling-and-so-could-you books. Yes, it does happen; rarely mind, that's why there are books about it. It's an extreme story – it *can* happen in sports betting. These people *do* exist. They might even exist in spread-betting – for those with inside knowledge. You never see a spread-bet millionaire wheeled out in front of the cameras! There were professional poker players long before the internet came along too. But you could invite all of these winners to your local pub and you'd still have space for a couple of pool tables – you could probably hire out a bucking bronco machine too. Please remember the pictures you *don't* see of the SB companies' executives leaning against the side of *their* Range Rovers with their massive houses in Surrey with their koi carp swimming around their fountains and their kids' hallmarked goldfish swimming around upstairs in their aquariums. Or those with a major stake in Partypoker.com or Jeremy's favourite, Foxybingo.com. or a hundred other such sites peddling bullshit. Don't forget there's a guy who regularly sweeps the table of all its chips from all those amateur poker players who have read the books and think they have the *cojones*. He knows what he's doing. You don't – even though you think you do. These companies fill their coffers at the click, click, click of *your* keyboard as you type in your three-digit security code. Security code! What security does it offer you! Might as well not have one if you're going to keep donating money to them!

Still watch Bloomberg or CNBC occasionally, for 'sentimental' reasons. A bit like visiting somewhere you used to go to when you were younger but when you think about it, you never enjoyed going there in the first place. The guests, if they are not bigging up themselves or their companies which the presenters encourage, are bigging up their own economic theory supported by some graph or another. Think you can find a chart to justify just about anything.

Your relationship to money has now changed forever. It might become difficult to go to work for a day when you will take home £100. This is what you can win in five minutes. So why work then? £100 is also what you can lose in five minutes. This strange relationship you have now developed with money due to gambling affects your ability to see wages and the effort you put in to receive your salary in the way that you used to. Even when you have quit and you are again focused on your work or are out shopping, you will get many, many occasions when you wonder what actually makes sense any more as you contemplate whether to spend 30 quid on something then realise you would do this without thinking when you were gambling. I used to do it with numbers into the thousands. But when you have something tangible in front of you, your mind drifts back to when you were younger, before you gambled, when money had a value in your mind. This is the strangest aspect of the post-quit gambler and one I still don't really understand how to deal with. You will never see money in the same way again. I still find myself excited by a bargain although the irony and contradiction with my previous life is something odd. I usually found myself laughing about it. But only to myself. I didn't want my partner asking what I was laughing about. Now she knows, everything changes – it makes it easier to stay stopped; now I have someone to talk to. Self-mockery works for me. In the end, I just went out and bought that John Parris cue that I'd been thinking about for years. Why not? I've lost this amount – much, much more than this amount sometimes in seconds. So just go and spend however much you want on something without thinking too much about how much it costs you. Isn't that what you used to do when you needed to fund your gambling for £500 or £5000? This is the true value of money at both ends; a dedicated craftsman gets a payment for creating something of beauty and elegance whilst at the other end I get to use such a thing after willingly paying my hard-earned cash for it. That's what money is for – not to risk it on dumb-ass ventures. Risk and reward? The latter is only for the bookies. And there is no 'risk' as this implies there could be a positive outcome.

I had my bike stolen during the time I was gambling. Yes, someone stole something of value of mine – rather than me giving it away, which I was doing a lot of. A few years before I would have been devastated to lose a one-year-old €600 bike. But now I would lose €600 in seconds spread-betting, it didn't seem such an issue. Still, losing €600 as a tangible asset that I loved seemed much harder than losing €600 in a SB account. It did make me think again what the fuck I was doing spread-betting when €600 really is a lot of money. But this realisation that money does have real value didn't last. I was still gambling and keeping an eye on market numbers when I turned up at the police station to report the theft.

Those SB bookies or poker sites or online bingo halls might even be 'award-winning'. You can win a prize too! Whenever I fly back from London, there is always a guy or attractive girl, flogging expensive raffle tickets to win the Ferrari or Porsche or Maserati they are standing in front of. Yes, if people want to try to win one at £50 a ticket or whatever price you have to pay then fair enough. But how stupid are the buying public if they believe that if you buy one ticket and get a second one free that increases your chances of winning! Even I'm not *that* stupid! No, I am *that* stupid. I fell for something with no chance of winning me a Ferrari. Gambling is like some Charlie Chaplin routine where you think you see the winning ticket lying on the ground, only for it to be whipped away by some joker who's tied a string to it. The gambling industry always pull the strings – and it wasn't even a winning ticket anyway.

My then soon-to-be wife told me how she did a week at medical school before she decided it was not for her. Her classmate carried on and is now a doctor but my partner has no regrets. I tell her one of my classmates also went to medical school and then specialised in rectal surgery. Now he is a brain surgeon. She believed me, which is fair enough. But when I said, 'Yeah, everyone has to start at the bottom', she might have twigged. She didn't. It's not her native language, after all. And I never bothered coming clean. When this book is out in paperback, I'll be coming clean to everyone about my previous life (far cleaner than that bloke who drinks windscreen wash!). At least I needn't have to sit there and explain unlike so many men who really do have a lot of explaining to do. They can just read it for themselves if they want. As your life also bears uncanny similarities, you could just give her the book too. You have not been taken from us like the much-missed Amy Winehouse or George Michael. You will not suffer the shame and embarrassment of Max Mosley. You have most likely committed no crime, nor cheated on you wife (not sexually, at least). All you have lost is time and money and you will experience some negative emotions as will some around you; but you are not a bad person and you still have your health. Stay strong and recover.

There are no books in Waterstone's or WHSmith on overcoming gambling addiction. Shelves of books on overcoming a smoking addiction but not gambling. Found a few on Amazon but you can find anything on Amazon. But these are either incredibly short, related to some minor celebrity or someone who found God or just predate the internet. If it ain't in Waterstone's, then this problem is still hidden. People need to know that they are not alone. Yes, even the middle-class can be conned, even those with an education so don't be too embarrassed or ashamed!

If you didn't gamble then you wouldn't have to work so long and could spend more time doing things you really enjoy, like spending time with the wife and kids or just at the golf club away from the wife and kids. You will work more efficiently and effectively, your mind will be clearer, your relationships at work better, career prospects improved and you will end up earning more money. You will be less stressed and also less likely to cause accidents at work; how guilty will you feel when it is your fault for injuring a colleague as your mind was on something else – 3.15 from Kempton, online casino loss from the night before, where the FTSE is now – or you're tired from being up until the early hours trying to win back your online poker losses. You can feel now how your mind is fogged up and unfocused; even when you try to concentrate you subconsciously think, plan and worry about gambling. Everyone has the image of the late-night poker player with a ciggy hanging between his lips; not so cool when you're losing though and chain-smoking your way through the whole packet due to nervousness and frustration. If you are bored or frustrated with life, gambling will not be the answer. If you are using gambling as a diversion, then find a different one. If you are doing it to make money, then you are delusional; you need to focus on your job or proper investments. We all need to get our kicks somewhere. Sherlock Holmes took cocaine and opium (and played the violin) between cases to relieve the tedium of life. The need to get away from the mundane is not fiction. Gambling is not the answer. Would be like someone who decides that the best way to remove all those tattoos all the way up their arm would be to chop it off. Problem solved, just that you have now created an even bigger one.

I still get flashbacks all over the place, just like someone who's been eating magic mushrooms or acid and keeps seeing things long after the drugs have supposedly worn off. When my phone is charging and the percentage is going up through the 80s and then the 90s, I actually *feel* good, the same feeling I had when my SB account went up. I must actually believe for that split second that it *is* my SB account.

We all seem to spend the first half of our lives fucking it up somehow, usually with the help of others; these others are sometimes our parents. Then we try to get on with our lives but still fuck it up as we are still tainted by what happened before, even though we are either unaware of this or just try to ignore it. We spend the second half of our lives trying to recover from the first half. For all the gambling losses, it was the feeling of being used and deceiving myself that got me - and how I deceived someone else. My only consolation is that I was born a gambler, I started spread-betting before I met my future wife and then, unsurprisingly, I just couldn't shrug it off.

Suicide is often thought of as affecting the mentally disturbed or angst-ridden teenagers or just people thought of as misfits or weak in some way. But suicide runs across all social classes, and a male in his 40s is a high-risk group. That would be me then. You will not be the sports star or pop star that you wanted to be. You have not fulfilled your dreams and it ain't gonna happen now, is it? You might be a successful accountant but it's hardly rock and roll. This is not what you want. And you can't just quit your job and become a hippy. You have too many responsibilities and you have always looked down on these beatniks. Now you sometimes envy them. You went to university, took the 'milk round' seriously and got that graduate trainee job that you wanted. Now look where you are. You might be frustrated in your chosen career but you can't choose an alternative now. So what do you do? Jump in front of that commuter train you've taken for the last 20 years? Some do. You could buy that Harley and try to relive your youth although you never had a Harley in your youth and nor did anyone else so how is buying one going to help? You are trying to relive a youth you never had but what you really want is just to be 18 again. Buying something big and powerful is not what being young is about. Being young is about being carefree. It is not about shopping around to get the best insurance deal on that Harley of yours. We get 20 years of bottled-up frustration that we hadn't even noticed had been bottling up. We suddenly realise that life ain't gonna begin at 40 and we seek alternatives. These involve reverting back to what we always wanted to do as a teenager but had neither the money nor the confidence. So now we have both, we have sex with anyone, take risks with fast cars, gamble like some high-roller. All comes down to self-restraint and finding something meaningful and exciting that ain't gonna kill you or hurt others emotionally or physically. Find yourself a challenge, a lifestyle that you are happy with. It won't involve spending hour after hour giving someone you don't know your money at an ever-increasing speed. You think you will win. They *know* they will win. Gambling time is dead time. You have achieved zero. This is also the final destination for your bank balance.

Our gambling addiction and culture is not a peculiarly British thing; it is similar across Europe as you can see from football shirts: Real Madrid 2014 'bwin', Atletico Madrid 2016 'Plus500', Juventus 'Betclic', Hertha Berlin 'Bet-at-home'. But to explore Europe and the rest of the world properly I'd need to write another book.

Gambling gives us that warm feeling inside. You feel 'at home' as soon as you walk through the bookies doors, even just online. But I will not be going there again as it may at first feel as comfortable as the sofa I sit on – but then I set fire to it! Now, for the first time in my life I have it under control. I will not be going on any benders. I have recognised myself for what I am. Writing this book has been my therapy, my confessional, my support partner. I hope reading it can be yours.

Gambling results for the last four years: £45. Profit too – not that it makes a lot of difference. So I'm now down only £129,955 then. I have wagered £12 gambling and spent around 40 minutes of my time doing it – in four years. My exit strategy has worked so far. 'Gambling is good, huh?' said John from Louis' gambling documentary. Changed his tune within a day after he lost his winnings then went more into the negative than he was ever in the positive – just like the rest of us. We all want to achieve something meaningful in life as Antonius Block in *The Seventh Seal* reminds us. You won't achieve this through gambling, whatever side of the screen you are on. And if you spend time on the same side as I inhabited, you won't get rich either.